The American Heritage Library

WORLD WAR II

By C. L. Sulzberger

Houghton Mifflin Company · Boston

This 1987 edition published by Houghton
Mifflin Company by arrangement with
American Heritage, a division of Forbes Inc.,
is a reprint of *The American Heritage Picture History
of World War II,* published in 1966.

Library of Congress Cataloging-in-Publication Data
Sulzberger, C.L. (Cyrus Leo).
    World War II.
    Includes index.
    1. World War, 1939–1945.   I. Title.
II. Title: World War 2. III. Title: World War Two.
D743.S74422   1985   940.53   85-3978
ISBN 0-8281-0331-3 Pa

Cover design: Paul Perlow
Cover painting: Ogden Plessner,
    U.S. Army Center of Military History

Printed in the United States of America

FFG 12 11 10 9 8 7 6

Table of Contents

I
The March to the Abyss

From the remnants of the German Army left
by World War I arose a formidable and
well-disciplined war machine, exemplified
by these goose-stepping troops.

Triumph in battle offers twin trophies to the victors. Their writers can impose on history their version of the war they won, while their statesmen can impose the terms of peace. In each case the opportunity was missed after the 1914–18 conflict. Ernest Hemingway later called it "the most colossal, murderous, mismanaged butchery that has ever taken place on earth," and the treaty-making assumptions of Allied leaders almost all proved falsely based. Those leaders, gathered around Paris in 1919 to draft the security they had pledged the world, found themselves trapped by secret promises they had made one another and by slogans they had uttered to hearten their mud-bound troops. When the machine guns subsided in November, 1918, there was actually less chance of a safe and democratic earth than when the slaughter started, more than four years earlier.

The series of treaties signed in Paris's agreeable suburbs—Versailles, St. Germain-en-Laye, Neuilly-sur-Seine, Trianon, and Sèvres—spoke of dreams and ignored realities. For better or worse, they imprisoned Germany, isolated Austria, fragmented Turkey, chopped up Hungary and Bulgaria, and overlooked murmurous Russia. Their harsh decisions might have provided a stable order, had they not been based on numerous miscalculations: that the United States would help police international justice; that Britain and France would enhance their strength and maintain the will to use it; that Russia would stay weak and Germany supine.

No one realized that Woodrow Wilson's idea of self-determination, leading toward "complete independence of various small nationalities now forming part of various Empires," would inflame Asia and Africa and sap the colonial vigor on which the European victors relied to keep the peace. Colonial markets for goods manufactured in Manchester and Lille faded as hitherto enfeoffed peoples began asserting their industrial freedom; and slowly, over subsequent decades, the general staffs of Britain and France became aware that soon they would be deprived of their famous regiments of Sikhs, Marathas, Tonkinese, and Goumiers.

Among the diplomats who gathered in Paris to blueprint a happy future were a few outstanding figures: Wilson, the tigerish Georges Clemenceau, David Lloyd George, and Eleutherios Venizelos, the scrappy Greek who captivated everyone and led them to another war. Ah, how soon again the troops began to march: Rumanian, Polish, Greek, French, British, and Turkish, and German and Italian freebooters. They all moved east. Germany set off on a secret search for power, and Russia began its devious negotiations.

Since those days we have raced from pit to pit. Wilson discovered that to make a world truly "safe for democracy" requires a knowledge of democratic processes at home. Misjudging the strength and temper of his political opposition, he saw the United States Senate spurn the Versailles Treaty and the League of Nations. Vladimir Ulyanov, a conspirator who took the name Lenin after his brother was hanged by Czar Alexander III, consolidated the revolutionary control he had seized in Russia. France relaxed, on the assumption that its wounded Army, despite a wracking mutiny in 1917, was Europe's finest. Britain's "balance of power" policy dwindled as Britain's decreased vitality became manifest. Slowly, accompanied by economic disaster, political apathy, and the rise of revolutionary dynamists, pleasant auguries dissolved.

The empires of eastern Europe had been destroyed, and the empires of western Europe were ailing. But burning ambitions had not left Europe's heart. There remained that dreadful verity discerned by Julius Fröbel, a leader of the 1848 revolution: "The German nation is sick of principles and doctrines, literary existence and theoretical greatness. What it wants is Power, Power, Power: and whoever gives it Power, to him will it give honor, more honor than he can ever imagine."

The German General Staff was not destroyed by the Treaty of Versailles. It merely changed its name, becoming the *Truppenamt* of the *Heeresleitung* office. The *Truppenamt* saw that World War I's most signal creation had been a renascent Russia, and it was there the German generals sought sustenance. They were the first to realize that the principal event of World War I was the rise of Russia, just as the principal event of World War II was to be the rise of China.

In 1920, Enver Pasha, a romantic Turkish revolutionary, wrote from Moscow to Hans von Seeckt, head of the *Heeresleitung*, who had resolved to build an army far exceeding anything envisioned at Versailles and also to explore the possibility of partitioning the new Polish state with Russia. Enver told Seeckt that Trotsky, Lenin's War Commisar, would welcome German instructors and arms collaboration. Seeckt wanted a remote hinterland in which to experiment beyond Allied supervision. He created "Special Group R" to negotiate with the Kremlin and signed an agreement without even confiding in his Government. Once again the world would learn, as Mirabeau had written in the eighteenth century, that Germany was "an army in search of a country."

By 1922, when the Berlin Government arranged the Treaty of Rapallo with Moscow, German officers had already made dispositions to manufacture tanks, shells, aircraft, and even poison gas in the Soviet towns of Lipetsk, Saratov, Kazan, and Tula. At Lipetsk, the famous Stuka dive bombers and all-metal aircraft were developed, ten years before they appeared on Allied drawing boards. Picked Soviet commanders, selected by the brilliant Marshal Mikhail Tukhachevski, were trained in German military academies and eventually made mass experiments with armored and airborne forces. The arrangement suited both Versailles pariahs. Seeckt told Lenin's secret envoy, the journalist Karl Radek: "You missed your chance in 1919 and 1920. It is possible that Germany, allied with your Red Army, may fight a war against France, but not," Seeckt added as a warning, "with a German Red Army."

The victors found that the pernicious anemia produced by bloodletting, imperial dissolution, and political misjudgment also had horrid economic symptoms. The new century's early economic expansion was totally disrupted. European investments in Russia became worthless; England, the world's banker, was supplanted by the United States; competitive industries arose in Asia.

The European Allies, with little economic logic, hoped to make the losers foot an impossible bill. Initially they sought $56,500,000,000 in German reparations. This claim was pared down, then postponed by a moratorium during which France occupied the Ruhr. Charles G. Dawes, an American financier who later became Vice-President, negotiated a formula whereby Germany would settle its debt through a series of escalating annual payments, but even his compromise vanished in 1932 in the midst of world depression.

Germany was engulfed by the most dismal inflation. At the end of the war, the mark was worth about twenty-five cents; by November, 1923, the value of the mark had shrunk dramatically.

With desperate shortages of fuel in Germany,
women and children glean bits of coal
in the dump heap of a mine in 1922. The
hysterical joy of the 1918 armistice was
soon blunted for all of Europe by hunger,
unemployment, inflation, and devastating
war-bred epidemics of influenza and typhus.

Workers in Essen took their pay home in barrels, and three hundred paper factories and one hundred and fifty printing establishments were unable to turn out notes fast enough to keep the economy off a barter basis. Eventually, Hjalmar Schacht, later Hitler's Minister of Economy, introduced a device called the *Rentenmark*, based, theoretically, on a mortgage of all Germany. This device created a new currency but did not salvage the ruined and embittered middle class.

Preceded by an atmosphere of uncertainty abroad and fostered by overconfidence at home, Wall Street's abysmal collapse hit at the end of 1929. For a decade, America had been entranced by the idea of being a leading economic power. American soldiers returned home believing they had made a new world. Optimism was the prevailing theme of American life. Absorbed in becoming ever more prosperous, the American people built a never-never land on Wall Street that lasted until shortly after Labor Day, 1929. All through a hot Indian summer there was an uncertain scramble for securities. Then, on Thursday, October 24, panic began. Almost thirteen million shares were unloaded. Tuesday, October 29, was, in the words of Professor John Kenneth Galbraith, the most devastating day in our financial history. Within weeks, investors lost thirty billion dollars—almost what the nation had spent on World War I. And prices kept on dropping until June, 1932. By 1933 there were some twelve million unemployed. Men retired wealthy and awoke paupers. Banks failed; mortgages were foreclosed, farm families evicted. Mines and factories ground to a halt. Shantytowns, known as Hoovervilles, grew like fungus around the edges of cities, and incredible as it may now seem, *Business Week* reported that some one hundred thousand Americans were seeking jobs in Russia.

The effect of the Wall Street disaster was felt throughout Europe. On May 11, 1931, Vienna's powerful Credit-Anstalt Bank collapsed. On September 21, England abandoned the gold standard. World trade dwindled. Wages shrank fantastically, and Europe's growing numbers of unemployed workers joined the ruined bourgeoisie in following the Fascist, National Socialist, and Communist movements, which thrived on despair.

In 1933, the pattern of leadership among the world's three most powerful nations was set for the next dozen years with the arrival in office of Roosevelt in Washington and Hitler in Berlin and the

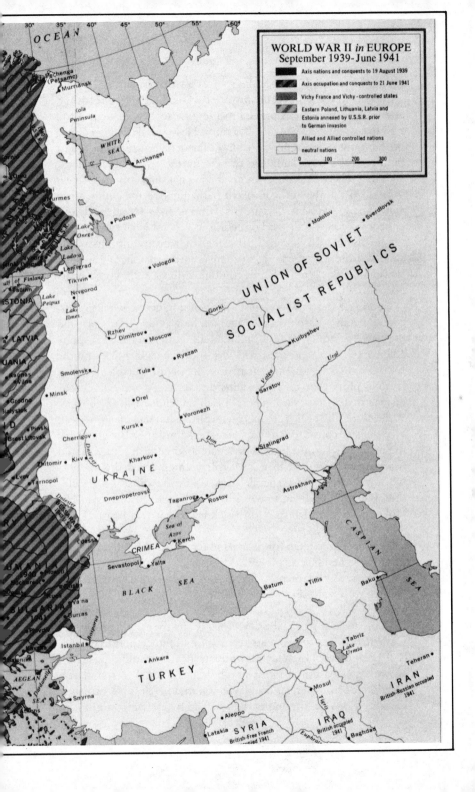

WORLD WAR II *in* EUROPE
September 1939-June 1941

Axis nations and conquests to 19 August 1939
Axis occupation and conquests to 21 June 1941
Vichy France and Vichy-controlled states
Eastern Poland, Lithuania, Latvia and Estonia annexed by U.S.S.R. prior to German invasion
Allied and Allied controlled nations
neutral nations

0   100   200   300

OCEAN

UNION OF SOVIET SOCIALIST REPUBLICS

Pechenga (Petsamo)
Murmansk
Kola Peninsula
WHITE SEA
Archangel
Pudozh
Molotov
Sverdlovsk
Lake Onega
Lake Ladoga
Vologda
Leningrad
Tikhvin
Gulf of Finland
Tallinn
Novgorod
Lake Peipus
Lake Ilmen
ESTONIA
Gorki
Kuibyshev
LATVIA
Rzhev
Dimitrov
Moscow
Ural
UANIA
Ryazan
Kaunas
Vilna
Smolensk
Tula
Saratov
Grodno
Minsk
Orel
Bialystok
Voronezh
Volga
Pinsk
Brest Litovsk
Cherrigov
Kursk
Dnieper
Don
Stalingrad
Lvov
Zhitomir
Kiev
Kharkov
Astrakhan
Tarnopol
UKRAINE
Dniester
Dnepropetrovsk
Taganrog
Rostov
Bug
Odessa
Sea of Azov
Kerch
CASPIAN
UMANIA
CRIMEA
Sevastopol
Yalta
Bucharest
Pruth
BLACK   SEA
Batum
Tiflis
Baku
SEA
BULGARIA
Burgas
Danube
Istanbul
Tabriz
Lake Urmia
Teheran
Salonika
Ankara
Mosul
IRAN
British-Russian occupied 1941
AEGEAN
SEA
Smyrna
TURKEY
Tigris
Aleppo
IRAQ
British occupied 1941
Athens
Cape Matapan
Latakia
SYRIA
British-Free French occupied 1941
Euphrates
Baghdad

consolidation of Joseph Stalin's Moscow despotism.

Roosevelt came in on promises of immediate relief, recovery, and improvement. His makeshift New Deal grew in a curiously effective way, revitalizing the economy. He lowered tariffs, repealed prohibition, relieved pressure on the farmers, revalued gold. Vast public works were launched to take up the employment slack. Exuding self-confidence and galvanizing national faith, Roosevelt brought a number of competent, imaginative men into office and almost haphazardly, in his famous first Hundred Days, concocted a new style and direction in Federal Government that would do more to change life in America than any administration since Wilson's. By the time Hitler succeeded in detonating another world war, the United States, though still not fully cured of its economic illness, was again on its feet.

Roosevelt was a great man. Hitler was not; but he was a genius, an evil genius. With infallible acumen he was able to discern and use powerful traits in the Germanic soul. Hitler had had a respectable corporal's career in World War I, during which he won the Iron Cross. After the 1918 armistice, he became involved in the furious plots that fermented inside Germany and joined the disgruntled World War I general Erich Ludendorff in an abortive 1923 *Putsch* in Munich. Robert Murphy, who was the American vice-consul, consulted the papal legate, Monsignor Pacelli, about the incident's significance. The legate assured him Hitler would never again be heard from. Murphy remembered this in 1944 when, as adviser to General Mark Clark, he called on Pacelli, then Pope Pius XII, in newly liberated Rome. "Bob," said His Holiness, patting Murphy on the knee, "that was before I was infallible."

Tried and convicted for his part in the *Putsch*, Hitler spent nine months in Landsberg prison, during which time he wrote his brutally frank testament, *Mein Kampf*, a book that too few foreigners read with any care, and too many Germans both read and believed.

Germany, using Schacht's *Rentenmark* and the essential fact that, while it had lost the war, its territory had remained unravaged, had recaptured much of its industrial and trading position. However, it harbored bitter psychological complexes of defeat and thirsted for revenge. By playing on middle-class resentments, the ambitions of the industrialists, and a fear of communism that was fanned by monarchists, officers, and the Church, Hitler and his hodgepodge National Socialist (Nazi) party seized power. Not much more than one German out of three voted for the party in 1933, yet Hitler gained control of the Reichstag.

During the astonishing six years between his accession in 1933 and the outbreak of World War II, Hitler made himself dictator and made Germany Europe's strongest military power, while the victors of World War I looked on in confusion. He brought into the open the remilitarization program that Seeckt had started secretly in 1921, putting the unemployed and discontented into uniforms. He smashed democracy, dispossessed (and ultimately liquidated) Germany's cultivated Jewish population, and crushed party dissidents through terror or sometimes outright murder. He cowed the General Staff and assumed direction of foreign policy. The rich Saarland, temporarily removed by the Allies from German administration, voted in 1935 to rejoin the Reich. On March 7, 1936, Hitler sent his troops into the demilitarized Rhineland and began to fortify it. The Allies did nothing but mumble. Next he sent agents to subvert Austria, and in March of 1938, with the help of armed Austrian Nazis, he added that mountain land and more than six and a half million people to the German Reich. Again the Allies did nothing; and Hitler announced he wanted no more territory.

Hitler reckoned that France and Britain would leave Germany alone so long as their interests were not directly threatened. Initially, he was more concerned with Italy and Russia. In 1921, Benito Mussolini, a renegade Socialist, had developed an antidemocratic party from restless elements and, dressing them in black shirts, had used them to take over Rome from a flabby parliamentary regime. Mussolini was personally more attractive than Hitler. He was flamboyant, cultivated, with a literary flare and a way with women; and, like Hitler, he dreamed of empire. However, the huge army he created was backed neither by economic sinews nor by national will.

There was no formal military alliance between Berlin and Rome when Hitler seized Austria on Italy's frontier. He forced an Austrian showdown despite Mussolini's vaunted "8,000,000 bayonets," which failed to protect a country whose independence was vitally important to Rome. After that, Hitler knew he could bind

Mussolini, in a 1938 photograph, leads a
parade of militiamen. Nicknamed the
twentieth-century Caesar, he talked grandiosely
about building Fascist Italy into a modern
Roman Empire. After taking over the German
goose step, he renamed it the "Roman step."

Italy to the German juggernaut. On March 11, 1938, he explained to Mussolini why he had grabbed Austria, and on September 29, they signed the Munich Agreement, which gave Hitler a free hand in eastern Europe, gave Mussolini nothing, and gave the world war.

Stalin, meanwhile, was consolidating his power by purging Russia's peasants, Army officers, and intellectual elite. A rock-like personality, devoid of humanity or fear, he was sustained by the same icy faith as the Spanish inquisitor Torquemada, who could do horrible things and then sleep like a child. Stalin's small frame, his withered left arm and pocked face, concealed a mixture of strength, vision, and ruse. He wrote dismally and spoke dully in heavy Georgian accents. Yet Mustapha Kemal said that "when the fame of all other dictators will have vanished," history would single out Stalin as the century's most important international statesman. Stalin was a brutal realist. After he had liquidated or starved millions of peasants, he remarked: "It is ridiculous to expatiate today on the expropriation of the kulaks. We do not lament the loss of the hair of one who has been beheaded."

While Stalin murdered and repressed, he also molded the apparatus for eventual war. He feared Germany, but even more, he feared a German alliance with the West. He permitted the Comintern to proclaim: "The conquest of power by Hitler does not signify a defeat for the Communist party." It is possible this assertion contained the first hint that Stalin wished to renew the old Seeckt-Lenin tie and make a deal with Hitler. There is evidence that Stalin sent Radek (who had dealt with Seeckt) in 1936 to discuss Polish partition with one of Hitler's secret-service colonels. Marshal Tukhachevski, the erstwhile collaborator with Seeckt, had prepared contingency plans for preventive war against the Nazis. Stalin's agents framed Tukhachevski and then executed him to betoken Moscow's desire for accommodation with Berlin.

While these murky events were taking place, the League of Nations was in the process of dissolution. Sixteen of its sixty-four members quit before World War II. And, starting with Greece's invasion of Turkey in 1920, wars again became commonplace. In 1931, a newly industrialized, bellicose Japan took advantage of a trumped-up "incident" on the South Manchuria

Railroad to conquer that wealthy portion of North China. A courageous United States Secretary of State, Henry Stimson, unsuccessfully sought international intervention. The Japanese created a puppet state called Manchukuo in the conquered province, and then, in 1937, invaded China proper, capturing its principal cities. In the summer of 1938 Japan's headstrong Army even clashed with Russia on the Manchukuo frontier. These Asiatic incursions saw the most brutal fighting and the most vicious savagery experienced by the world since 1918. They also exposed the frailty of international peace machinery and, while particularly horrifying the American people, reinforced the shelter of America's isolationist cocoon.

Mussolini, anxious to prove his new Fascist troops and to expand his new Roman Empire in Africa, provoked a border skirmish at Walwal, near the border of Ethiopia, in December, 1934. Although Emperor Haile Selassie appealed for help to the League of Nations, the League could do nothing because the Great Powers refused to intervene. On October 3, 1935, the attack came. Mussolini's own son-in-law, Count Galeazzo Ciano, led a bombing raid on Aduwa, and a carefully prepared expeditionary force then marched inland from Eritrea and Somaliland, strafing, gassing, and shelling Haile Selassie's ill-equipped tribal warriors. Britain left the Suez Canal open to Italian troop ships. Fascist forces, helped by a remarkable engineering corps, marched across mosquitoed swamps and craggy mountains to Addis Ababa; and Haile Selassie fled the country. The war lasted only six months and was marked by terrible atrocities. Vittorio Mussolini, the conqueror's son, wrote enthusiastically of an air attack: "One group of horsemen gave me the impression of a budding rose unfolding as the bomb fell in their midst and blew them up."

The wildest, bloodiest, and most heartrending of these lesser conflicts was the civil war in Spain, where Germany, Italy, and Russia tested weapons, tactics, and commanders. On July 18, 1936, a handful of well-financed right-wing generals, headed by forty-four-year-old Francisco Franco, led a military revolt against the weak Republic. Communists and liberal groups throughout the world joined to support the Republican militia, while Fascists and conservatives backed Franco. The Germans sent him tanks, planes, and ten thousand men; the Italians, another seventy-five thousand. The Russians sent planes, tanks, and ammu-

On July 18, 1936, Francisco Franco led
the army into military revolt against
the young Spanish republic. Hitler and
Mussolini sent weapons and troops to aid
the Fascist-led rebels. Although Russia
forwarded weapons and technicians to the
Loyalists, Britain, France, and the United
States maintained a strict neutrality.
Not surprisingly, Franco triumphed and
promptly joined the Rome–Berlin Axis.

nition to the Republican forces, plus some of their best officers, operating under aliases.

Spain aroused infinite passions and came to represent, in some weird prevision, the ideological fanaticism of World War II, so soon to explode. Before their own bodies and souls were torn on far greater battlefields, millions of people were caught in the emotional and symbolic Spanish vortex. Picasso painted his greatest picture, "Guernica," after Hitler's *Luftwaffe* first practiced mass bombing on that city. Hemingway wrote his finest novel about Republican guerrillas. Miguel de Unamuno, Spain's famous author, died of a broken heart, and the poet García Lorca was murdered. Georgi Dimitrov, later head of the Comintern, and Josip Broz, now called Marshal Tito, gained conspiratorial experience working for the Republican cause. André Malraux led an air squadron against Franco. Yet what the Spanish War lacked was another Goya. Only a Goya could describe the horrors committed by both sides: burned churches, raped nuns, massacred labor leaders, tortured intellectuals; the slaughter in a bull ring, the shooting of prisoners on the cold Castilian killing ground of Cuenca; the savagery of Spaniards against Spaniards, in the name of ideologies that were foreign to Spain.

While German tanks, bombers, and tacticians were being tested, Hitler turned his attention to the great Slavic plains that the Teutons long had coveted as living space, or *Lebensraum*. By seizing Austria, he managed to outflank a ring of fortifications that conglomerate Czechoslovakia had erected around its curved western frontier. Then, using the large German minority in the Czech Sudetenland, the *Führer* applied massive new pressures. A schoolteacher named Konrad Henlein, who much admired Hitler, succeeded brilliantly in Nazifying the Sudeten German minority, or *Volksdeutsch*. When Eduard Beneš, the solemn little soccer-playing Czechoslovak President, turned for help to his French allies and British friends, they cynically ignored him.

Initially, Beneš was resolute. I was in Prague as a newspaperman much of that fateful summer of 1938, and I remember how, on one hot afternoon in his baroque palace, he unrolled a large map and with pointer showed me which German cities he intended to bomb if Hitler invaded. He recited impressive military production figures from his famous Skoda and Tatra ordnance works. But Paris and London were more impressed by Hitler.

This picture of Chiang Kai-shek was taken
in November, 1936, just a month before
he was kidnapped and forced to join with
the Communists against the Japanese. After
1927 Chiang had adopted a policy of civil
war against the Communists, even though he
had once been chosen for training in Moscow,
and he did not, until coerced, waver from
this policy, even after the Japanese began
their aggressions in Manchuria in 1931.

Unctuous French statesmen, cautious generals who hoped to gain strength with time, and pro-German pressure groups in the British establishment persuaded Premier Daladier and the umbrella-toting Chamberlain to appease the Germans at Munich, sell out the Czechs, and proclaim that they had preserved peace. An argument still is heard that the twelve months purchased had value, but I agree with Churchill, who then commented: "You have gained shame and you will get war."

Axis dynamism thrust eastward. Mussolini invaded impoverished Albania on Good Friday, 1939, and King Zog, a tribal chieftain, fled into Greece with his family and all available gold, leaving behind a tiny rear guard.

That March, Hitler had already blandly violated pledges to make no further claims on the Czechs. He partitioned the rest of the country, installing his own satraps. Too late, the French and British issued territorial guarantees to Poland and Rumania and started negotiations with Russia. But by midsummer Stalin was not interested.

Thanks to his purges, the Soviet Army was in a state of confusion. The Red Air Force was no match for the *Luftwaffe*, which had developed so impressively from its Russian incubator. Furthermore, Stalin had lost all respect for the willpower of the West. He suspected that the inner intention of Daladier and Chamberlain was to encourage Hitler's embroilment with Russia by urging his attentions eastward across Czechoslovakia. He decided to reverse that political strategy and urge Hitler westward, hoping to see his capitalistic enemies destroy themselves against each other.

Hitler also was attracted by the thought of another German-Soviet deal, in the tradition of the Seeckt arrangements and Rapallo. He could eliminate potential threats from eastern Europe by partitioning it with Stalin, and then invade the West. On August 23, 1939, Molotov and Joachim von Ribbentrop, Hitler's Foreign Minister, signed a nonaggression pact in Moscow that arranged to divide Poland, granted Russia eventual sovereignty over the Baltic states, conceded a potential Soviet sphere in Finland, and gave Moscow a free hand to take Bessarabia from Rumania when it wished. Under a further secret protocol, Russia promised to supply Germany with raw materials and to join in suppressing Polish "agitation" after that country had been occupied.

World War II, already inevitable, was thus made imminent. A Polish boy born Armistice Day, 1918, when Poland was re-created, was not old enough to be killed fighting the German or Russian armies that would soon roll once again across his country.

August spun swiftly to September. There was tense anticipation in Berlin and stunned astonishment in Moscow. The French people marched wearily to their comfortable Maginot fortifications. Gloom and disappointment swept London. But in the United States, the cynosure for most eyes was the New York World's Fair, with its trylon and perisphere, its "Town of Tomorrow," its General Motors show, and a Japanese Shinto shrine enclosing a replica of our Liberty Bell, made of diamonds and pearls. The news from Europe was indeed dark, but Europe was, after all, a distant continent from which the United States had sensibly withdrawn.

II

Blitzkrieg

A German soldier heaves a "potato masher" grenade at resisting Poles.

By 1939 both Hitler and Stalin wanted war—although for different reasons. Until then, Hitler had judged correctly that he could attain his goals without fighting. He believed that France and Britain no longer had the will to risk another generation on the battlefield and that they would cede what he wished. "Why should I demoralize him [the enemy] by military means," he asked, "if I can do so better and more cheaply in other ways?"

Nevertheless, the *Führer* became giddy with success and determined to shed the "corrupting" influence of peace. Prior to Munich, the German General Staff had warned that an attack on Czechoslovakia would mean war with the West, and that defeat in such a war would be a certainty. But when Western resolve collapsed at Munich, Hitler interpreted the Munich pact as permission by Paris and London for him to drive eastward with a free hand. The Anglo-French guarantee of Poland seemed a deception. Therefore he resolved to smash the West—with Russia's tacit help.

Stalin, for his part, was resolved to do nothing to help the inept Paris and London Governments. He proclaimed that Moscow would not be drawn into "conflicts by the warmongers who are accustomed to have other countries pull the chestnuts out of the fire for them." On March 10, 1939, when the likelihood of war was mounting, he told his Eighteenth Party Congress that he intended "to allow the belligerents to sink deeply into the mire of war . . . to allow them to exhaust and weaken one another; and then, when they have become weak enough, to appear on the scene with fresh strength, to appear, of course, in the interest of peace and to dictate conditions to the enfeebled belligerents." He was therefore ready to accept Hitler's bribe of eastern Poland, the Baltic States, and Bessarabia in exchange for pledging the security of the German rear in any confrontation with the West. The fact that hundreds of thousands of anti-Nazis from these bartered territories were eventually sent by Moscow to German concentration camps, while hundreds of thousands of anti-Stalinists were sent by Berlin to Soviet concentration camps, disturbed neither dictator.

All spring and summer of 1939, while his agents were feeling out Russian intentions, Hitler made plans for a lightning assault on Poland. By April 3, he had already issued his directive for the attack, known as Case White. There was no longer much effort to obscure extensive military preparations. Arms and Nazi thugs disguised as tourists were dispatched to the Germanic free city of Danzig, on the Baltic.

Poland was a particularly desirable target. About a third of its population was of non-Polish stock. Its leaders too often showed excessive ambition and limited talent. Its flat, fertile fields, protected by antiquated matériel, offered optimum conditions for the Germans to experiment with their new blitzkrieg—lightning war.

Huge German armies were concentrated on two sides of the chosen victim, in Pomerania, East Prussia, Silesia, and subdued Czechoslovakia, and a series of armed incidents and provocations was carefully orchestrated to inflame the border. Although the Pope, President Roosevelt, and the King of Belgium appealed for peace, the Germans merely prepared a sixteen-point ultimatum that they knew to be unacceptable and published it before allowing the Poles to turn it down. At 4:45 A.M., September 1, they attacked. Two days later France and Britain declared war on Germany, and Ribbentrop invited the Soviet Government to move into Poland from the east.

Fifty-six German divisions, nine of them armored, rumbled toward Warsaw, Bialystok, Cracow, and Lvov, under a galaxy of generals whose clumsy Teuton names, like mortar crumps, were soon to be feared from the Caspian to the Channel: von Küchler, Guderian, von Kluge, von Reichenau, List, von Bock. The brave but antiquated forces of Marshal Edward Smigly-Rydz, the Polish commander, were squeezed to death in one gigantic pincer. Fifteen hundred *Luftwaffe* planes, including Stuka dive bombers with their terrifying whistles, smashed gravely baroque Polish towns and wooden villages festooned with harvest symbols. The Poles fought bravely, but their old-fashioned infantry, lancers, and armor proved useless. The Polish Government fled Warsaw to Lublin on September 6. On the seventeenth, surrounded by thousands of refugees riding everything from barrows to fire engines, the Government crossed the Rumanian border near Cernăuti (now incorporated in the Soviet Union). Eventually it established itself in Paris and then London, the first of those pitiful exile cabinets to become so commonplace in World War II.

Poland was squashed like an egg. Britain and France, although they proclaimed belligerency, did nothing helpful. On September 17, the day the German pincer snapped shut south of Warsaw,

German troops demolish a border barricade
at the start of the invasion of Poland on
September 1. Clearly superior, Hitler's
forces waged their assault with unwarranted
brutality. The Polish Army and Air Force
were antiquated; those of Germany were the
most modern in the world. The valor of
the Poles proved futile, as on one occasion
when a brigade of horse cavalry armed with
lances attacked a Nazi tank column.

the Polish ambassador in Moscow was handed a note announcing that the Soviet-Polish nonaggression pact was void. The explanation was curt. "A Polish state no longer exists," and the Red Army was moving in "to protect White Russian and Ukrainian minorities in Poland."

Isolated Warsaw fought with exemplary fortitude. There was no bread; the bakers had been mobilized. A few barrage balloons were hoisted above the smoking city, and trenches were dug in the outskirts. Surrounding roads were encumbered by peasant carts and by corpses. Day after day the radio broadcast Chopin's "Military Polonaise" and appeals for "the quickest aid" from France and Britain.

Walter Schellenberg, chief of Hitler's espionage service, described Warsaw after its surrender on September 27: "I was shocked at what had become of the beautiful city I had known—ruined and burnt-out houses, starving and grieving people. The nights were already unpleasantly chilly and a pall of dust and smoke hung over the city, and everywhere there was the sweetish smell of burnt flesh. . . . Warsaw was a dead city."

The end came on September 28, when Warsaw, Modlin, and a few scattered military units in the hinterland gave up. That same day, in Moscow, Ribbentrop and Molotov signed a treaty, completing Poland's fourth partition. Germany took some 71,000 square miles; Russia, about 75,000. The Germans admitted to having lost 10,572 killed and claimed 450,000 prisoners. The Russians suffered almost no losses. They rounded up a huge Polish force, whose officers were incarcerated. Most of them were later murdered in the Katyn forest. Temporarily freed from preoccupation with the East, the *Wehrmacht* turned its attentions westward. Britain and France found themselves faced at last with war.

Then, a sudden new explosion burst on the distant Baltic. Russia, intent on securing every advantage offered by its cynical pact with Hitler, decided to subdue Finland. Provocation was nonexistent, and the formula was blunt. The Soviets invited Helsinki to send a negotiator to the Kremlin, October 5, 1939, to discuss Moscow's demand for cession of territory on the Karelian Isthmus, exchange of woodlands in the north, and the right to establish a Russian naval base in the Finnish gulf. The suggestions were not acceptable to the Finns, and on November 30, after denouncing another nonaggression pact, Soviet planes bombed Helsinki and Viipuri. The Red Army rumbled across Finland's border at five different points. The vapid League of

Nations responded by expelling the Soviet Union.

It was evident from the start that Stalin's myrmidons must win this patently unequal conquest. But the Finns proved to be hardy warriors, while the enormous Soviet Army showed itself badly trained, ill equipped, and above all, poorly led. Purges in the Red Army officer corps had upset the command structure. Furthermore, the Russians, deceived by their own propaganda, had expected to be hailed as liberators by an enthusiastic proletariat. Instead, they were slaughtered by careful artillery barrages and expert rifle marksmanship. Their loosely organized supply lines were easily severed by Finnish ski patrols. White-uniformed Finnish infantry knifed Soviet patrols in the long nights and blocked off entire battalions on the edges of frozen lakes. There the Russian troops congealed into awkward agonies of death. One eyewitness wrote: "For four miles the road and forest were strewn with the bodies of men and horses. . . . The corpses were frozen as hard as petrified wood."

Despite their valor, the Finns could expect but limited aid from the slow-moving Allies and the wary Scandinavian neutrals. The Swedes transgressed their neutral affirmations by sending eager but limited numbers of volunteers; the British and French permitted a few adventurous handfuls to participate; the Americans cheered lustily; and the Russians won. The sheer weight of their matériel, of their massive if clumsy gunnery and their aerial onslaught, plus the bravery of their bewildered infantry, managed an ultimate penetration. Helsinki capitulated. It granted Moscow even greater concessions than those originally asked.

The Russians both lost and gained by this dismal experience. They lost in the sense that Finland was thrust uncomfortably into German arms, but they won in that they were forced to realize their own defects. Old-fashioned officer ranks were restored, after years of experimentation with less formalized discipline. Attention was paid to the need for modernizing equipment and training and, above all, for revising fundamental concepts of strategy. The costly and humiliating Finnish campaign in a sense could be said to have saved Russia from absolute disaster when the final Nazi onslaught came in 1941.

The Finland episode shifted the attention of the main adversaries to Scandinavia. The Norwegian port of Narvik, which was linked by a railroad over the mountains to Sweden's iron mines, had been used in a small way to supply the Finnish armies. With

The Nazis execute a captured Pole, whose
corpse will fall into the pit containing
his fellow dead. Conquered Poland had
disappeared from the map and sunk into a
nightmare of Nazi barbarism, in which the
people, contemptuously deemed "sub-human"
by their captors, were enslaved, brutalized,
and often exterminated. No other occupied
country suffered as much as Poland.

British strategic interest beginning to focus on Germany's industrial dependence on Swedish iron, the Admiralty studied means of blockading this route, unaware that Hitler had been tentatively planning the occupation of Norwegian bases as early as October of 1939. By April 8, when London and Paris proclaimed they had mined the area south of Narvik, a Nazi invasion was already secretly under way. The very next night, Hitler's forces landed in Norway while the *Wehrmacht* rolled unopposed across Denmark.

Although the German fleet was no match for the Royal Navy, by stealth and efficiency it succeeded in landing sufficient troops in Norway, and the *Luftwaffe* achieved prompt superiority, enabling it to offset British naval power. The Norwegians showed an intense will to resist, fighting vigorously and sinking several Nazi vessels. But the Allies came late with little. Vidkun Quisling, a local Nazi, arose to help the insidious aggression, thereby adding his name to history's leaden roll of traitors.

The notable but miniature campaigns fought by British and French expeditionary forces at Namsos, Andalsnes, and Trondheim are today, outside Norway itself, remembered primarily on regimental rosters. The Royal Navy managed to land a considerable army around Narvik, but the R.A.F. was based too far away to provide the desperately needed cover. Resolute German defenses succeeded in first discouraging and then repulsing inexperienced Allied troops, who were pinned against the sea and eventually routed when Hitler overwhelmed France.

The Danish King Christian X yielded with dispatch and locked himself in his castle. The King of Norway, Haakon VII, fled with his Government to London. And the few French and British, aided by disorganized Norwegian bands, found themselves doomed along the northern fiords. Winston Churchill concluded: "We, who had the command of the sea and could pounce anywhere on an undefended coast, were outpaced by the enemy moving by land across very large distances in the face of every obstacle." Hitler's ruthless audacity succeeded in sealing off Europe's northern flank, insuring access to Sweden's invaluable iron, and closing off the Baltic.

From late summer, 1939, until late spring, 1940, the British and French gave the appearance of being removed from the conflict they had accepted. Britain, with all its sea power, mustered only small overseas land expeditions, for which it was able to grant only marginal air support. The French, comfortable in their casemates, sent a gallant group to Norway, talked of their audacious army, and waited for the inevitable showdown. President Roosevelt sought to intervene, but he found no peace.

On May 10, the so-called Phony War, eight months of watching and waiting along the principal Western front, came to a sudden end. Hitler attacked Holland, Belgium, and Luxembourg. On the same day, Winston Churchill became Britain's Prime Minister. "I was sure I should not fail," he wrote later. "I slept soundly and had no need for cheering dreams."

Case Yellow, as the Germans named their carefully devised plan for the swift defeat of France, called for an armored thrust through the Ardennes, past Sedan to the Channel coast at Abbeville, in which tanks, followed by motorized infantry and protected by Stuka dive bombers, would thrust forward to join paratroops landed behind the Allied lines. For this purpose, a gigantic force of about one hundred and seventeen divisions was disposed, seventy-five of which took part in the initial attack under Generals Fedor von Bock and Gerd von Rundstedt. The offensive depended on lancing north of the Maginot Line through nonbelligerent Luxembourg, Belgium, and Holland. Hermann Göring's airborne forces were assigned the task of reducing the Dutch, while armored wedges pierced Luxembourg, swung across Belgium, and entered France. The fortresses around Liège were captured with surprising ease by Nazi engineers and paratroopers who had trained for the assault against full-scale replicas of the Belgian defenses. At Fort Eben Emael, the most vital of these strongholds, some twelve hundred Belgian defenders capitulated to only eighty Germans.

The German juggernaut rolled through thirty-six British, French, and Belgian divisions while its sapper units constructed pontoon bridges across waterways. By May 19, the panzers, led by newly rising commanders such as von Kleist and Rommel, had smashed a great gap in the northwestern Maginot Line and joined a vast army grunting southward from Belgium.

On May 28, the Belgians surrendered unconditionally. King Leopold, refusing the appeals of his ministers to flee and carry on the fight, chose to capitulate and sought solitude in a quiet castle near Brussels, where he later married a beautiful Flemish girl. The Belgian surrender exposed the entire left flank of the Anglo-French defenses, and France itself was crumbling fast.

Cartoonist Herblock neatly satirized
Stalin's standard practice of claiming
self-defense as his excuse for attacking
a smaller nation. The Finns, although
tremendously outnumbered and at a severe
disadvantage in planes, guns, and tanks,
were able at first, through superior
tactics, leadership, and adaptability, to
fight their ponderous foe to a standstill
and inflict dreadful losses on them.

The *Wehrmacht* had accomplished a shattering triumph. Within a few weeks it had disintegrated a French army that considered itself Europe's finest; and this was done by superior quality of command, weapons, techniques, and soldiery, not by an advantage in quantity. Indeed, Hitler's armies actually were inferior in numbers and had fewer tanks. The combined Anglo-French forces alone disposed four thousand armored vehicles, against twenty-eight hundred for Germany. The French tanks were superior in both armor and gun caliber, although slower and more difficult to control. Only in the air and in the skill of handling troops were Hitler's forces superior. What a harvest they reaped from this advantage!

The battle of Dunkirk, which reached its peak May 30, was one of the remarkable moments of British history. By a miracle of improvisation an Allied army of 338,226, which appeared to be hopelessly cut off on the French Channel coast, was taken away by more than a thousand hastily mustered boats. Virtually every English ship afloat had been pressed into service by the Admiralty to save the men at Dunkirk. There were French fishing boats, coasters, paddle steamers, colliers, yachts, lifeboats from sunken ships. And these were manned by Royal Navy veterans and merchant seamen, by dentists, stevedores, taxi drivers, farmers, civil servants, and downy-faced Sea Scouts. Swung by tides, stranded in shallows beside the burning beach, harried by airplanes that hunted them by night with parachute flares and riddled them by day with tracers, this extraordinary flotilla headed across the cluttered Channel waters for a shore that was black with men—and took them off.

Dunkirk was typical of a British strategy that specializes in losing battles and winning wars. It was a dreadful affair, but the survivors—and their number was astonishing—became the heart of a new army that would one day march through London in the Victory Parade.

The total number of British troops either killed, wounded, or taken prisoner at Dunkirk came to 68,111. Field Marshal von Rundstedt, whose Army Group A held the British in its grasp, later said: "If I had had my way the English would not have got off so lightly at Dunkirk. But my hands were tied by direct orders from Hitler himself. While the English were clambering into the ships off the beaches, I was kept uselessly outside the port unable to move. I recommended to the Supreme Command that my five panzer divisions be immediately sent into the town

A mother and her children wander dazedly
through the ruins of a devastated landscape
after a German air raid over Belgium.
Despite powerful forces sent by France and
Great Britain to join the Belgian Army,
the Germans maintained their advantage with
blitzkrieg tactics and almost endless
rehearsals for the siege of Fort Eben Emael.

and thereby completely destroy the retreating English. But I received definite orders from the Führer that under no circumstances was I to attack. . . ."

Hitler had consigned the Dunkirk annihilation task to Göring's *Luftwaffe*, for several reasons. He feared the cost to his straining tanks of direct ground assault over difficult terrain while the French armies to the south had not yet been destroyed. He overrated the destructive power of air bombardment. And finally, he seems to have had vague thoughts that perhaps, once France had fallen, he could force a swift peace upon the British.

Of all Hitler's misjudgments, those concerning Britain were the most profound. He didn't think they would fight in 1939; he didn't think they would persevere in 1940; and until late 1942, it never occurred to him that the British might actually win.

Meanwhile France dissolved, militarily and morally. General Maxime Weygand, then seventy-three years old, replaced General Maurice Gamelin as supreme commander. Weygand, a fine fighting man, came too late. He attempted to stand on the Somme and Aisne rivers, but on June 5, the Germans hit this feeble line like a pile driver and drove through to the Seine. Nazi propaganda encouraged tales of terror and a mass flight of civilians, who blocked important roads to both the retreating French and the pursuing German armies. On June 12, Paris was declared an open city. Two days later the German forces entered, clattering down empty avenues. Only one cafe was open on the broad Champs-Élysées. Within hours, the swastika flew from public buildings.

Hitler thus obliterated the army he supposed to be his greatest enemy, at a cost of only 27,074 German dead. And in Rome, on June 10, on a balcony above the Piazza Venezia, protruding his jaw to obscure the fatness of his chops, Mussolini announced to the cheers of a huge crowd carefully assembled below that Italy had joined the fray. Ciano, his son-in-law and Minister of Foreign Affairs, whom Mussolini later ordered shot, confided to his diary: "I am sad, very sad. The adventure begins. May God help Italy." President Roosevelt said in a speech at the University of Virginia: "The hand that held the dagger has struck it into the back of its neighbor." A huge new army and a sizable navy and air force thus entered the war.

Once the Germans took Paris, it was evident that the conflict in western Europe was over. Even the silly old Kaiser, exiled in Holland, wired Hitler congratulating his former corporal on "the mighty victory granted by God." Premier Paul Reynaud and his

British soldiers on the beach at Dunkirk
fire at Nazi planes with their rifles.
The rescue of a third of a million Allied
troops succeeded through a combination
of fortuitous factors. Strangest of these
was Hitler's order that halted his panzers
short of Dunkirk, leaving the *Luftwaffe* to
contend alone with the trapped army.

Government fled south to Bordeaux and sent a junior cabinet official, Brigadier General Charles de Gaulle, to London to discuss ways of transporting forces to North Africa. De Gaulle was much impressed by the vigor of British resolve and even brought back to France an offer from Churchill for a Franco-British union with a joint defense program, joint economy, and joint citizenship for all Englishmen and Frenchmen. But the rot of despair had gone too far.

The offer was ignored. The Reynaud cabinet resigned on June 16, and Marshal Philippe Pétain, an august symbol of French glory whose body but not whose mind had survived World War I, took power. He was backed by the fleet commander, Admiral Jean Louis Darlan, and by Pierre Laval, a brilliant but unscrupulously ambitious politician who saw a future for France only as triumphant Germany's mistress. Pétain asked for an armistice, later claiming that he had thus "performed an act of salvation."

On June 22, 1940, the French surrender was formally signed at the same clearing in Compiègne forest, north of Paris, where Marshal Ferdinand Foch had dictated terms to Germany in November, 1918. The identical railway car, hitherto kept as a museum piece, was wheeled out of its shed to serve as the parlor for France's funeral. It was a lovely, warm day. Hitler stood with Göring and other gloating chieftains while General Wilhelm Keitel, chief of his Supreme Command, began reading out the conditions to the French delegation. Hitler didn't wait. Followed by Göring, Hess, Ribbentrop, and a strut of officers, he walked out of the rickety Pullman toward a French monument honoring Alsace and Lorraine. The band played "Deutschland über Alles" and the "Horst Wessel Lied," a Nazi party song commemorating an ignominious street-fighting thug.

The armistice provided that German troops would occupy more than half of France, including the entire Atlantic coastline. The French Army was demobilized and its fleet rendered immobile. France yielded its German prisoners and any German refugees Berlin wanted. French prisoners were left in the Reich. Hitler had three objectives: to establish a French Government in the unoccupied zone that would help him extract what he needed materially from France; to prevent Darlan's fleet from joining Britain; and to frustrate any support for Britain. He clearly hoped to turn the French slowly against the British if the latter refused to transact with him, a possibility he had been sounding out through an intermediary in Sweden.

The British, however, were resolute. Churchill expressed to the House of Commons "brotherly sentiment for the French people" but promised to fight on without mercy. And he was determined to keep alive the embers of resistance in smoking Europe. Here he was to find aid from a virtually unheard-of leader.

Charles de Gaulle, at forty-nine the youngest general officer in France, was little known except by military theorists. But Churchill appreciated his pugnacity and took the initiative in allowing him to broadcast an appeal to the French people. On June 18, a text of less than three hundred words was read aloud by "Moi, le général de Gaulle," summoning Frenchmen and Frenchwomen throughout the world to carry on the fight. There were only a few of them in Britain: veterans from the Norway campaign, refugees from Dunkirk, pilots, seamen, diplomats, and a purchasing mission headed by Jean Monnet. Inside dazed France, de Gaulle's words were heard by only a small number of people; among them were Pierre Mendès-France, a future premier, and Maurice Schumann, later a minister, who was in a railway station that was being bombed at that very instant. At Locminé, a small Breton town through which a German motorized unit was rumbling, a youth ran into the central square to shout: "A general has just spoken on the radio and said that we must continue to fight. His name was de Gaulle." An old woman, hanging to the arm of a priest, murmured, "It is my son." Twelve days later she died.

And so the preposterous first phase concluded. Stalin swiftly and brutally carried out the remaining privileges allotted him by his pact with Hitler. He sent an ambassador to Pétain's Vichy and ordered his troops into Latvia, Lithuania, and Estonia. In the wake of a hasty ultimatum, he took Rumania's Bessarabia and north Bucovina provinces. From the Black Sea across Poland to Finland and the Arctic, a huge band of territory, once czarist, was returned to Russian control. Although Moscow had arguable legal claims to the area, the method of expressing them was appalling.

Strangely enough, it was also in a grim sense the final payment for that deal with Seeckt that initially had permitted German militarism to revive, long before it waxed amid Allied lassitude. But the Kremlin's calculation that in revenge for inept Western diplomacy it could sit back while Europe tore itself to pieces and then move in as arbiter, proved wrong. The price that Russia eventually paid in blood was terrible and huge.

III
England Alone

A barrage balloon floats above London's
Tower Bridge in 1940. These balloons were
anchored by steel cables that discouraged
low-flying enemy planes.

Remember him, for he saved all of you: pudgy and not very large but somehow massive and indomitable; baby-faced, with snub nose, square chin, rheumy eyes on occasion given to tears; a thwarted actor's taste for clothes that would have looked ridiculous on a less splendid man. He wore the quaintest hats of anyone: tinted square bowlers; great flat sombreros squashed down on his head; naval officers' caps rendered just slightly comic by the huge cigar protruding beneath the peak. On grave and critical occasions he sported highly practical Teddy-bear suits few grown men would dare to wear in public. He fancied oil painting, at which he was good, writing, at which he was excellent, and oratory, at which he was magnificent. His habits were somewhat owlish (a bird he faintly resembled), and he stayed up late at night, often working mornings in bed with a lap tray for his desk. (Once, after the war, when I called on him at 11:00 A.M., he inquired whether I wished a drink, ordered me a whiskey and soda, then, reaching for the empty glass beside him, told his manservant: "And bring me another.")

This was the man, blooded at Omdurman and Cuba, among the Pathans and the Boers, long before most of those he led were even born, who guided Britain to victory in World War II—and, one might add, who was the guiding spirit for the whole Free World. For had Britain succumbed, as it had every logical reason to do in 1940, probably no successful coalition could have been formed.

Winston Churchill once complained that democracy is the worst system of government—except for all the others. And it was democracy, with its curious and lethargic workings, that, allied with its Russian antithesis, produced Hitler's defeat. One may argue that the *Führer's* strategic errors caused his ultimate downfall: that he allowed Britain's Army to escape him at Dunkirk; that he misjudged Germany's strength in attacking Russia; that he overextended himself both at El Alamein and Stalingrad. But it was not in the end the negative factor of Nazi miscalculation but the positive factor of democratic vigor that brought the German *Götterdämmerung*. This democratic vigor, freely voiced in a moment of bleak despair, produced Churchill as Prime Minister and a government resolved to win the war.

Even before France collapsed, an irate House of Commons had summoned the irresolute and gullible Neville Chamberlain

NATIONAL DEFENCE COMPANIES HOME DEFENCE

EX-SERVICE MEN

between the ages of 45 and 51
are required to enlist in the
NATIONAL DEFENCE COMPANIES
(Territorial Army Reserve)
FOR 4 YEARS
with the option of re-engagement

Personnel will be required to
perform a number of
DRILLS EACH YEAR
for which they will receive pay and
travelling expenses

When called up for service personnel
will receive a **BOUNTY of £5-**
TRAVELLING EXPENSES
to place of joining -
PAY at current **ARMY RATES**
and all usual allowances.

This poster urges Britain's ex-servicemen between the ages of forty-five and fifty-one to enlist in the home guards. After the fall of France, Britain rallied to prepare for what would likely be a fight for survival. Besides bolstering home defense, beaches were manned against invasion and London children were sent to the country, beyond the reach of the bombings that were certain to come.

to defend the conduct of the Norwegian debacle. It was no longer a party matter; the nation's life was evidently at stake. Clement Attlee, the Labor leader, said: "We cannot afford to leave our destinies in the hands of failures." Arthur Greenwood added: "Wars are not won by masterly withdrawals." The retired Fleet Admiral, Sir Roger Keyes, appearing in full uniform, thundered that the Norwegian disaster was "a shocking story of ineptitude which I assure the House ought never to have happened." And spry little Leopold Amery, a staunch Conservative, told the Government, in Cromwell's famous words: "You have sat too long here for any good you have been doing. Depart, I say, and let us have done with you. In the name of God, go!"

Churchill had loyally served Chamberlain as First Lord of the Admiralty and accepted ministerial responsibility for his share of the Norway mess. But even old Lloyd George, arising as it were from the grave of an earlier Great War, urged that "Mr. Churchill will not allow himself to be converted into an air-raid shelter to keep the splinters from hitting his colleagues." Chamberlain won an initial vote of confidence, but two days later, on May 10, as the Nazis launched their attack on the Low Countries, he resigned and designated Churchill to succeed him. Churchill named a national coalition government of all three parties and set his jaw in the bulldog expression that was to become so famous.

Although Hitler did not know it at the time, this political event was the single greatest disaster he would experience. Without Churchill's skill and determination, it is doubtful that Britain could or would have carried on the fight long enough for the German invasion of the Soviet Union and the Japanese bombing of Pearl Harbor to take effect. When Russia and the United States went to war, there was still a fortified island position bristling off the shores of occupied Europe and the remnants of a global empire bounded by the pulsing power of the sea.

This was a power with which Britain's new leader was entirely familiar. In his correspondence with Roosevelt he called himself "Former Naval Person." He had headed the Admiralty in World War I and the early days of World War II. In a long life of adventuring, he had seen how ships, properly deployed, could nourish beleaguered peoples, outflank armies, and frustrate the plans of even the most brilliant and successful generals. With a Royal Navy virtually intact; with a friendly United States led by another naval enthusiast; with the wealth and geographical facilities of empire; with the knowledge that the British people were thoroughly behind him; and with the suspicion that sulking Europe might eventually gnaw at its conqueror's vitals, Churchill took over, never doubting that he would succeed.

Britain's military preparedness at the war's start was sadly lacking, but the quantitative deficiency was made up for, in part, by a qualitative genius. A committee at the Air Ministry, under the scientist-educator Sir Henry Tizard, acted as broker to float new scientific issues, accelerating research and development. Relying on studies by the brilliant inventor Sir Robert Watson-Watt, Tizard rushed through a radar system far superior to similar German devices. The Nazis soon found their U-boats being bombed at night when they surfaced to recharge batteries, and their bombers being attacked in the darkness long before they had approached their targets.

While building up the protection of the home islands and strengthening their ties with bastions around the world, Churchill bottled up the French fleet and then began to nibble at boastful Italy. He refused to heed his admirals who counseled that Britain should abandon the east Mediterranean to Mussolini and instead slowly took the offensive there. He pushed convoys through to embattled Malta and across the hostile narrows on to Egypt.

At home, the British imagination had been busy picturing the horrors of aerial assault. *Ordeal*, a novel by Nevil Shute, published in 1939, depicted nerve-wracking days and nights of steady bombing, when civilians would be forced to live in backyard dugouts, with a shortage of food, polluted water, flooded sewers, and curtailed electricity and gas. Britain made ready for such a nightmare. A million and a half women and children were evacuated from the cities; blackouts were enforced; most people carried gas masks; hospitals were made ready for hundreds of anticipated victims.

After the fall of France there was a threat of immediate invasion. On July 16, the *Führer* ordered secret preparations for Operation Sea Lion, a landing on England's southern coast. Three days later, in an effort to avoid an amphibious campaign, which his generals warned against, Hitler publicly offered Churchill peace in exchange for recognition of Nazi domination of western Europe and a return of Germany's former colonies. The offer was ignored. After a heavy *Luftwaffe* raid on Channel convoys and southern British ports, it became clear that a new kind of battle, a purely aerial assault, had been launched against the resolute British.

The numerical odds were most adverse. Churchill's R.A.F.

The deep tunnels of London's subway system
provided air-raid shelter for hundreds of
thousands during the Blitz. Though German
bombing missions arriving under conditions
of good visibility usually aimed first
for the dock areas, airdromes, and other
strategic targets, all pretense of military
justification was soon dropped and the
bombings became an instrument of terror to
destroy the city and break civilian morale.

had but 704 serviceable aircraft, 620 of which were taut little Hurricane and Spitfire fighters. The Germans possessed 1,392 bombers and 1,290 fighters deployed for immediate action. All through July and August they intensified their attack on airfields and radar stations along the vulnerable south and east coasts. On August 15, a thousand German planes took part in various actions. Nine days later, Göring decided that 50 per cent of British Fighter Command had been destroyed, and he began to throw the *Luftwaffe* against London itself. With squadrons of up to forty bombers each, escorted by more than one hundred fighters, he hoped to smash the huge imperial center. And indeed, he nearly succeeded. When the *Luftwaffe* shifted to night bombing tactics on September 7, almost one fourth of the R.A.F.'s pilots had been lost.

This was a brave and extraordinary period in English history. All along the coast, metallic loudspeakers hollered: "Squadron. Red Section. Scramble"; and the little eagles climbed into the sky, aimed by the radar beams of Tizard and Watson-Watt. "This wicked man," said Churchill, ". . . this monstrous product of former wrongs and shame, has now resolved to break our famous island race by a process of indiscriminate slaughter and destruction." But the British responded to the challenge, and the *Luftwaffe* paid heavily. The R.A.F. lost 915 fighters during the 1940 Battle of Britain, but they claimed to have shot down 2,698 *Luftwaffe* planes.

By September 17, Hitler acknowledged the indefinite postponement of Sea Lion. Never, as Churchill was to say, had so many owed so much to so few—youngsters like Richard Hillary: "Then I was pulling out, so hard that I could feel my eyes dropping through my neck. Coming around in a slow climbing turn, I saw that we had broken them up"; or like Johnnie Johnson: ". . . the wicked tracer sparkles and flashes over the top of your own cockpit and you break into a tight turn. . . . You black out! And you ease the turn to recover in a grey, unreal world of spinning horizons. . . . You have lost too much height and your opponent has gone—disappeared."

When Hitler's aerial campaign failed to crush R.A.F. defenses, he changed it into a punitive assault on London, designed to break the spirit of the British people. The British turned from the Battle of Britain to what they dubbed "the Blitz," a terrifying, thunderous, brutal assault primarily on civilians. On August 24, 1940, the first German bombs struck London, and Churchill promptly ordered a retaliation raid on Berlin. Hitler furiously announced: "If they attack our cities, we will simply rub out theirs." And he tried. There was vast destruction along the blazing Thames, but neither the British Government nor the economic machinery of London was paralyzed. The population managed courageously to continue its daily functions while in its spare time beating out flames and minimizing destruction. "Disposal Squads" marked off and defused delayed-action bombs. Air raid wardens sanded or hosed incendiary blazes among toppling buildings from Coventry to Bristol.

The summer of 1940 was a historic moment for Europe. The abandonment of Operation Sea Lion, leaving an undefeated German Army stranded on the Channel beaches, marked the beginning of Hitler's defeat. The example and the success of Churchill served as a glowing reminder to occupied European peoples that, as in the days of Napoleon, a dictatorial land power need not succeed in ultimately triumphing over an intact sea power. And in secret, underground fashion, a susurrous continental resistance to the Nazis started.

To help this, the British in 1940 established an organization known as the Special Operations Executive. It began to organize subversion and sabotage in German-occupied lands, aided by skillful propaganda broadcasts by the B.B.C. with its clever Morse code signal, V—for Victory. Slowly but remorselessly, in Poland, France, Belgium, Holland, and Norway, a collection of agents and adventurers, mostly amateur, threw back into the teeth of the German General Staff the cautionary words of the great Prussian military theorist, General Karl von Clausewitz: "Armed civilians cannot and should not be employed against the main force of the enemy, or even against sizable units. They should not try to crack the core, but only nibble along the surface and on the edges." And as another reminder of Napoleonic days, the first of Lord Louis Mountbatten's famous Combined Operations and Commando units began to experiment with the tactics and mechanics of small amphibious assaults.

During this summer of Hitler's first frustration, Stalin decided to collect what was left on the bill for his German pact. In June he successively completed the occupation of the three little Baltic states, Lithuania, Latvia, and Estonia, and five days after notifying Germany of his intention, he seized Bessarabia from Rumania. Sir Stafford Cripps, Churchill's new ambassador to Moscow, sought to convince the master of the Kremlin that Hitler was a

In the bombing of Coventry, the cathedral
was completely gutted. This historic
city, which had aircraft and machine-tool
factories, became the first victim of
Göring's decision to destroy the great
Midlands industrial centers that produced
Britain's war materials. Although some
seventy thousand homes were laid waste,
Coventry's factories continued to operate
throughout the indiscriminate bombings.

danger "to the Soviet Union as well as England." He urged that the two countries should "agree on a common policy of self-protection," and he secretly offered a bribe—the promise to recognize Russia's claims in the Dardanelles and to give her a leading role in the Balkans. But Stalin turned a deaf ear.

It soon became evident that Germany was also looking to that part of eastern Europe it had not already conquered, where Russia was inching forward and where Italy, having entered the war without Hitler's permission and somewhat to his dismay, had staked its own claim. On August 30, 1940, Ribbentrop and Ciano signed an agreement in Vienna awarding 40 per cent of Rumania's Transylvania province to Hungary and the southern part of Rumanian Dobruja to Bulgaria. I accompanied the ragtag Hungarian army into Rumania as far as Cluj, where Admiral Miklós Horthy, Hungary's chief of state, balanced uneasily on a white circus horse at the head of a victory parade. I then joined the noisy Bulgarian troops as they poured into Rumania from the south, winding up in the hot streets of Balchik, where gypsy children begged for handouts. King Carol, the dissolute Rumanian monarch, loaded a train with his mistress, his closest friends and courtiers, and all the valuables he could pack, and fled.

On October 28, again without asking Hitler's advice, Mussolini attacked Greece from Albania, expecting a swift and easy victory. But the courageous Greeks forgot their political differences and astonished the world by beating back the Italians and invading Albania themselves. I was also with that army, whose gallantry and conceit were formidable. Rickety trucks bounced to the front over impossible roads, bearing Hellenic fishermen and farmers. They rode to death and glory with garlands over their ears and their rifle muzzles stuffed with flowers, shouting "On to Rome." Antiquated mountain artillery was trundled along ridge combs to shell the Fascists in the valleys. Evzone guard patrols attacked with their knives and teeth, biting the scared little Italian infantrymen. I visited a forward prisoner's cage that included dozens of frightened Fascists with tooth wounds in their shabbily bandaged necks. The *Duce*'s highly touted air force, furthermore, proved inaccurate and timid and was soon largely offset by a handful of British planes rushed to Greece from the Middle East. Churchill sent Sir Anthony Eden and General Sir John Dill to Athens to investigate the possibility of opening a land front against the Axis in Europe. He cautioned them: "Do not consider yourselves obligated to a Greek enterprise if in your hearts you feel it will only be another Norwegian fiasco. If no good plan can be made please say so." I talked with Eden at length; he was sufficiently impressed by the chances to take the gamble. Early in 1941, Britain began to move troops from Egypt into Greece.

In the long run, this decision was to have a profound and helpful strategic effect on the war, even though the British expeditionary force was smashed successively in Greece and Crete. Hitler had already reached the basic conclusion that since he could not use his Army directly against England, he would strike at Russia. As an initial step, he had begun moving divisions eastward from France into Poland and had signed a "transit agreement" allowing him to send troops into Finland, although that country had been cynically allotted to the Soviet sphere. The *Führer* then sent Rumania what was called a military mission. I pointed out in dispatches that this "mission" was headed by the same general who had led the Nazi military "mission" that had destroyed Rotterdam earlier that year, and that it comprised many regiments. Those days in Bucharest, it was hard to shove one's way to the bar and order a drink among all those fat-necked, stodgy Nazis talking openly about the coming war with Russia.

The Rumanian "mission" was followed by an accord permitting Germany to send troops into Bulgaria. This surrounding pressure understandably frightened the Yugoslavs. Their cultivated and gentlemanly regent, Prince Paul, sought to stave off trouble by permitting his Government to sign an accord with Hitler. But the example of Greece and exaggerated rumors of British strength there, rumors ably guided by British intelligence agents, encouraged the Yugoslav Royal Guard and Air Force to revolt. On March 27, 1941, they ousted Paul and his regime. General Dušan Simović was installed as dictator, and Guards officers forged the boy King Peter's name to a declaration assuming power. This was read on the radio amidst wide rejoicing by the warlike Serbs. When Yugoslavia collapsed a month later, the Air Force general who arranged the coup escaped to Cairo, where he was given two-star rank in the British forces, although he did not speak English.

Hitler was infuriated at this insult to his prestige. He ordered a swift assault on Yugoslavia and embattled Greece. The invasion began early in the morning of April 6, 1941. Throughout the preceding night, under a full moon, I had watched peasant boys march into the old fortress at the tip of Belgrade, where the

Prime Minister Winston Churchill makes
one of his frequent walking tours of London
streets, inspecting bomb damage and giving
a boost to morale. Armed with skill,
determination, an indomitable spirit, and
the complete support of the British people,
he never doubted that he would succeed.

Danube and Sava rivers meet, pick up their uniforms and guns, and trundle out behind oxcarts, singing: "Oh my love, the German is again at our frontiers and there again he will meet the Serbian bayonet." Within hours the capital was shattered by the *Luftwaffe*. German tanks and motorized infantry rolled in, aided by the Hungarians and Bulgarians, who had been bought by the Vienna award; and the Italians launched their own offensive from Albania.

Yugoslavia was riddled with fifth-column movements among its Croatian, Albanian, and German *Volksdeutsch* minorities. Defections among the non-Serbs were manifold, and the Yugoslav armies were torn apart before they had even been deployed. The Germans captured Skoplje two hours after its commander assured me it was safe and poured across the undefended Monastir Gap into Greece. From Bulgaria they hammered southward against Greek pillbox positions in Thrace. The colonel commanding one of these, Fort Rupel, summoned his garrison and told them: "We will hold them with our teeth." When the Germans finally broke in, they found, written with chalk on a wall above the dead: "At Thermopylae, the three hundred were killed. Here the eighty will fall defending their country."

Greece, in an agony of despair and bitter confusion, collapsed. The Government fled to Cairo. The British defended themselves stubbornly, especially—and appropriately—in the area of Thermopylae, and managed to salvage a considerable part of their expeditionary force. But on April 17, Yugoslavia capitulated, and six days later, Greece did the same.

Initially, this seemed but another dreadful Nazi victory. The British lost fifteen thousand casualties against fifty-three hundred for Germany. The Germans captured two hundred thousand Greek and three hundred thousand Yugoslav prisoners. They partitioned Yugoslavia, taking some bits and giving pieces to Hungary, Italy, and Bulgaria, while establishing puppet states in Croatia and Serbia. They allowed Mussolini, in theory, to take over Greece, after awarding a portion to the Bulgars.

And on May 20, 1941, history's first fully airborne invasion was launched against Crete with remarkable efficiency. The combined British, Commonwealth, and Greek forces on Crete made the Germans pay a heavy price; yet by the end of the month, the legendary island was in German hands. All the Mediterranean's northern shore and central bastions were under Axis control, save for Gibraltar and beleaguered Malta, which at one time was defended principally by three old Gladiator biplanes called "Faith," "Hope," and "Charity." The Balkans had been lost; Turkey was trembling; and there were rumors of an impending invasion of Cyprus and the Middle Eastern Arab states.

Nevertheless, Hitler paid dearly for this improvised and impressive Balkan victory. It has been argued by his own generals that the time lost in conquering Greece and Yugoslavia delayed by two or three critical weeks the eventual assault on Russia. As a consequence, despite the mauling they suffered in June and early July, the Russians were able to check the *Wehrmacht* at Smolensk, to hold them at Moscow, and then to drive them backward into the bitter Russian winter. Had Hitler not run up a swastika on the Acropolis, he might have succeeded in draping it upon the Kremlin.

At approximately this point, a curious incident occurred. Forty-seven-year-old Rudolph Hess, the number three man in the Nazi hierarchy, flew secretly to England in an unarmed plane that he had persuaded the aircraft designer Willi Messerschmitt to lend him. Hess was seeking out the Duke of Hamilton, whom he had met at the Berlin Olympic Games in 1936. He hoped the Duke would help him get in touch with British leaders so that he could propose conclusion of a peace that would guarantee the integrity of Britain's Empire and leave Hitler free to attack Russia, thereby bringing about the end of bolshevism. Hess broke his ankle while parachuting to Scotland, was captured by a farmer with a pitchfork, and then was locked up as a prisoner of war. Hitler was baffled and furious. He denounced Hess as being in "a state of hallucination," which was perhaps not wholly inaccurate. Hess was known to have been ill and psychologically disturbed. British propaganda made the most of this unexpected opportunity to create the impression of confusion in the highest Nazi ranks. The arrival of this haunted-looking enemy at a moment of bleak despair was a heaven-sent gift to England.

None of these dramatic events, including a new Axis offensive in North Africa and the failure of German efforts to hold Syria with Vichy French collaboration and to seize Iraq in a conspiracy, served to deflect Hitler from his main preoccupation, the forthcoming Russian campaign. Once he realized that his enormous Army, perched on the Channel, was doomed to an indefinite period of idleness, he decided to march it eastward against Stalin. This, after Dunkirk and the failure to invade Brit-

In this 1938 photograph Hitler stands beside
Rudolph Hess, an old and trusted friend. It
was Hess to whom the future *Führer* dictated
most of *Mein Kampf* after they were both
sent to prison in 1924. In 1941, Hess secretly
embarked on his own bizarre one-man peace
mission to England, but was captured before
he could attempt any negotiations. Hitler,
infuriated, had Hess declared deranged due
to World War I injuries.

ain immediately, was Hitler's second major strategic error. The Stalingrad campaign and the failure to bolster Rommel in North Africa came later.

But Hitler's decision to invade Russia was prompted by more than military stalemate in the west. Not only did he hate both bolshevism and the Slavs; in July, 1940, he summed up his credo: "*Russia is the factor by which England sets the greatest store. . . . If Russia is beaten, England's last hope is gone.* Germany is then master of Europe and the Balkans. . . . *Decision: As a result of this argument, Russia must be dealt with. Spring 1941.*"

On July 29, 1940, General (later Field Marshal) Alfred Gustav Jodl, Chief of Staff of the Armed Forces High Command, informed a select group of *Wehrmacht* planners of the *Führer*'s "expressed wishes" for an attack on Russia. On August 9, the first directive for an offensive was issued. Sunday morning, June 22, was set for the massive Soviet invasion—far later that Hitler's customarily prudent generals wished.

Because of the very immensity of the project—the building of the German Army to three hundred divisions, the concentration of vast forces from Finland across Poland to Rumania on the Black Sea—and because of inevitable indiscretions coming from such preparations, it was hardly a secret that a new assault was coming. Both London and Washington advised Stalin of the impending attack, but he refused to credit such warnings from the West, and he remained persuaded of the rocklike firmness of the Red Army.

On June 22, 1941, the greatest campaign of World War II began, and with it came the final and thunderous denouement of all those devious Russo-German dealings, started after World War I by Seeckt and Trotsky and continued well into World War II. Sir Stafford Cripps, a cold vegetarian teetotaller with the face of a seventeenth-century Puritan, was in London at the moment, believing his mission to Moscow had failed. Churchill called in his ambassador to help prepare a speech to the Russian people. The old Tory strode up and down, chewing a cigar. Cripps told me later he was startled to see that as the Prime Minister, who for so many years had berated the Soviets, began to dictate melodious phrases about suffering Russia, tears rolled down his cheeks.

IV

Arsenal of Democracy

Roosevelt and Churchill join in shipboard
church services on August 10, 1941, in
Argentina Bay, during the meetings that
produced the Atlantic Charter.

There are often confusing gaps in United States foreign policy between what we say we are going to do and what we actually do. As Gertrude Stein observed, Americans are brought up "to believe in boundlessness." This is manifest with respect to the behavior of our Government in matters outside its jurisdiction and therefore outside its control. In foreign policy we sometimes make laws in one way and apply them in another.

Our obsession for avoiding entanglements with the countries from which our forefathers escaped to a new society derived from both history and philosophy. In 1794, we passed our first Neutrality Act to escape involvement in a continental war between England and France. Two years later, George Washington warned in his Farewell Address against "interweaving our destiny with that of any part of Europe." Americans considered ours a noble and moral experiment, removed from the corruption and decay of other lands; and they wished to preserve it untarnished. But the consequent desire for total isolation did not become a real problem until early in this century, when we became a world power.

During World War I, most Americans supported the Allies. There were, to be sure, many who did not, especially among those of German, Irish, and Jewish ancestry who cherished anti-British or anti-Russian sentiments. Thousands of such Americans actually left the United States to fight for the Kaiser. Nevertheless, the nation as a whole fervently hoped to stay out of the conflict, even though many leaders clearly saw that should the Allies lose, the United States might become an island of democracy in a militaristic world.

Soon, however, reports of the brutal behavior of German troops in Belgium and France, exaggerated by Allied propaganda, began to stir American anger. At the same time, we rather arrogantly expected the Germans to accept our own special definition of neutrality: we committed ourselves to protect United States citizens on the high seas even when they traveled on belligerent ships. Thus when Berlin proclaimed unrestricted submarine warfare, it became inevitable that we would soon be involved in the war Woodrow Wilson had sworn to shun.

After peace came, isolationism still ran strong in the national bloodstream. In 1935, Congress enacted a law authorizing the President to stop arms shipments and prohibit United States citizens from traveling on foreign ships except at their own risk. Then, in 1936, Congress declared all loans to belligerent nations illegal. When civil war broke out in Spain, the 1936 legislation was extended to prevent American aid of any kind to either side.

But another Neutrality Act in 1939 repealed the arms embargo contained in previous measures and authorized a so-called "cash-and-carry" system designed to help our Allied friends while keeping us out of the conflict. Once again, as in 1916, we were determined to have our cake and to eat it. We began selling arms to Britain and France, despite protests from the leonine Senator William E. Borah, Midwestern isolationists, and right-wing followers of the reactionary radio priest, Father Charles E. Coughlin. Again we set out to maintain a neutral position that could continue only if one belligerent side, the Axis, accepted its paradoxical terms.

Even President Roosevelt admitted, when Hitler started World War II, that neutrality of thought was a different matter from neutrality of policy. After the Nazis overran nearly all of western Europe, he counseled: "Let us have done with both fears and illusions." When France fell, the United States Government was faced with the bleak reality that only Britain stood between America and the *Führer*'s European fortress. Within a year after the Nazis struck the Lowlands, Congress appropriated $37,000,000,000 for rearmament and aid to the Allies, a sum larger than the total cost of World War I. But we had started very late. It was reckoned by military experts that the United States would not have an adequate air force until 1943, and it would be another two years before we possessed a two-ocean army.

Furthermore, the nation was still riven by vigorous debate between outright interventionists and outright isolationists. William Allen White, the renowned editor of the Emporia, Kansas, *Gazette*, organized the Committee to Defend America by Aiding the Allies. He wrote Roosevelt urging that we become Britain's nonbelligerent ally and warned the President: "As an old friend, let me tell you that you may not be able to lead the American people unless you catch up with them." Robert Sherwood, a brilliant and ardently Anglophile playwright, took the lead by running a newspaper advertisement headed "Stop Hitler Now!" Nevertheless, various groups fought the current. The America

First Committee preached a mixture of isolationism, pacifism, Anglophobia, and anti-Semitism and gained the support of many distinguished citizens, including Charles A. Lindbergh, Senator Burton K. Wheeler, and the Chicago *Tribune*'s powerful publisher, Colonel Robert McCormick. This was still the era of the Hitler-Stalin pact; pro-Fascist and pro-Communist groups joined in urging that we mind our own business.

President Roosevelt, who had begun a personal correspondence with Winston Churchill when Churchill was still First Lord of the Admiralty, began to prepare the country for a more active anti-Axis role. In his famous June 10 speech at Charlottesville, Virginia, he warned in his flat, reedy voice that we could not afford to become "a lone island in a world dominated by the philosophy of force." What is more, he promised to "extend to the opponents of force the material resources of this nation." Later, on July 29, he announced our protection over all Latin America and thus blocked the Nazis from assuming control of French or Dutch colonies. The United States then pooled defenses with Canada, a nation already at war, and in September inaugurated the draft with a call-up of eight hundred thousand men. In July Churchill had cabled Roosevelt that the British had lost eleven destroyers in ten days and urgently requested help. The President responded by transferring fifty United States destroyers to hard-pressed Britain. All but three of them were antiquated four-stackers that had been in mothballs for eighteen years. Roosevelt called this "an epochal and far-reaching act of preparation for continental defense in the face of danger," since in return we had received ninety-nine-year leases on seven British bases from Guiana to Newfoundland. The United States was fast becoming a boundlessly unneutral neutral.

The problem of preparing the country for war itself was, however, appallingly difficult. Our regular Army, prior to the draft, had been legally limited to three hundred seventy-five thousand men. Our factories needed to be retooled, and many of our workers required retraining before the nation could turn from civilian to military production. But by August of 1940, the Battle of Britain was on, shocking the United States out of its lassitude. On September 8, Roosevelt declared a state of emergency. An Office of Production Management was created to coordinate defense output and speed aid to Britain in every way

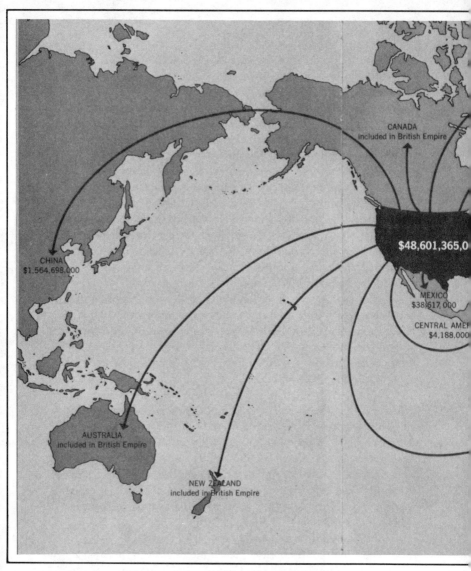

CANADA
included in British Empire

$48,601,365,0

MEXICO
$38,617,000

CENTRAL AME
$4,188,000

CHINA
$1,564,698,000

AUSTRALIA
included in British Empire

NEW ZEALAND
included in British Empire

The Lend-Lease bill authorized United
States military aid, shown in monetary
value on this map, to anti-Axis countries.
Despite "the Great Debate" of 1940–41 that
raged between the traditional isolationists
and the so-called interventionists, the
United States eased steadily away from
neutrality and finally plunged into the war.

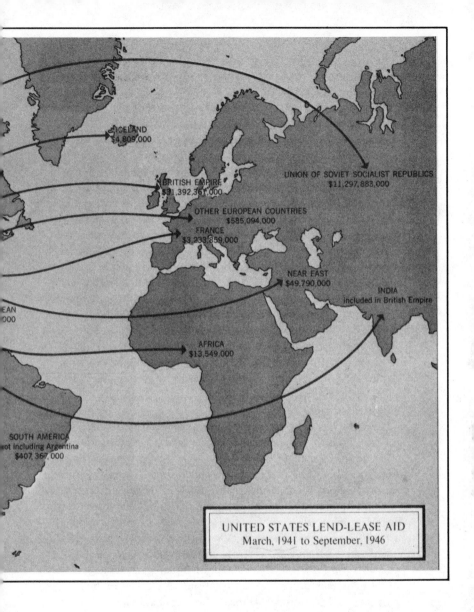

ICELAND
$4,609,000

BRITISH EMPIRE
$31,392,361,000

UNION OF SOVIET SOCIALIST REPUBLICS
$11,297,883,000

OTHER EUROPEAN COUNTRIES
$585,094,000

FRANCE
$3,233,859,000

NEAR EAST
$49,790,000

INDIA
included in British Empire

EAN
000

AFRICA
$13,549,000

SOUTH AMERICA
not including Argentina
$407,367,000

UNITED STATES LEND-LEASE AID
March, 1941 to September, 1946

"short of war." At the same time, a National Defense Research Committee, established the previous year under Dr. Vannevar Bush, was taking steps that would ultimately lead the United States—and the world—into the atomic age.

War was the major issue of the presidential election that November. Roosevelt took the unprecedented step of running for a third term on the grounds that there was a world crisis. Like Wilson before him, he ran on a platform pledging that while we would help those fighting against aggression, we would not participate in foreign conflicts or send military forces outside America except in case of attack. The Republicans, despite the many influential and vocal isolationists in their party, finally nominated a liberal, pro-British Wall Street businessman, Wendell L. Willkie. His program promised "Americanism, preparedness, and peace." Willkie had a hard time campaigning. It was evident that he agreed on fundamentals with the man he wished to defeat, and he pledged himself to "outdistance Hitler in any contest he chooses." Republican propagandists depicted Roosevelt as a "war candidate." The Democrats called their rivals isolationists and appeasers, which Willkie, for one, was certainly not. The contest was uneven. Roosevelt received four hundred forty-nine electoral votes and Willkie only eighty-two.

By the time 1940 drew to a close, our self-confidence, our growing sense of self-interest, our admiration for British courage, and our increasing detestation of the Nazis had combined to produce a new national mood. In early December, Roosevelt went off on a two-week fishing trip in the Caribbean and returned with the ingenious—indeed revolutionary—idea that we keep Britain going with what he called a Lend-Lease program. There was no time to be lost. Britain was going broke and could ill afford our cash-and-carry terms for arms. She had begun the war with about $4,500,000,000 in gold, dollars, and United States investments; the money was almost gone. A week after the President returned from the Caribbean, he introduced his novel concept at a White House press conference. "Now, what I am trying to do," he said, "is to eliminate the dollar sign. That is something new in the thoughts of everybody in this room, I think —get rid of the silly, foolish old dollar sign. Well, let me give you an illustration. Suppose my neighbor's home catches fire, and I have a length of garden hose. . . ."

On January 6, 1941, Roosevelt went before Congress and made

the position of the United States entirely clear. "Today, thinking of our children and their children," he said, "we oppose enforced isolation for ourselves or for any part of the Americas." He called for a world that would be founded upon "four essential freedoms": freedom of speech, freedom of worship, freedom from want, and freedom from fear. It took no seer to recognize that this was a world in which Adolf Hitler had no place.

In the same speech, the President asked Congress to legislate Lend-Lease. The bill was cleverly presented. Its proponents argued that there was historical precedent, an 1892 statute enabling the Secretary of War to lease Army property "when in his discretion it will be for the public good." The bill went up to Congress under the happily patriotic designation of HR-1776 and was vigorously supported by the War Department. Its terms authorized the President to sell or lease military material to any anti-Axis country in return for any kind of direct or indirect payment "which the President deems satisfactory." The bill was savagely debated for two months. Isolationists, quite rightly, said its enactment would destroy what was left of our 1939 neutrality position. Robert M. Hutchins, the outspoken and respected president of the University of Chicago, regarded the entire concept as national suicide. But Churchill's strong voice pleaded from burning London: "Give us the tools and we will finish the job." In March, HR-1776 became law.

Never before had an American President received such immense discretionary authority. Within two weeks an initial appropriation of $7,000,000,000 was authorized by Congress. By the close of the war the total exceeded $50,000,000,000. Military goods started to flow across the Atlantic with maximum speed and minimum red tape, and Churchill at last felt able to make what he called "long-term plans of vast extent." United States military leaders began to discuss joint preparations with the British and exchanged scientific, military, and intelligence information, from which we benefited greatly. R.A.F. pilots came to America to train. American warships helped shepherd Lend-Lease convoys and were soon tangling with U-boats in an undeclared shooting war. All but the figment of neutrality was gone.

This deliberate intrusion into the European conflict was mirrored in our relationship with Japan. Since 1931, when Secretary Stimson had sought unsuccessfully to muster international opposition to the Japanese invasion of Manchuria, the United States had found itself increasingly at odds with the dynamic Pacific nation that had so brilliantly imitated and improved on Western industrial ideas. Japan's assault on inchoate China and its subsequent accord with Hitler had brought it increasingly into the ranks of those we considered our enemies. After Germany's triumphs in Europe, it was clear that the only potentially effective opposition to Japanese expansion in Asia was that of the United States.

Pressure to curb Japan in the East more or less paralleled pressure inside the United States to bolster Britain in the West. In the summer of 1940, Washington initiated its first ban on sales of strategic materials to Tokyo. The embargo was rapidly extended, hurting the Japanese and producing an increasingly militant reaction among their military and political leaders. On September 27, 1940, Japan joined Germany and Italy in a Tripartite Pact that obliged the signatories to support each other should the United States enter the war. And the following April, Tokyo sought to insure itself against such a contingency by negotiating a neutrality pact with Russia, at that time still Germany's passive partner.

It is possible that the tightening American blockade accelerated the evident Japanese intention to expand. At any rate, fifty thousand Japanese troops seized Indochina from the Vichy French regime on July 2, 1941. Roosevelt promptly warned Tokyo to keep out of the Dutch East Indies, and the United States and Britain froze all Japanese funds under their control. By October the few remaining voices of moderation inside the Tokyo regime grew still. On the seventeenth the bellicose General Hideki Tojo was named Prime Minister, and it became more and more obvious that Tokyo, suffering especially from a freeze on petroleum imports from America, source of 90 per cent of its supplies in 1940, was preparing for imminent war before its stockpiles diminished. Indeed, we now know that the Japanese high command had started planning the attack on Pearl Harbor the preceding January—more than ten months before the event. That same October, a war council, in the presence of the Emperor, fixed the date for opening hostilities.

As the United States became more and more directly involved in the menacing problems of both the Atlantic and Pacific, American diplomacy became increasingly active. Harry Hopkins, a lean, sickly social worker who enjoyed Roosevelt's particular confidence,

Blindfolded Secretary of War Henry L.
Stimson, on October 29, 1940, draws the
first of the numbers to determine the
order in which men would be called under
the new Selective Service law. A little
more than a month earlier Congress had
passed the first peacetime military draft
in American history.

served him as personal envoy on extraordinary missions. In July of 1941, Hopkins flew to England and talked to Churchill about a proposed conference with Roosevelt. At the end of his stay in London, on the night of July 25, Hopkins cabled Roosevelt: "I am wondering whether you think it important and useful for me to go to Moscow. Air transportation good and can reach there in twenty-four hours. I have a feeling that everything possible should be done to make certain the Russians maintain a permanent front even though they be defeated in this immediate battle. If Stalin could in any way be influenced at a critical time I think it would be worth doing by direct communication from you through a personal envoy." Roosevelt agreed.

The following Monday, wearing a grey Homburg Churchill had lent him after he had lost his own battered fedora, Hopkins climbed aboard a PBY Catalina that took him on a hasty and highly secret mission to Moscow. He bore a letter from Roosevelt to Stalin that said: "Mr. Hopkins is in Moscow at my request for discussion with you personally and with such other officials as you may designate on the vitally important question of how we can most expeditiously and effectively make available the assistance which the United States can render to your country in its magnificent resistance to the treacherous aggression by Hitlerite Germany. . . ."

The shift in attitude toward Russia, Hitler's colleague in the partition and plundering of Poland, was as dramatic and significant as the shift away from our originally proclaimed neutrality. Stalin bluntly suggested to Hopkins that the United States enter the war. Instead, Roosevelt sent Averell Harriman to Moscow together with Churchill's special agent, Lord Beaverbrook. On October 1, 1941, they signed a protocol with Molotov listing the supplies America and Britain would send to the Soviet Union. Roosevelt later authorized a Soviet Lend-Lease credit of up to $1,000,000,000.

And so, gradually but immutably, with a growing national awareness of what lay at the end of this unfamiliar road, the United States became ever more deeply committed to protect its friends and those who were at least the enemies of its enemies.

As we drew nearer and nearer to the edge of war, Roosevelt decided the time had come to meet Churchill personally. From August 9 to 12, 1941, the two leaders conferred with their staffs at Argentia Bay, Newfoundland, exchanging visits aboard their battle-camouflaged warships, *Prince of Wales* and *Augusta*. Thus began a personal and official relationship between the gallant cripple and the tough old artist-adventurer. No past President had ever been on such terms with the head of another Government. As Robert Sherwood later wrote, "It would be an exaggeration to say that Roosevelt and Churchill became chums at this conference. . . . They established an easy intimacy, a joking informality and moratorium on pomposity and cant—and also a degree of frankness in intercourse which, if not quite complete, was remarkably close to it." Each clearly respected the other not only for what he represented but as an individual. Roosevelt cabled Churchill shortly afterward: "It is fun to be in the same decade with you." And Churchill recalled in his memoirs: "I felt I was in contact with a very great man who was also a warm-hearted friend and the foremost champion of the high causes which we served."

The Newfoundland conference was remarkable in that it produced a joint statement by the leader of a belligerent state and the leader of a nonbelligerent state, outlining the principles for which World War II was being fought—even before the war's greatest power had actually entered the fight. This statement, known to history as the Atlantic Charter, postulated certain basic tenets for the postwar world. It was drafted by Churchill and modified by the two statesmen together. On January 1, 1942, after Churchill visited Washington, it was incorporated in a Declaration of the United Nations.

And so, in a most extraordinarily curious way, primarily through the willpower and political genius of one man, Franklin Roosevelt, often inadvertently and sometimes only by executive order, the United States became deeply involved in history's greatest conflict without actually joining the war. In the East we helped China and squeezed and threatened Japan, more or less pushing her to do what she had planned to do anyway. In the West we armed first Britain, then Russia. We dispatched envoys to see what matériel was needed, and warships to insure that it was safely delivered. There is no doubt that we deliberately violated any internationally accepted concept of neutrality for eighteen months before we became belligerents. There is also no doubt that had we not done so, first Britain and then Russia would have lost the war. The isolation so many Americans craved would then have become both total and disastrous.

V

Japan Strikes

The infamous attack of December 7, 1941,
left the battleship *Arizona* mortally
wounded—she still lies today, with most of
her men, at the bottom of Pearl Harbor.

During the last half of the nineteenth century, after Commodore Matthew Perry's "black ships" opened the self-isolated feudal nation of Japan to American trade, a group of militant and nationalist young samurai inspired an industrial and political revolution that by the early part of the twentieth century had placed a new kind of Japan squarely in competition with the West. Big business, a big army, and a big navy combined with native Japanese energy to produce a dynamism that eventually gave rise to massive expansion, first in Manchuria in 1931, then across the Pacific and deep into China.

The thrust into China began in the summer of 1937, when the so-called War Lords of Japan provoked several "incidents" and then invaded. They were censured by the League and received strong protests from the United States—all of which seemed only to reaffirm the Tokyo militarists' argument that war with the West was inevitable, and that the next step should be to preempt the oil and minerals of southern Asia. The principles of such bold expansion had been outlined ten years earlier in a secret memorandum called the Tanaka Memorial, a blueprint for military conquest that even included the conquering of Europe. But after Hitler overran Europe in the spring of 1940, Japan signed a Tripartite Pact with Germany and Italy to secure a free hand in the Orient.

Friction between Japan and the United States increased rapidly. In July, 1940, President Roosevelt froze all Japanese assets in the United States, and later a commercial blockade of Japan was put into effect. A moderate Prime Minister, Prince Fumimaro Konoye, urged restraint and tried to find some basis for a bargain with the United States. But his cabinet was dominated by General Hideki Tojo, known as "Razor Brain." Not long after, Konoye was almost murdered for his views, and on October 17, 1940, Tojo became Prime Minister. A United States Navy Department memorandum concluded that the "jingoistic military clique" was now supreme. Tojo resolved on war, arguing that "rather than await extinction it were better to face death by breaking through the encircling ring to find a way for existence."

From these impulses had already grown "the Greater East Asia Co-Prosperity Sphere," an economic and political program for a Japanese empire that would extend all the way from Manchuria and China to Thailand and New Guinea. In theory the program endorsed the anticolonial aspirations of Asian nationalists, but in practice it merely substituted one form of imperialism for another.

Unlike the Germans, the Japanese had a finite and audacious scheme, whose first postulate was the crippling of the United States Pacific Fleet—and specifically the battleships—at Pearl Harbor. Thereafter, in concurrent moves, it envisioned the rapid seizure of Thailand, Burma, Malaya, and Singapore, and also the Philippines and Dutch East Indies archipelagoes. The idea was to achieve an impregnable position before America was ready to hit back. The program was endorsed at a Supreme War Council on September 6, 1941.

Five months earlier, British and American staff representatives had met in Washington and agreed on a defensive plan in the event of an Asian war. Known as ABC-1, it called for a concentrated effort against Germany and a holding operation in the East. The United States expected to hang on to the Philippines, especially after General Douglas MacArthur was named Far East commander that July. The possibility of an assault on Pearl Harbor was not considered. This was strange, since Joseph Clark Grew, our ambassador in Tokyo, had reported in January, 1941, that the Japanese might "attempt a surprise attack on Pearl Harbor using all their military facilities."

Even at the end of November, when we had managed to break the Japanese secret codes, nobody suspected that Honolulu might be in danger. Aircraft on Hawaiian bases were parked wing-to-wing to protect them from local sabotage; and it was only mere chance that three carriers were absent from Pearl Harbor when the attack came. Analysis in Washington was unimaginative; intelligence was faulty; communications were slack and mixed up.

Undoubtedly part of this muddleheadedness came from over-confidence. Ernest Hemingway later wrote: "All through the Pacific and the Far East in 1941 I heard about the general incapacity and worthlessness of 'those Little Monkeys.' Everywhere I heard what we would do to those little monkeys when the day of the great pushover came. One cruiser division and a couple of carriers would destroy Tokyo; another ditto Yokohama. No one ever specified what the little monkeys would be doing while all this was going on. I imagine they were supposed to be consulting oculists trying to remedy those famous defects in vision which kept them from being able to fly properly. Or else trying to right all those battleships and cruisers which would capsize in a beam sea."

Specific plans for the Pearl Harbor attack were put together by a staff working under Admiral Isoroku Yamamoto, Commander in Chief of the Japanese Navy, an excellent officer and by no means an extreme jingo. Six carriers, protected by a heavy screen of surface vessels and submarines, were assigned to the task. The idea of surprise raised no moral problem, as such surprise is even recommended in *Bushido*, feudal Japan's code of honor.

By November the project was proven ready. Yamamoto assembled his commanders on the *Nagato* and told them that without a triumph at Honolulu, Japan could neither make war nor aspire to great-power rank. But he warned his subordinates: "The Americans are adversaries worthy of you." On December 2, the fleet received the coded message ("Climb Mount Niitaka") that irrevocably ordered the attack. Officers and pilots listened to their instructions, then bowed in prayer before the Shinto shrines aboard their carriers. On December 7, they struck.

That December, I was in Kuibyshev, temporary capital of war-torn Russia. Two days before Pearl Harbor, the confused provincial Soviet cable service delivered to me by mistake an enormously long cable in what was patently Russian code. It had been sent from Tokyo and was addressed to the Foreign Commissariat. I struggled through the snow to deliver the message to an embarrassed official. I have long since wondered what forebodings that ambassadorial message contained. In any case, it was clear that the news of Pearl Harbor was welcomed by Stalin; at last, as Lenin had predicted, Japan and the United States had "turned their knives against each other," and the Soviets could relax along their edgy eastern frontier. Three Japanese correspondents shared a room across the corridor from me in Kuibyshev's modest Grand Hotel. Affable fellows, they knocked on my door and told me, with happy smiles, how sorry they were that the United States Fleet had been destroyed. To my horror, I found that what they said was true.

World War II became truly global only in December, 1941; the majority of Latin America joined the United States in declaring war on the Axis, and the number of belligerents rose to thirty-eight, of whom only ten were on the Axis side. The sphere of operations extended from Ethiopia to the Aleutians and Papua, and from the Arctic Circle to the Tropic of Capricorn.

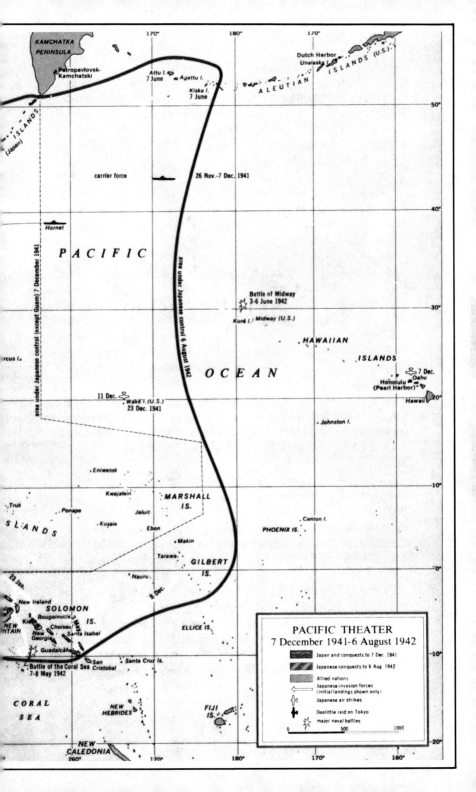

KAMCHATKA PENINSULA

Petropavlovsk-Kamchatski

Attu I. 7 June • Agattu I.

Kiska I. 7 June

Dutch Harbor Unalaska ALEUTIAN ISLANDS (U.S.)

ISLANDS (Japan)

carrier force 26 Nov.-7 Dec. 1941

Hornet

PACIFIC

area under Japanese control (except Guam) 7 December 1941

area under Japanese control 6 August 1942

Battle of Midway 3-6 June 1942

Kurē I. Midway (U.S.)

HAWAIIAN

OCEAN

ISLANDS

7 Dec. Oahu Honolulu (Pearl Harbor)

Hawaii

rcus I.

11 Dec. Wake I. (U.S.) 23 Dec. 1941

Johnston I.

Eniwetok

Kwajalein

MARSHALL IS.

Truk • Ponape

Jaluit

Kusaie

Ebon

Canton I.

PHOENIX IS.

SLANDS

Makin

Tarawa

Nauru

GILBERT IS.

9 Dec.

23 Jan.

New Ireland

SOLOMON IS.

Bougainville

NEW BRITAIN

Kieta Choiseul

New Georgia Santa Isabel

Guadalcanal

San Cristobal

Santa Cruz Is.

ELLICE IS.

Battle of the Coral Sea 7-8 May 1942

CORAL SEA

NEW HEBRIDES

FIJI IS.

NEW CALEDONIA

160° 170° 180° 170° 160°

PACIFIC THEATER
7 December 1941-6 August 1942

- Japan and conquests to 7 Dec 1941
- Japanese conquests to 6 Aug 1942
- Allied nations
- Japanese invasion forces (initial landings shown only)
- Doolittle raid on Tokyo
- major naval battles

0   500   1000

The abrupt change from unneutral neutrality to full belligerency came with shocking surprise to the incautious American high command. Since mid-November, Tojo's special envoy, Saburo Kurusu, had been in Washington to assist Ambassador Kichisaburo Nomura in seeking—or pretending to seek—a negotiated settlement. Kurusu and Nomura began negotiations with Secretary of State Cordell Hull on the seventeenth, almost two weeks after the Japanese fleet had received secret Operational Order No. 1, which led to Pearl Harbor. At 2:05 P.M., December 7, Kurusu and Nomura again called upon Secretary Hull—twenty minutes late for their appointment. They arrived just after Roosevelt had telephoned Hull to tell him of the attack on Honolulu. The handsome, tight-lipped Secretary coldly accepted the document presented by his visitors, which outlined the Japanese formula for a Pacific settlement. When he had finished reading it, he said: "In all my fifty years of public service I have never seen a document that was more crowded with infamous falsehoods and distortions —infamous falsehoods and distortions on a scale so huge that I never imagined that any government on this planet was capable of uttering them."

At that moment, early in the morning by Pearl Harbor time, the American fleet was smoking in disaster. Three hundred and fifty-three Japanese bombers, torpedo bombers, and fighters had within a few moments knocked out half of the entire United States Navy.

The surprise was total. Soldiers were taking their Sunday ease outside their billets; sailors were sauntering along the decks of their moored vessels. When the first enemy aircraft swept out of the morning haze above Diamond Head, few people paid attention. Passengers on an incoming American liner were pleased to be able to witness what they thought to be remarkably realistic preparatory exercises. Then the intruders leveled off. The torpedo planes, armed with special shallow-running devices, headed for the moored battleships, their prime targets. High-flying bombers blasted crowded Hickam Field. A group of unarmed United States planes coming in from the mainland found itself caught in the melee.

Six great battleships—*West Virginia, Tennessee, Arizona, Nevada, Oklahoma,* and *California*—were sunk or seriously damaged. Our Air Corps was left with only sixteen serviceable bombers. American striking power in the Pacific was virtually paralyzed. Tokyo newspapers proclaimed that the United States had been reduced to a third-class power. The American people were stunned. The next day, President Roosevelt told a joint session of Congress that December 7 was "a date which will live in infamy," and the Senate voted unanimously for war. There was one dissent in the House—from Montana's Jeannette Rankin, a pacifist who said she wanted to show that a "good democracy" does not always vote unanimously for war. Three days later, Germany and Italy declared war, and Congress passed a joint resolution accepting the state of war "which has been thrust upon the United States."

The Japanese onslaught continued with simultaneous attacks against Hong Kong, Malaya, and the Philippines, where the American Far East Air Corps was crippled in a catastrophe almost as bad as that of Pearl Harbor and one for which there was even less excuse, for there had been sufficient and accurate advance notice. General MacArthur had reason to expect an assault on at least Luzon. Nevertheless, Japanese planes succeeded in destroying eighteen of the thirty-five Flying Fortresses at Clark Field, as well as fifty-six fighters and twenty-five other planes. They lost only seven aircraft in the process. Within three weeks, strong amphibious forces under Lieutenant General Masaharu Homma had landed on the northern and southern shores of Luzon and were driving on Manila. The United States Asiatic Fleet withdrew with large convoys of merchant shipping to safer and more southerly waters. By January 2, 1942, Manila had fallen, and American and Philippine troops were retreating to the Bataan Peninsula.

While the United States reeled from these savage blows, the Japanese unleashed a multiple offensive on the Asian mainland. The Indochinese colonies of defeated France had already been occupied; now it was Britain's turn. Native populations under the Empire were restive, if not actually hostile, and as the hitherto dominant white tuans faltered, the Asiatic peoples proved willingly subject to Japanese propaganda. The Royal Navy adhered to obsolete tactics. Hong Kong was entirely isolated and fell on Christmas Day. Singapore, vaunted island citadel of the Orient, had all its guns and fortifications facing seaward and lay open to the Malayan land side, from which the attack developed.

Wearing sneakers, carrying small sacks of rice, venerating their Emperor and believing implicitly in their commanders, some two hundred thousand Japanese soldiers rushed like lizards through the Malayan jungle. The British kept falling back, only to find their enemy already installed behind them. "It's like trying to build a wall out of quicksand," said one despairing officer. Within six weeks the Japanese had taken the peninsula. The British withdrew into Singapore, swarming with refugees, but Sir Arthur Percival, the commanding general, found himself outnumbered and outmaneuvered. With more than seventy thousand men, he surrendered on February 15, 1942. It was the worst military disaster ever suffered by any European nation in the Orient.

Even before that great island city fell, Britain suffered an unmitigated naval disaster. A flotilla of six ships, including the heavy cruiser *Repulse* and the powerful new battleship *Prince of Wales*, was cruising openly in Malayan waters, hoping to deter Japan. There was no aircraft carrier in the flotilla, and its commander, Sir Tom Phillips, an old-fashioned "battlewagon admiral," easily reconciled himself to the lack of support from land-based planes. When the Royal Air Force notified him, "Regret fighter protection impossible," Phillips merely remarked to an officer on the bridge, "Well, we must get on without it." Soon he found himself being shadowed by Japanese observation planes. By the time he turned back, it was too late. On December 11, the *Prince of Wales* and the *Repulse* were both sunk by Japanese bombers and low-flying torpedo planes. Phillips went down with his ships. Churchill told Parliament: "In my whole experience I do not remember any naval blow so heavy or so painful. . . ."

Already established in French Indochina with the helpless permission of Vichy's Governor General, the Japanese swarmed southward across Malaya toward the Dutch East Indies and far-off Australia, and westward over Thailand to Burma and the edge of India. In Burma the British were aided by a Chinese force under Chiang Kai-shek's chief of staff, the redoubtable American general "Vinegar Joe" Stilwell. But his troops were soon cut off and had to make a difficult forced march out of Burma to northeast India. Stilwell confessed in his usual unabashed fashion: "The Japs ran us out of Burma. We took a hell of a beating!" The Burmese, like many other Asians, were pleased to see the Western overlords defeated. A Tokyo newspaper, commenting on the extent of collaboration in Mandalay, observed:

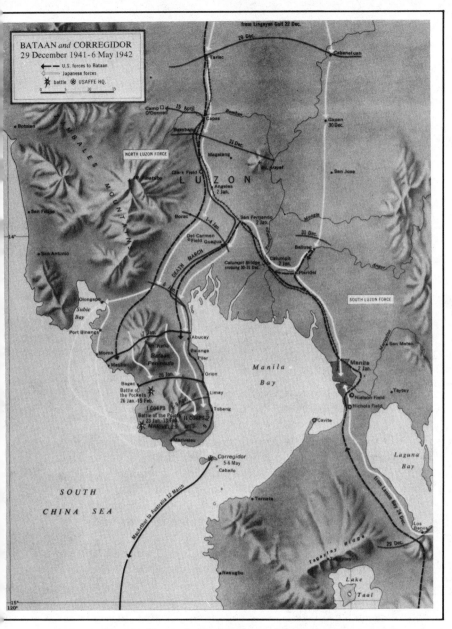

BATAAN *and* CORREGIDOR
29 December 1941–6 May 1942

→→ U.S. forces to Bataan
→→ Japanese forces
✶ battle ⊛ USAFFE HQ.

0   5   10   15

from Lingayen Gulf 22 Dec.

29 Dec.

Cabanatuan

Tarlac

Camp O'Donnell 15 April
Capas
Bamban
Bamban 31 Dec.
NORTH LUZON FORCE Magalang

Gapan
30 Dec.

Mt. Arayat

Clark Field San Jose
LUZON
Angeles 2 Jan.

Borac 1-4 Jan.

San Fernando
2 Jan.
Del Carmen
Field Guagua 31 Dec.
DEATH MARCH Baliuag

Calumpit Bridge
crossing 30-31 Dec. Calumpit
1 Jan.
SOUTH LUZON FORCE
Plaridel

San Mateo

ZAMBALES MOUNTAINS

Botolan

San Felipe

14°

San Antonio

Olongapo
Subic
Bay
Port Binanga
Moron
Mauban Abucay
Mt. Natib Balanga
Bataan Pilar
Peninsula
26 Jan. Orion
Bagac
Battle of Limay
the Pockets
26 Jan.-15 Feb.
I CORPS Tobeng
Battle of the Points
23 Jan.-13 Feb. II CORPS
MARIVELES Mariveles

Manila
Bay
Manila
2 Jan.

Nielson Field
Nichols Field
Cavite

Taytay

Laguna
Bay

Corregidor
5-6 May
Caballo

SOUTH

CHINA SEA

MacArthur to Australia 12 March

from Legaspi Dec. 24

Tarnate

Tagaytay Ridge

Nasugbu

Los
Banos

29 Dec.

Lake
Taal

15°
120°

Despite Bataan's ideal defenses of jungles,
mountains, and swamps, MacArthur's embattled
forces faced hunger, sickness, a scarcity of
everything and, finally, surrender.

"We do not have to reward our friends with posts in the government. They had taken them before we arrived."

The Japanese fleet meanwhile penetrated the Indian Ocean and hammered Ceylon. Admiral Jisaburo Ozawa captured the Andaman Islands in the Bay of Bengal, sank 112,000 tons of merchant shipping, and cruised menacingly along the coast. It seemed as if India, threatened by sea and by land from Burma, was about to disintegrate. Subhas Chandra Bose, a popular Bengali nationalist, began organizing an Indian army to fight the British. Radio Tokyo lauded the historic culture of Hindustan and called for rebellion against the alien masters. In March, 1942, Churchill sent Cripps, his Socialist ambassador to Moscow, on a special mission to Delhi to promise the Indians postwar independence. Mahatma Gandhi remarked, "They are offering us a postdated check on a bank that is obviously crashing"—and was put in jail.

But then, to the astonishment of the Allies, the Japanese high command, considering the Indian Ocean of but secondary importance, ordered its triumphant admirals eastward back to Singapore. Neither Ceylon nor India was ever again seriously threatened. The extreme danger that the Germans might come from Russia and Iran and the Japanese from Burma and India to join in a monstrous victory embrace was gone.

One of the principal objectives of the Japanese strategic plan was that wealthy colonial prize, the Dutch East Indies (now Indonesia). Japan desperately needed petroleum, and after Holland's occupation by the Nazis, Tokyo had applied increasing pressure on the Dutch colonial administration in Java. Even before the fall of Singapore, the Japanese landed troops near the Borneo oil fields, and shortly afterward, a massive invasion of Java began. To oppose this, the Allies assembled a small flotilla of American, Australian, and Dutch ships, which met the Japanese on February 27, 1942, in the three-day Battle of the Java Sea. The Allied force was entirely destroyed. By March 9, the whole archipelago was gone, and nearly one hundred thousand prisoners were marching off to Japanese concentration camps. In four weeks the Dutch lost an empire that they had owned for nearly four centuries.

One consequence of this sensational advance was to expose the entire continent of Australia to invasion. The Japanese pushed across the mountains of neighboring New Guinea and bombed

Darwin, the northern Australian port. A landing seemed imminent. A member of parliament at Canberra warned: "We are facing the vile abomination of a Jap invasion." The country was placed on a total-war footing, but there was a dangerous shortage of troops because of the units sent to North Africa.

Australia looked to the United States for help, but we were hard put to shoulder any added responsibilities. Pearl Harbor was paralyzed, and Wake Island, deep in the Pacific, had been lost to amphibious assault two days before Christmas. In the Philippines, a tough, efficiently commanded Japanese force had bottled up MacArthur's defenders on the peninsula of Bataan. His first line of defense was crushed by a redoubtable infantry thrust in which Japanese hurled themselves on barbed-wire entanglements, permitting their comrades to cross upon their writhing bodies. Then, as MacArthur fell back on a second line, a Japanese battalion landed behind him.

On February 22, 1942, following Churchill's advice, Roosevelt ordered MacArthur to abandon his force and go to Australia. On March 11, the handsome general and his family and staff quit Corregidor by PT boats. At Mindanao they transferred to two Flying Fortresses that flew them to Darwin, Australia, where MacArthur issued his famous statement: "The President of the United States ordered me to break through the Japanese lines and proceed from Corregidor to Australia for the purpose, as I understand, of organizing the American offensive against Japan, a primary purpose of which is the relief of the Philippines. I came through and I shall return."

Meanwhile, under MacArthur's successor, General Jonathan Wainwright, the defenders of Bataan fought on with great courage but small hope. Their rations had been halved in early January. Now they were foraging for any kind of flesh: dogs, pack mules, monkeys, iguanas, snakes. Ill fed, ravaged by tropical diseases, totally isolated, the troops composed their own war song:

We're the battling bastards of Bataan;
No mama, no papa, no Uncle Sam;
No aunts, no uncles, no nephews, no nieces;
No pills, no planes, no artillery pieces.
. . . and nobody gives a damn!

On April 8, Wainwright ordered the abandonment of Bataan. After destroying its ammunition dumps, the General and a few defenders retreated to the island fort of Corregidor; the rest surrendered. General Homma, the Japanese commander, then concentrated his artillery and bombers on the tunneled fortress, silencing its big guns one by one. On May 6, it too yielded.

The Japanese displayed particular callousness toward the American and Filipino soldiers they captured at Bataan, marching them sixty-five miles to a railway junction from which they were to entrain for an internment camp. Dazed and weak from thirst and starvation, the prisoners were formed into columns of fours, then driven forward under a blinding sun. Thousands of them died from disease or exhaustion or from Japanese brutality in what became known as "the Death March."

Despite the immense emotional pressures engendered by successive blows to American prestige in the Pacific, President Roosevelt and his Chiefs of Staff held to the strategy that had been fixed with Churchill well before Pearl Harbor. The first objective was still the defeat of Nazi Germany. In the Pacific, American planners emphasized the strategic triangle embracing Alaska, Hawaii, and Panama, thus implicitly accepting the loss of Wake, Guam, and the Philippines.

Both by his military strategists and by the officials chosen to mobilize the nation's industrial potential, Roosevelt was excellently served. Under their supervision, young men were drafted into the armed forces; women enlisted for noncombat duties; labor's work week was lengthened; a War Production Board took charge of America's immense factory potential. Between July 1, 1940, and July 31, 1945, the United States produced 296,601 aircraft, 71,060 ships, and 86,388 tanks. By the time peace came, over 15,000,000 Americans had served in the country's forces, 10,000,000 in the Army alone.

All the internal dissension occasioned by the lingering debate between isolationists and interventionists vanished after Pearl Harbor. Even Senator Wheeler said: "The only thing now to do is to lick the hell out of them." Colonel Lindbergh asked to be reinstated in the Air Corps; and since Hitler had attacked Russia, the Communists and other left-wing pacifists were now enthusiastic warriors. The Government saw to it that the pro-Nazi German-American Bund Organization was dissolved, but a wholly unjust penalty was paid by the Nisei, Americans of Japanese ancestry, who were forcibly relocated from the West Coast be-

This sign appeared in the window of a small
Oakland, California, store on December 8,
1941, but the owner, though a University of
California graduate and a U.S. citizen, was
later moved with other Japanese Americans to
a relocation camp. Some protectionist groups
that advocated relocation were probably
more interested in eliminating the Japanese
American as a business competitor than as
a possible spy or saboteur.

cause of exaggerated spy fears. Those Japanese Americans who later fought in the United States Army compiled a superb record for courage and endurance. I remember when at Cassino, as a Nisei battalion was moving into a particularly difficult position where it suffered heavy losses, some German prisoners simultaneously marched to our rear. One of the puzzled and astonished Germans asked an American lieutenant: "But aren't those Japanese?" "Yes," said the lieutenant. "Didn't you know they were on our side? Or do you believe all that stuff Goebbels tells you?"

If there had been any doubts about the fighting spirit of the American people, they were quickly dissolved. But for all the national energy and purpose, the Red Cross volunteers, the Irving Berlin songs, the speeches, and the hurry, hurry, hurry, the fact was that the first part of 1942 was a very dark time indeed. The news was nearly all bad. U-boats were sinking American ships with terrible regularity. The Japanese, hitherto held in contempt, had smashed our best fleet in Hawaii, defeated our best general in Luzon, destroyed Britain's finest warships, captured her most impregnable fortress, and seized a huge empire in one incredibly swift campaign. It was clearly necessary for Americans to prove to themselves that they were capable of hitting back, and to prove to the Japanese that they would suffer for their impudence. Out of this determination was born the bombing raid on Tokyo led by Colonel James Doolittle.

The idea originated with a submarine staff officer, Captain Francis S. Low, who submitted a plan for using Army bombers from aircraft carriers. General "Hap" Arnold, head of the Army Air Corps, asked Doolittle to study the project. Doolittle ascertained that, properly modified, B-25 medium bombers could carry one-ton bomb loads and still manage the risky, short takeoff. Sixteen planes with specially selected five-man crews were prepared for the dangerous mission and loaded aboard the carrier *Hornet*. On April 18, 1942, some 670 miles from Tokyo, they flew off one by one, in a strong wind that helped lift them from the short deck. Their orders were to strike the enemy capital and head for a small airfield deep inside unoccupied China. The resolute bombers swung in over Japan, spending some six minutes over the target, where, ironically, a practice air raid drill was going on. All but one of the planes later crashed or were abandoned in China or off the coast of China; one landed at Vladivostok, and its crew were interned by the Russians; two came down inside enemy territory, and three of their crewmen were later shot in reprisal for American bombing of Japanese residential areas. Of the eighty flyers on the mission, seventy-one eventually returned to the United States.

Tokyo had a hard time figuring out where Doolittle's planes had come from. President Roosevelt facetiously announced that they had taken off from Shangri-La, the Himalayan retreat of James Hilton's novel, *Lost Horizon*.

Doolittle's feat was audacious and psychologically important, even if, having inflicted minimal damage, it had little effect upon the course of the war itself. All that spring, the Japanese war machine continued to grind out victories.

It was only later, near the little island of Midway, in June, 1942, that the tide began to turn.

VI

War at Sea

British seamen battle ice and high seas
in the North Atlantic, 1943.

When Hitler began his onslaught in 1939, he reckoned that sea power was not a crucial military matter. Unlike the favored *Luftwaffe*, the German navy was ill prepared. Not even Germany's redoubtable U-boat fleet was ready for a long campaign. But it was the sea—the narrow English Channel—that inevitably thwarted Hitler's ambitions for total domination of Europe and led him to turn his armies eastward into the disastrous Russian snows. In North Africa, where Rommel almost broke the British on the verges of the Nile, failure to control the Mediterranean narrows cost the Germans still another important triumph. And ultimately, from across the seas, came a huge American armada. As time passed, even the U-boats began to lose their efficacy.

Japan made no such basic miscalculation. As a sea people, the Japanese were instinctively aware of the maritime key to victory, and they boasted a massive fleet that included the world's two largest battleships, the 72,908-ton *Yamato*, and the *Musashi*. The flaw in Tokyo's thinking was the belief that an initial advantage attained at Pearl Harbor would gain sufficient time to insure an impregnable economic and military position, and that this in turn could ward off eventual counterattack. As General Marshall reported in 1945, such assumptions proved erroneous because "the Japanese had reckoned without the shipyards of America and the fighting tradition of the United States Navy."

In 1939, when the conflict started, the world was accustomed to regarding Britain as the great maritime power, but the Royal Navy was no longer that Queen of the Seas that had dominated the nineteenth century. Despite admirable equipment made available by British scientists, it was not sufficiently strong for the immense combination of duties it had to face. Despite fifty destroyers that the United States had made available at Churchill's request, and despite a concentrated building program, the entire British battle fleet by the end of World War II was no larger than the single U.S. Task Force 77 in the Pacific.

Had the Germans produced a thoroughly rational and consistent strategy, they might have capitalized upon British weakness; but Hitler began full-scale naval preparations only in 1939. Admiral Erich Raeder, commander in chief of Hitler's navy, had hoped there would be no conflict before 1942, by which date he planned to have ready a prodigious fleet that would include two hundred and fifty U-boats, thirteen battleships, and four aircraft carriers. When the *Führer* precipitated war, Raeder was forced to abandon this program and concentrate on the immediate construction of submarines.

Because the British were spread so thin and because the German fleet was inadequate, the naval potential of Italy and France assumed heightened importance. The Italians had fast ships but showed more dash in maneuvers than in battle. They were never able to control the eastern Mediterranean, even when British power was at its ebb. Had the Axis gained the use of the French Navy, however, the balance might have been dangerously turned. After France's capitulation, those of its vessels to join Britain had little importance. Other units, seized in Alexandria harbor, were interned according to their wish. The main strength lay in Toulon, with substantial forces also anchored at the Mers-el-Kebir base of Oran in Algeria. On July 3, 1940, unwilling to risk the possiblity that these might help the Axis, the British sent an ultimatum to the Oran flotilla. When the French commander failed to respond within six hours, the British then attacked and seriously damaged three battleships, a seaplane carrier, and two destroyers.

The Oran battle between the vessels of two allies was a difficult and heartrending affair (more than a thousand French sailors were killed); but it was made necessary by British determination to retain the upper hand at sea. Inflammatory Nazi propaganda stressed this tragic engagement and sought to persuade the French to join the campaign against Britain. Nevertheless, as Churchill later and generously recalled in his history of the war: "The genius of France enabled her people to comprehend the whole significance of Oran, and in her agony to draw new hope and strength from this additional bitter pang. General de Gaulle, whom I did not consult beforehand, was magnificent in his demeanour, and France liberated and restored has ratified his conduct."

The first dramatic confrontations of the war at sea were between conventional surface vessels. The earliest of these was the hunting down of the *Graf Spee*, third and last of those German pocket battleships so neatly designed to get around the regulations of the Versailles Treaty: fast, light, heavily gunned and armored. When hostilities started, it dashed for the southern Atlantic to prey on Allied shipping and soon sank nine cargo vessels off the coast of Latin America.

On December 13, 1939, the *Graf Spee* appeared near Uruguay, where it was surprised by three British cruisers, *Exeter*, *Achilles*, and *Ajax*. For fourteen hours the ships pounded away at one another. Then the *Graf Spee* turned away through the phosphorescent offshore seas and sought haven in Montevideo. It was summarily ordered out by the neutral Uruguayans. On December 17, the *Graf Spee* blew itself up in the broad River Plate while three hundred thousand spectators lined the shore to watch. Captain Hans Langsdorff, a veteran of the famous World War I encounter at Jutland, was interned in Argentina with his crew. Three days later, he draped around him the old German Imperial Naval flag, ignoring Hitler's swastika, and shot himself dead.

For the British people, the end of the *Graf Spee* was a comforting victory that their propaganda services were able to dramatize with some effect. The Germans, somewhat puzzled, sought to play down its importance. At the time, I was in Slovakia, the Nazi puppet state carved from the murdered Czechoslovak Republic, traveling with Edward Kennedy, an Associated Press reporter. We were arrested by the Gestapo and, despite United States neutrality, accused of espionage—a charge we easily refuted. The scuttling of the *Graf Spee* coincided with our release, and all the local press covered its front pages with accounts of the presence of two "English spies," Kennedy and myself. News of the River Plate battle occupied only a few brief inside paragraphs.

A second great sea encounter came in the spring of 1941, when the German dreadnought *Bismarck*, accompanied by the cruiser *Prinz Eugen*, sailed from occupied Poland through the British blockade, intent on sinking as much tonnage as possible on the cold, gray North Atlantic. Six U-boats were assigned to help the mighty surface raider. The British first spotted the *Bismarck* when it was refueling at Bergen, Norway, on May 21 and began to mark its passage through fog and clouds. Three days later, in clear weather, the powerful *Hood* and *Prince of Wales* found their enemy and opened fire. The *Hood* was destroyed by a formidable salvo; the *Prince of Wales*, badly damaged, limped away. But the *Bismarck*, also seriously wounded and leaving a steady oil trail, turned back, at reduced speed, to seek haven at Saint-Nazaire in occupied France.

On the morning of May 26, a Royal Air Force flying boat once again spotted the great ship, still seven hundred miles from

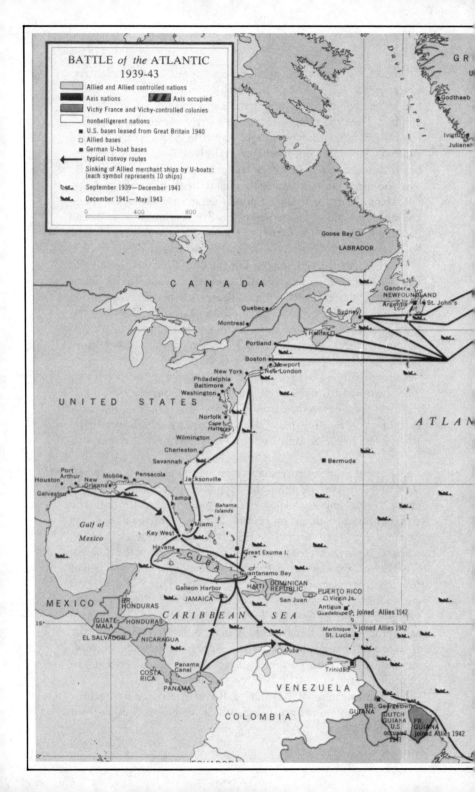

BATTLE of the ATLANTIC
1939-43

Allied and Allied controlled nations
Axis nations ▨▨▨ Axis occupied
Vichy France and Vichy-controlled colonies
nonbelligerent nations
■ U.S. bases leased from Great Britain 1940
□ Allied bases
■ German U-boat bases
← typical convoy routes
Sinking of Allied merchant ships by U-boats:
(each symbol represents 10 ships)
🦅 September 1939—December 1941
🦅 December 1941—May 1943

0   400   800

GR

Godthaab

Ivigtut
Julianeh

Davis Strait

Goose Bay □
LABRADOR

C A N A D A

Gander
NEWFOUNDLAND
Argentia   St. John's

Quebec

Montreal

Sydney

Halifax

Portland

Boston
Newport
New London

New York

Philadelphia
Baltimore
Washington

U N I T E D   S T A T E S

Norfolk
Cape
Hatteras

ATLAN

Wilmington

Charleston

Savannah

Jacksonville

■ Bermuda

Port
Arthur
New
Houston Mobile Pensacola
Galveston   New
Orleans

Tampa

Bahama
Islands

Gulf of
Mexico

Key West

Havana   C U B A

Great Exuma I.

Guantanamo Bay

Galleon Harbor
JAMAICA

HAITI
DOMINICAN
REPUBLIC
San Juan

PUERTO RICO
□ Virgin Js.
Antigua ■
Guadeloupe joined Allies 1942

M E X I C O   BR.
HONDURAS

GUATE-
MALA   HONDURAS
EL SALVADOR NICARAGUA

C A R I B B E A N   S E A

Martinique joined Allies 1942
St. Lucia ■

COSTA
RICA
PANAMA

Panama
Canal

◇ Aruba

Trinidad

VENEZUELA

COLOMBIA

BR. Georgetown
GUIANA
DUTCH
GUIANA
U.S.
occupied
1941
FR.
GUIANA
joined Allies 1942

ECUADOR

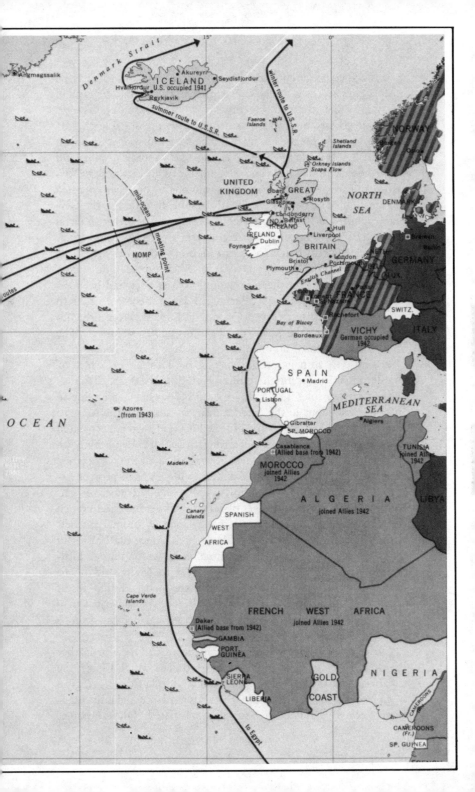

the French coast, and the British sent torpedo planes to delay its escape. *Bismarck* was struck twice, once in the rudder. Its captain knew now that the end was not far off. His antiaircraft crews were out of ammunition, so he dropped them alongside on rafts and made ready for the inevitable. The next morning a squadron of British ships encircled their victim like yapping hounds and opened concentrated fire. The were unable to pierce the *Bismarck's* armored deck or destroy its engines, but one by one they smashed the machinery of its turrets. Finally, unable to proceed, the German captain scuttled. In a strategic sense this was a British naval triumph because Hitler lost his greatest and irreplaceable battleship. But in the process Britain also lost its most powerful vessel, the *Hood*, and suffered damage to two other battleships, a destroyer, and many planes. Furthermore, much of its fleet had been diverted from important Mediterranean assignments in order to encompass the elusive *Bismarck's* end, and this weakened the defense of Crete at the moment of its invasion on June 1. The victory proved to be an expensive one.

Second only in naval importance to the Home Fleet's task of supplying and guarding the United Kingdom itself was Britain's Mediterranean role. The lovely inland sea served as a lifeline to British possessions in the Middle East, to Suez and the route to India, and to the Army of the Nile, which had been concentrated in Egypt in 1939. From the start, the British depended heavily on France to police the western Mediterranean, and they weakened their own forces in the east by withdrawing ships to protect Atlantic convoys when Mussolini initially failed to declare war. However, the combined effect of Italian belligerency and French collapse suddenly altered the relative balance. With fewer vessels at their disposal, the British suddenly had to face the Italians in the eastern Mediterranean and assume in the west a burden hitherto left to the French. From Gibraltar to Malta and on to Alexandria, their bases were now directly menaced. The result was the War Cabinet order to attack France's Oran naval base and carry out a series of aggressive actions against Mussolini's speedy but inept fleet.

Admiral Sir Andrew Cunningham, a tough, hell-for-leather sea dog, first struck a large force of Italian warships off the Calabrian coast. He drove another Italian flotilla from the region of Cape Spatha, northwest of Crete. His hard-pressed units managed to convoy badly needed supplies to isolated Malta, and then,

The *Graf Spee* explodes off Montevideo, where
she had been trapped by British cruisers.
Armed with six 11-inch guns, eight 5.9-inch
guns, and eight torpedo tubes, she was one
of Hitler's deadliest weapons. Captain
Langsdorff, the commander, scuttled her
rather than risk having her fall into
British hands. Later, after his crew was
safely interned in Argentina, he felt
honor-bound to follow the fate of his ship.

on November 11, 1940, he thrust a carrier raid at Taranto, on Italy's heel, while all Mussolini's battleships were in port. Heavy damage was inflicted by obsolete Swordfish aircraft. When the smoke cleared, the *Duce* found his battle force had been halved. Of his six mightiest ships, one never sailed again, and two others were out of action for months. Taranto was abandoned as a fleet base when the surviving vessels scurried for Naples. News of this famous victory was broadcast through embattled Greece, and the vivacious Greeks went mad with joy.

Until Sicily was successfully invaded by the Allies in 1943, the Mediterranean was constantly ripped apart by sea and naval-air battles. To gain the upper hand, Hitler's high command conceived a plan called Operation Felix, designed to bring Spain into the war and block the Gibraltar straits. However, Franco demurred, and ultimately the idea was dropped. Instead, the Germans first sent a mechanized Afrika Korps to help the Italians in the Libyan Desert and then rescued Mussolini's bogged-down Army in Albania by crushing Yugoslavia, Greece, and Crete. Malta, as a result, was more cut off and threatened than ever before. *Luftwaffe* squadrons were moved into the Mediterranean, and Alexandria and the Suez Canal came under immediate danger. To supply its Middle East forces, Britain was now forced to send convoys by the long and costly route around the Cape of Good Hope. The Navy was further weakened during the Battle of Crete and the consequent need to evacuate British and Greek troops when that island fell. The Admiralty grimly notified the War Office that if it were to lose Cyprus after Crete, it could expect no further succor.

The next and immensely difficult naval task was to hold on to Malta and from that rocky base hamper the flow of Axis supplies from southern Italy to North Africa, where Rommel had begun to threaten the Nile Valley. British losses en route to Malta were enormous. In April, 1942, Churchill urged Roosevelt to make the carrier *Wasp* available to fly in help. The request was granted, and some sixty Spitfires were dispatched. Within a few days, all were destroyed. Nevertheless, the tough little island held out and kept Rommel pinched for supplies. Once again the *Führer* paid dearly for Italy's weakness.

The Mediterranean naval war was a desperate and hemmed-in affair in which land-based aircraft played an increasingly prominent role. But at least it had the advantage of being fought in an agreeable arena. When men jumped from their sinking ships, they stood a good chance of surviving. The war in the Atlantic was another story. There a dreary, lengthy, and far more strategically vital battle was fought to decide whether Britain would survive and become the marshaling point and base for the ultimate European assault. Britain was the node between triumph and disaster; and its safety, as it had for centuries past, relied on its ships.

The Battle of the Atlantic endured through two stages. In the first, before Pearl Harbor, Britain—with increasing United States support—fought to keep its supply channels open against the savage and expert U-boat hunters and to track down any German surface vessels that ventured out to open water. During the latter part of this stage, American warships, violating all technical definitions of neutrality, helped to escort convoys across the northern arc from Newfoundland to the Irish Sea. On the last day of October, 1941, more than a month before Pearl Harbor, the first United States warship was sunk: the *Reuben James*. A trim but obsolete American destroyer, "the Rube" was helping out the shorthanded British in the protection of a convoy west of Ireland when its direction finder locked on U-boat signals. Moments later, it was hit by a torpedo. The magazine exploded, and the ship was blown in two. More than one hundred men, including the captain and all of its officers, were lost.

After Pearl Harbor, Hitler launched a submarine offensive against the North American seaboard. Eastern ports such as New York, Boston, and Norfolk had to be protected with mines, nets, and booms. Coastal convoys were established, blackouts ordered, and ship radios restricted after U-boat packs, operating initially in northern waters off Newfoundland and then moving south to warmer bases in the Caribbean, achieved astonishing initial success.

In the first seven months of 1942, German submarines sank an appalling total of six hundred and eighty-one Allied ships, at small cost. Nevertheless, as American radar and American planes came increasingly into play, the ratio changed to Germany's disadvantage. Long-range aircraft operating from Newfoundland, Northern Ireland, and Iceland hunted down enemy raiders and blasted them into the depths. As the Nazis lost their best submarine commanders, replacements proved less expert and less resolute. By late spring, 1943, Admiral Doenitz was forced to conclude:

Although the American Navy repelled the
Japanese invasion force in the Battle of the
Coral Sea, it lost a destroyer, an oiler,
and, most grievous of all, the *Lexington*
(above). Converted from a battle cruiser,
she was a tough ship, and it appeared for
a time that she would survive the torpedo
damage. Then internal explosions rent
her, and she had to be abandoned and sunk
by an American destroyer.

"Losses, even heavy losses, must be borne when they are accompanied by corresponding sinkings. But in May in the Atlantic the destruction of every 10,000 tons was paid for by the loss of one U-boat. . . . The losses have therefore reached an unbearable height." And Churchill proudly reported to the House of Commons that at sea, June "was the best month from every point of view we have ever known in the whole forty-six months of the war." Moreover, Roosevelt and Churchill, honoring their promises to Stalin, managed to start convoying vast amounts of matériel along the so-called Murmansk Run, a dangerous route from Scotland, north of Nazi-occupied Norway, and on to the northern Russian ports of Murmansk and Archangel.

The Atlantic battle was a dirty, cold, grueling business. Nerves were constantly on edge, whether in the quivering, claustrophobic submarines, dodging among depth bombs, or aboard the destroyers zigzagging overhead, always on the alert for telltale sonar signals. Vessels were generally sunk by submarine shellfire if they had not been finished off by the first torpedo salvos, and at times, during the early part of the Atlantic battle, before the Allies had perfected their defenses, U-boats even attacked from the surface. In those days, when crews escaped in lifeboats, they were sometimes overhauled, questioned on their destinations and cargoes, offered provisions and cigarettes, and told with bluff bonhomie to send the bill for damages to Roosevelt or Churchill. But such hearty comradeliness soon was to disappear. More and more frequently, survivors were machine-gunned as they tried to swim through viscous oil slicks, ducking to escape the searing flames, or as they floundered about, clinging to rafts or life preservers. The Battle of the Atlantic became brutal and merciless.

It was apparent quite early that the United States was unprepared for the combined responsibilities of a naval war in two oceans, and this disadvantage was dreadfully emphasized by the disaster at Pearl Harbor, which crippled our Pacific striking power. In July, 1940, Congress had passed a "Two-Ocean Navy" bill, designed to make our fleets all-powerful by 1944. We were far from such a condition in early 1942, yet our productive capacity was able to keep well ahead of our initial losses. Shipyards began turning out a destroyer in five months instead of twelve. Big carriers were launched within fifteen months instead of three years. By the end of World War II, despite heavy casualties, the

United States had six more battleships, twenty-one more aircraft carriers, seventy more escort carriers, and one hundred and twenty-seven more submarines than in 1941. United States industrial know-how and production wholly upset the calculations of both Japan and Germany, which reckoned respectively on surprise massacre and steady U-boat attrition to restrict America's capacity to fight overseas.

At Mare Island shipyard in California, the longest assembly line in the United States was established. Over twelve hundred miles inland, in Denver, Colorado, vessels were constructed in sections and sent by rail to the sea. Prefabricated landing craft were shipped in pieces and assembled abroad for attacks on distant shores. Andrew Higgins developed an amphibious assault boat that was used on almost every invasion beach from Guadalcanal to Normandy. Donald Roebling invented a tracked landing vehicle that could crawl from the water like a turtle. And both the Navy and the Marine Corps perfected ingenious encircling strategies and tactics of envelopment by land, sea, and air that ultimately enabled them to bypass the tremendous range of Japanese positions on the long route to Tokyo.

But the greatest innovation in naval fighting during World War II was the aircraft carrier. This then relatively novel weapon was given its first major test in the Pacific during the Coral Sea battle of May, 1942. General MacArthur, heeding Roosevelt's orders to protect Australia, decided to base his defense north of that helpless continent. He chose the little town of Port Moresby on New Guinea as the hub for his strategic maneuver. The Japanese had been trying to take Port Moresby by land, but New Guinea's treacherous mountains seemed impassable. Therefore they decided to attack by water and sent a huge invasion fleet down past the Solomon Islands and into the Coral Sea. To insure success, they ordered in a carrier force commanded by Vice-Admiral Shigeyoshi Inouye, who was met by Australian and American warships under Rear Admiral Frank Fletcher. Fletcher had at his disposal the two big flattops *Yorktown* and *Lexington*. The result was the first of those famous sea-air confrontations that became a phenomenon peculiar to the Pacific between 1942 and 1945.

Almost as if blindfolded, the two admirals groped toward each other, each dependent upon his pilots to tell him what was happening. Conventional naval artillery was silent during the engagement because the ships never came close enough to exchange

In naval uniform, Emperor Hirohito (front row, center) poses with the officers of the giant battleship *Musashi*. Japanese morale was riding high in the spring of 1942, despite minor setbacks in the Coral Sea. The Emperor's Navy would seem invincible until its crushing defeat at Midway, the battle that marked the end of their long, impressive sea offensive.

fire. But antiaircraft guns blazed, and bombs and torpedoes came flashing out of the tropical sky. The unprecedented battle continued for two days. Consequent losses were rather evenly balanced, with both the great Japanese carrier *Shoho* and the *Lexington* sunk. But the Japanese assault force was turned back; Australia remained inviolate; and Port Moresby soon became the starting point for the long, island-hopping campaign that took MacArthur back to the Philippines and onward to Japan.

At this point the Japanese high command decided that it was time for a dramatic move. Admiral Yamamoto had convinced his colleagues at Imperial Headquarters that a single major naval engagement would prove decisive for the course of the rest of the war. The little-known island of Midway, situated some one thousand miles northwest of Honolulu, was selected as the focal point for the attack, and an armada of over one hundred warships plus transport and supply vessels was marshaled to deal the knockout blow. Yamamoto reasoned that the capture of Midway would mean Japanese penetration of Hawaiian waters, giving Japan a base in the eastern Pacific from which to harry and shake the American people. He ordered a diversionary attack against the Aleutian Islands of Alaska and fixed an operational date of June 7. Then he dispatched a coded order: "Commander in Chief Combined Fleet, in cooperation with the Army, will invade and occupy strategic points in the Western Aleutians and Midway Island."

The force assigned to this task was the most powerful in Japan's naval history. It included eight carriers and eleven battleships. Yamamoto himself took command of this combined fleet. Vice-Admiral Chuichi Nagumo was given the vital carrier striking force. Yamamoto was relying once again on secrecy and surprise, but he was still unaware that the United States had broken the Japanese codes. This time the advantage was properly interpreted. Admiral Chester Nimitz in Honolulu knew of Yamamoto's intentions and began his countermeasures. Later he admitted: "Had we lacked early information of the Japanese movements, and had we been caught with carrier forces dispersed . . . the Battle of Midway would have ended differently."

Vice-Admiral Jinichi Kusaka, a staff officer in the operation, thought it was merely a matter of bad luck that an American seaplane spotted the enormous fleet as it gathered up a convoy of assault troops from Saipan, some twenty-six hundred miles west of Midway. But Nimitz had ordered that sweeping searches be made, and two task forces under Admirals Spruance and Fletcher were deployed to meet the armada. Their strength, even in carriers, was not equal to the Japanese; but they relied on the support of land-based planes from Midway itself and ultimately from Honolulu.

The fighting started June 4, 1942. Japanese planes swept off from their carriers to hit the little island target, and American planes retaliated by seeking out the invasion force. During four entire days, furious fighting raged. Again, as in the Coral Sea, aircraft battered ships that were always too distant from each other to fire their customary broadsides. One group of fifteen American torpedo bombers continued to press home their attack until all had been shot down by a curtain of antiaircraft fire thrown up around the huge Japanese carriers. Only one man survived to tell the tale. But four of Yamamoto's carriers were so heavily hit that they became blazing hulks. The captain of the *Akagi* ruefully noted: "We were unable to avoid the dive bombers because we were so occupied in avoiding the torpedoes." As one by one the Japanese flattops were crippled, their planes flew off helplessly and dropped into the warm Pacific.

Yamamoto finally decided to turn homeward before his entire force vanished. As it was, he had suffered a smashing defeat, losing four carriers and a heavy cruiser plus many damaged vessels. The Americans lost one carrier, the *Yorktown*, one destroyer, and more than one hundred planes. But this was a small price to pay. The Japanese Navy had forced a showdown with superior strength, and it was decisively beaten. Instead of threatening Hawaii and the West Coast, Japan suddenly found itself upon the defensive for the first time.

From that historic instant, the American counteroffensive began to gather force and to move relentlessly toward the home islands of Japan. Midway was one of World War II's critical battles, ranking in importance with Dunkirk, El Alamein, and Stalingrad. The tiny atoll group was, indeed, properly named, for the contest marked a dividing line in strategy if not in time. Everything before Midway was an immense Japanese success, and everything after, a failure. At Midway the Rising Sun that had shone so suddenly and so ferociously over all Asia slowly began to set.

VII
The Desert War

A cross-grained terrain of tank and tire
tracks and this disabled panzer mark the
traffic of Montgomery's passage to Tripoli.

Shepheard's Hotel in Cairo was World War II's most singular hostelry. There, amid unaccustomed luxury, red-tabbed British colonels back from the fighting in Libya vied for a place at the bar. Brigadiers were allotted beds at the favor of a Swiss concièrge, who cured one such officer of incipient alcoholism by rooming him with a subaltern who kept a crocodile in the bathtub. From the terrace, one could see passing on the street below a cinematic panorama of war: tough Australian sergeants advising enraged majors, "We ain't saluting today"; Free French subalterns; Greek commandos; Poles and Yugoslavs; vociferous English Cockneys; huge South Africans from the veld; and bearded Indian Sikhs.

The view from Shepheard's was romantic—and deceptive. It was easy to forget that the power implied by soldiers of so many nations had in fact been driven out of Europe, back to Stalingrad and to the very borders of the Nile. And yet, from the Egyptian capital, for all its tenuous neutrality, its good food and its belly dancers, its ancient monuments and its golf courses, a vast and patient strategy evolved.

Working according to the best of British imperial and naval traditions, this strategy slowly squeezed off victories in salients as far removed as Madagascar, Tripolitania, and the Dodecanese. From Cairo headquarters stemmed Colonel Orde Wingate's remarkable Ethiopian foray, against bravely commanded Italians, that succeeded in restoring Haile Selassie to his throne. Cairo pried a small corps out of the Western Desert and dispatched it on a hopeless mission to Greece. Cairo arranged the seizure of Italian Somaliland and of vital Eritrea, on the Red Sea. With armies that were little more than paper organizational tables, Cairo headquarters ran German sympathizers out of Iran, Iraq, Syria, and Lebanon and coordinated Balkan guerrillas. Cairo was the base for two daring British raiding officers who jumped into Crete and kidnapped the commanding German general. And Cairo was the base for a good-natured bunch of thugs assembled under a Belgian guerrilla who called his gang Popski's Private Army and led it from Alexandria to the Alps. Using a maximum of panache and a minimum of effectives, the sprawling, overstaffed Cairo command regained control of more square miles of hostile territory than it had soldiers to deploy.

When the war began, Britain had assembled in Egypt a force vaingloriously named the Army of the Nile, under the overall command of Sir Archibald Wavell, a one-eyed general who boasted diplomatic skill and strategic talents more lavishly admired by his contemporaries than by history. It was Wavell who planned the first success in the famous Western Desert campaign.

In September, 1940, Marshal Rodolfo Graziani had penetrated Egypt at Sidi Barrani, but the Western Desert campaign really began that December, when the vastly outnumbered British attacked the Italian Army and drove it into Libya.

The December, 1940, campaign was an unqualified British victory. While the Greeks were making mockery of Mussolini's invasion from Albania, Wavell took a series of Libyan citadels from the *Duce*'s badly commanded African army, penetrating deep into Cyrenaica and capturing enormous quantities of matériel and some one hundred and thirty thousand prisoners, including a red-bearded little general named Bergonzoli, who had been nicknamed "Electric Whiskers" by his troops and who had become something of a legend for his prowess at losing battles but always escaping.

As a result of Italy's humiliations in Albania and Libya, Hitler was forced to spread his forces by dispatching aid. General Marshall later concluded that this overextension "subsequently became one of the principal factors in Germany's defeat." The *Führer* sent his *Fliegerkorps* X to stiffen the Italian Air Force. Then, along with a German armored corps, he sent in Rommel.

Erwin Rommel, who had once, if briefly, been a Nazi bullyboy, soon became Hitler's favorite general, a place he held until, suspected of helping plot the *Führer*'s downfall, he was ordered to commit suicide and so save his family from Gestapo torture. A keen, brave man, he became a master of armored warfare, leading his units into combat from the turret of his tank, exploiting the slightest opening presented. His men idolized him, and even Churchill said, "His ardor and daring inflicted grievous disasters upon us. . . . [He was] a great general."

Rommel opened his first offensive March 24, 1941, a few weeks before Hitler overran the Balkans. He drove into Egypt, leaving an isolated British garrison sealed off in the Libyan port of Tobruk. From bases in Tripolitania and Sicily, the *Luftwaffe* started to raid Alexandria, Port Said, and Suez and intensively mined the canal, thus cutting off the main route to India and hampering Wavell's normal supply lines. But the improvised fortress of Tobruk held out on Rommel's flank. It was reinforced by General Sir Alan Cunningham of the newly named Eighth Army. (The overall commander for the Middle East was now General Sir Claude Auchinleck. In June, Churchill had decided that Wavell needed a rest from desert campaigning and had sent him to India.) All through the summer and autumn of 1941, coastal ships from Alexandria scurried along the dangerous North African shore to strengthen the besieged port.

During the fourteen months following Rommel's arrival in Libya, the Desert War was a seesaw affair. There were lengthy advances and retreats but no crucial victory in what the Tommies called "miles and miles and bloody miles of absolutely damn all." Soldiers learned to navigate like sailors, reckoning the featureless spaces by map, compass, speedometer, and stars. At night, formations of each side would encamp, unsure just where the other's hull-down tanks lay. Acres of flatness were marked by countless tracks left by the treads and tires of past battles, littered with piles of jerry-cans and discarded tins of food, swarming with insects. Drivers sought to steer to the windward of each other and thus escape the dust. From desert shoes to goggles, they were generally covered by a beige coating compounded of sand, dust, and sweat. Supply services were hard pressed to provide enough water for the thirsty vehicles and men.

From the start of this extraordinary campaign, the naval-minded British realized the critical importance of Malta to the desert fighting. They kept the island bastion alive, losing vast shipping tonnage in the process. But the price was not too heavy; Rommel's need for supplies and reinforcements could not be satisfied so long as Axis convoys were being smashed from Malta. Hitler and Mussolini therefore agreed on a full-scale amphibious and airborne assault on the island, called Operation Herkules. But when Tobruk was finally taken from the besieged British in spring, 1942, the Malta attack was called off and the assault forces were allotted directly to Rommel instead. This was a capital strategic error. Despite the heavy cost to reinforcement convoys from Gibraltar and Alexandria, Spitfires, submarines, and destroyers from Malta kept on hammering Axis supply lines. Rommel's eventual defeat owed as much to these pilots and naval crews as to Montgomery's Desert Rats.

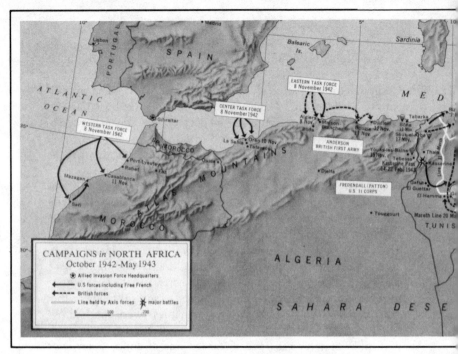

CAMPAIGNS in NORTH AFRICA
October 1942 - May 1943

✹ Allied Invasion Force Headquarters
→ U.S forces including Free French
◄--- British forces
------ Line held by Axis forces ✗ major battles

0   100   200

Phase three of the war in North Africa
(detailed in the map below) began in
the fall of 1942, when the British and
Americans invaded Morocco and Algeria.
The British Eighth Army, now commanded
by General Bernard Montgomery, struck at
El Alamein and sent the Axis armies falling
back on one of the longest retreats in
history. In eighty days Rommel traveled
seventeen hundred and fifty miles, or about
as far as from Paris to Moscow. Behind
him he left a desert strewn with burnt-out
tanks and thousands of dead and wounded.
At the end of his retreat, he ran into the
British First Army and the Americans coming
in from the west. The map at right shows
the battle of Kasserine Pass, where Rommel,
reinforced with new armor, drove a "bulge"
into the Allied lines and gave the American
Army its first real taste of German fire.
The weight of the attack had caught the
Allies by surprise, and some twenty-four
hundred green GIs surrendered.

104

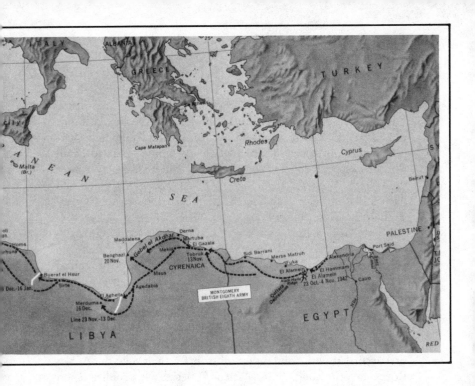

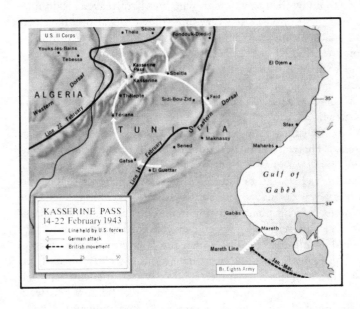

In August, 1942, Churchill flew to Cairo in order to weigh the military prospects before meeting Stalin for the first time. Rommel by then had established a new forward position deep inside Egypt. The British Prime Minister, in one of his most significant military decisions, reorganized his command. He named General Sir Harold Alexander to replace Auchinleck as head of all Middle Eastern forces. Then, to take over the Eighth Army after the officer slated for that post, W.H.E. ("Strafer") Gott, had been killed in an airplane crash, he picked Lieutenant General Bernard L. Montgomery.

Monty, as he became known to his soldiers, was a highly debatable figure, detested by many officers. At that moment he was fifty-five years old, lean, tough, conceited, insolent, and as yet relatively unknown. His tastes were plain; he was a stern disciplinarian who forced his staff to keep strenuously fit, frowned on smoking and drinking, fired many of the commanders he had inherited, and injected into his dispirited army a sudden surge of confidence. His troops began to cherish the label Desert Rats, first accorded with contempt, and stole for their own the Afrika Korps' favorite song, "Lili Marlene." Because his soldiers soon came to know their new leader, who wisely displayed his double-badged beret on visits to every unit, they came also to have personal faith in his craft and wisdom. He insisted on refraining from the offensive until he had overwhelming weapons superiority. And with such superiority, his army soon presented him with a massive string of victories.

Monty was a lonely man and in some respects a priggish puritan, a latter-day Cromwell. He was fascinated by his own homilies and had a habit of repeating them at least twice for the sake of stress. "There are only two rules of war," I have heard him say, "only two rules of war. Never invade Russia. Never invade China. Never invade Russia or China." Eisenhower believed that Montgomery was an inadequate strategist. At a French golf club he demonstrated his point, drawing maps on paper cloths and marking divisions with salt and pepper cellars to show how Monty should have fought at El Alamein and later at the Falaise Gap in France. Hans Speidel, at one time Rommel's chief of staff, insists that Montgomery understood only two maneuvers, a left hook and a thrust through the center, and that because he always telegraphed his punches, the Germans knew in advance what he planned to do. This may be, but he gave heart to a disheartened army at a critical moment. He combined the stern talents of Cromwell with the persistence of Wellington. If he is not accepted as Britain's greatest ground commander since the Iron Duke, at any rate, he never lost a battle. Let that be his epitaph.

Montgomery was aware that Rommel was then preparing his final push toward Alexandria and the Nile, but he was not dismayed. He propped Rommel's photograph in his headquarters and, with characteristic immodesty, remarked: "Give me a fortnight and I can resist the German attack. Give me three weeks, and I can defeat the Boche. Give me a month and I can chase him out of Africa." As it was, Monty spent two months just getting ready for the chase.

Fate threw these two great captains against each other sixty miles west of Alexandria, in an ugly, arid patch called El Alamein. To the north lay the Mediterranean flank, covered by the Royal Navy, and to the south gaped an impassable rock canyon named the Qattara Depression. Thus the battlefield was a narrow passage that restricted the customary wide, high-speed flanking movements of desert warfare. The passage itself was strewn with mines and packed densely with guns and tanks. It was impossible for infantry to dig in on the rock-studded terrain. Rommel was intent on punching through this gap before his opponent could thicken his own defenses. In August he said: "We hold the gateway to Egypt with full intention to act. We did not go there with the intention of being flung back sooner or later."

And indeed, his power seemed inexorable. Were he to penetrate, the entire Nile Valley would be exposed to the fanning out of his tanks and self-propelled guns. The British moved masses of stores from the neighborhood of Cairo, flew out dependents, and established distant contingency headquarters. Hitler ordered medals struck to honor the expected triumph of his Afrika Korps; Mussolini sent his favorite white charger to Libya so he could ride through Cairo in a victory parade. But the British lines held. In September, Rommel flew to Germany to report to Hitler, complaining at the *Führer*'s East Prussian headquarters that R.A.F. bombers were destroying his panzers with American 40-mm. shells. "Quite impossible," Göring observed. "Nothing but latrine rumors. All the Americans can make are razor blades and refrigerators." Rommel replied: "I only wish, *Herr Reichsmarschall*, that we were issued similar razor blades!"

During the Western Desert campaign against
the Italians, General Archibald Wavell's guns
pounded Derna, a key seaport along the
route to Tripolitania. War on the rock-hard desert,
where there was no cover and few landmarks
to take bearings on, was more like a sea fight
than anything else, which may have been
one reason why the British were so good at it.

Rommel was resting at a German sanatorium when in late October, 1942, Montgomery at last felt strong enough to launch his own offensive. On October 23, Montgomery announced to his troops: "When I assumed command of the Eighth Army I said that the mandate was to destroy Rommel and his Army, and that it would be done as soon as we were ready. We are ready NOW!"

Thunderous artillery pieces, to the clattering counterpoint of mortars and machine guns, suddenly smothered the advance German positions with their blast, and that night, under a shining moon, the famous foot soldiers—Britons, Australians, New Zealanders, Indians, South Africans, Highlanders probing forward beside their kilted pipers—began to move into the mine fields. When these were partly cleared, the British tanks rumbled through. The Germans were outnumbered, outweaponed, and overwhelmed. General Georg von Stumme, Rommel's replacement, fell dead of a heart attack, and two days after the assault started, Hitler's youngest field marshal was back, surveying the wreckage of his burned-out panzers. Hitler sent him a desperate message: "In the situation in which you now find yourself, there can be no other consideration than to hold fast, never retreat, hurl every gun and every man into the fray. . . . You can show your troops no other way than that which leads to victory or death." This was the same counsel the *Führer* would give to Friedrich Paulus, his Stalingrad commander. Rommel was smarter. At last, later than he would have wished, he started a massive retreat. General Ritter von Thoma, when captured in full uniform by the British, expressed the feeling of the entire Afrika Korps command by assailing Hitler's order as "unsurpassed madness."

In the long rout from the Nile borders and westward across the Libyan frontier, Rommel helped protect his disciplined German troops by posting Italian rear guards and using their transport for evacuation. He lost approximately sixty thousand men as well as most of his guns and tanks before, under cover of a rainstorm, he managed to establish a temporary holding position. And then, on November 8, came word of an Allied landing in French North Africa. Not only was Egypt irrevocably lost; now an enormous pincer started to close in.

The Afrika Korps and its Italian allies were trapped just as it became clear that another huge Nazi army was caught in the snowy wastes of the Volga bend at Stalingrad, and that the Americans were striking back against Japan in far-off Guadalcanal. Autumn of 1942 was the turning point of the war. As Churchill said, "Up to Alamein we survived. After Alamein we conquered."

The serious planning for Operation Torch, the Anglo-American landing in Morocco and Algeria, did not begin until early August, 1942. A still-obscure American lieutenant general, Dwight D. Eisenhower, had been sent to England by Marshall and was given overall command of the expedition. A formal directive to proceed was sent to him only on August 13, after full consideration had been made of the strain the operation would place on Allied resources. Endorsement of Torch meant that in the Pacific the United States would be confined to holding a Hawaii-Midway line and preserving communications to Australia. In Europe it meant cancellation of Operation Sledgehammer, a diversionary attack across the Channel into France that Marshall had hoped to launch that same year. But it also put a period to Hitler's dream of joining in the Middle East the Egyptian and Russian salients of his astonishingly advanced armies.

The Torch invasion was made up of three separate forces: thirty-five thousand Americans embarked from the United States for French Morocco; thirty-nine thousand Americans embarked from England to take Oran in western Algeria; and a third force of ten thousand Americans and twenty-three thousand British also sailed from Britain to seize Algiers. All were transported and protected by the U.S. and Royal navies. Eisenhower wrote of this extraordinary undertaking: "The venture was new—it was almost new in conception. Up to that moment no government had ever attempted to carry out an overseas expedition involving a journey of thousands of miles from its bases and terminating in a major attack."

The operation was further complicated by the confused situation of France itself, part occupied, part under Pétain's Vichy regime, part in a colonial limbo. Some French officers in North Africa were loyal to General de Gaulle's movement in England; others were conspiring to back General Henri Honoré Giraud, who had just escaped to France from a German prison camp; still others were pledged to their Pétainist commanders; and there were those who were merely waiting to see how the war would go. In October, 1942, Eisenhower sent his deputy, Major General

Mark W. Clark, with a handful of specialists, to visit Algeria secretly by submarine and confer with the State Department's Robert Murphy, who had spread an intelligence network throughout North Africa on direct orders from Roosevelt. De Gaulle, who was disliked in Washington and suspected in London of indiscretion by incautious talk, was excluded from all planning, an insult he never forgave.

Just eleven months after Pearl Harbor, at 3:00 A.M. on November 8, 1942, a series of convoys numbering more than eight hundred war vessels and transports began to assemble along the African coast between Morocco to the south and Algeria to the west, disembarking troops on the Atlantic and Mediterranean shores. The Axis was taken wholly by surprise, not knowing, when the convoys were first spotted, whether they were bound for Malta, for Egypt, or for where. Spain did not interfere by attempting to pinch off the Mediterranean straits, and the venture succeeded with relatively few casualties. The only serious fighting was at Oran and at Casablanca, where French naval units shelled the attackers until put out of action by bombing.

Eisenhower rapidly built up his armies and a huge stockpile of equipment. Pétain, senile and embittered, ordered French North African forces to resist and severed diplomatic relations with Washington. For a brief time the position of the fourteen French divisions remained uncertain. In the hope of finding a figure to whom the French would rally, the Allies had smuggled General Giraud out of France to Gibraltar, where he agreed to take part in the operation but at the same time arrogantly demanded command of the entire expeditionary force. Instead he was flown to Algiers, where, to everyone's surprise, the archcollaborationist Admiral Darlan had arrived to visit his sick son and was caught by the invasion. On November 10, after negotiations with Robert Murphy, Darlan ordered all French commanders to cease resistance. Eisenhower, seeking to establish some kind of order, made Darlan the French political chief for all North Africa and Giraud the military chief. This anomaly soon resolved itself. On Christmas Eve, Darlan was assassinated by a young French royalist. Giraud, a brave, vain, but somewhat inept and politically inexperienced officer, was soon outmaneuvered by the cunning and furious de Gaulle and found himself gradually stripped of all but the costume of authority. De Gaulle assumed real power over the gathering elements of Free France.

Despite their astonishment, the Germans reacted swiftly and effectively to the landings. Long before Eisenhower managed to get his inexperienced forces moving, the Germans and Italians occupied Tunisia and, benefiting from its proximity to Sicily, built up impressive strength, especially in aircraft. Winter rains turned the roads into quagmires, bogging down the Allied eastward advance, and for the first time, the Americans were pounded by Stuka dive bombers and the remarkable German 88 artillery piece, which astonished the Allies by its deadly effect against troops, tanks, and even planes. On November 23, Eisenhower transferred his headquarters to Algiers, and that white, hilly city, surrounded by orchards, slowly assumed the role hitherto played by Cairo.

In February, 1943, the Germans made a sudden thrust at the uncoordinated Allied advance and hurled the Americans back through the Kasserine Pass. Major General George S. Patton, Jr., a formidable United States commander whose name, genius, and eccentricities were soon to become renowned, was blocked further to the south near El Guettar, where his troops met unexpectedly stubborn resistance from Italian infantry. At this point Eisenhower summoned an old West Point classmate, Brigadier General Omar Bradley, to serve as his "eyes and ears" and stimulate the faltering United States Army.

The American fighting man soon proved, however, that he was competent, crafty, and courageous. He learned the arts of camouflage, the value of digging, and the need for coordinated patrolling. Professional officers, national guard divisions, and drafted replacements were rapidly welded into an efficient, weather-beaten force. On Eisenhower's orders, Patton began to look forward to a new invasion, this time against Sicily, and before the North African campaign ended in the summer of 1943, General Clark had been assigned to develop and train a new Fifth Army in Morocco for the eventual assault on Italy itself.

By March it was apparent even in Berlin and Rome that the Allied pincer arms extending toward each other from Cairo and Casablanca could not be kept apart. Rommel was recalled by Hitler. The British, under Montgomery, moved on Tunisia from the east, aided by Jean Leclerc's tiny, glamorous French force

In London on October 29, 1942, Churchill
fumed: Why was there no news from Egypt?
What was Montgomery doing? But at El
Alamein, as this picture taken on the same
day so dramatically suggests, the tide
had already turned. Rommel, bitterly
obeying Hitler's "victory or death" order,
was bombed day and night, hit by swarms
of fast new tanks, and slashed by infantry
and artillery that seemed inexhaustible.

that had fought its way up from the Chad Territory, and the British and Americans closed in on Tunisia from the west. On April 23, the final attack began. Montgomery had already pierced the Mareth Line between Libya and Tunisia and now swept up toward Tunis as the United States II Corps overran Hill 609, blocking the road to Bizerte, and the British First Army, under Eisenhower's command, took bloody Longstop Hill, the last great natural barrier. On May 7, Tunis and Bizerte fell, and the final line of Axis retreat on the Cape Bon Peninsula was severed.

The North African campaign, which succeeded beyond any original hope, was the largest pincers movement ever successfully applied in war, joining forces from the Nile Valley to the Atlantic. Its timing was superb. The coincidence between Montgomery's El Alamein breakthrough and the Moroccan-Algerian landings was carefully foreseen, but that impact, already immense, was enhanced by the simultaneity of triumphs at Stalingrad and Guadalcanal, the latter being of special political and morale importance to the United States.

All told, North Africa cost the Germans and Italians 349,206 in dead and prisoners. Apart from extensive losses at sea, they were deprived of nearly two hundred thousand tons of matériel. Italy's Field Marshal Alessandro Messe and Germany's General Jürgen von Arnim were among those taken. When it was suggested to Eisenhower that he receive the latter, Eisenhower refused, believing himself engaged in a "crusade" against "a completely evil conspiracy." (It was a policy he would stick to for the rest of the war.) Mussolini's vision of a new Roman Empire dissolved in blood where Rome had once obliterated its Carthaginian enemy; soon the *Duce* would lose Italy itself. And for Hitler it was a catastrophe. Montgomery analyzed the *Führer*'s strategic error accordingly: "From a purely military point of view, the holding out in North Africa once the Mareth Line had been broken through could never be justified. I suppose Hitler ordered it for political reasons; it may sometimes be necessary, but they will generally end in disaster."

Rommel commented on the crucial El Alamein battle with justifiable acerbity: "The fact is that there were men in high places who, though not without the capacity to grasp the facts of the situation, simply did not have the courage to look them in the face and draw the proper conclusions. They preferred to put their heads in the sand, live in a sort of military pipedream and look for scapegoats whom they usually found in the troops or field commanders. Looking back, I am conscious of only one mistake —that I did not circumvent the 'Victory or Death' order twenty-four hours earlier."

The African victory gave resurgent confidence to the weary British. The experience proved the effectiveness of a new team of United States commanders and broke in an American army. It forged an alliance that, at Eisenhower's insistence, was led by an integrated, international staff. And, finally, it prepared the foundation for a liberated, Gaullist France. For de Gaulle, ignored in planning the invasion, then thrust aside in favor of Darlan and Giraud, forced his way by willpower and artful maneuver to the leadership of French North Africa. From there he moved into France, carrying all his bitter memories.

VIII

The War in Russia

The partisans behind the lines, like
these two watchful Russians crouched
waiting in the hay with their weapons,
played an important role in the war.

The cynical military collaboration between Nazi Germany and Communist Russia came to a bloody end June 22, 1941, when Hitler hurled against Stalin the most powerful army ever seen. Between the Arctic Ocean and the Black Sea, more than two hundred and fifty divisions rumbled across the long Soviet frontier and headed for Moscow, Leningrad, and Kiev. Not quite four years later, their journey ended in the ruins of Berlin.

On July 29, 1940, General Alfred Jodl, chief of German operations, had told a conference of staff officers that the *Führer* had decided "to attack the U.S.S.R. in the spring of 1941." Two days later, Hitler himself revealed this plan to his leading generals. General Franz Halder took down Hitler's words at the briefing: "Wiping out the very power of Russia to exist! That is the goal!" That November, Stalin sent Molotov to Berlin to demand further extension of Soviet influence in eastern Europe. The request only reaffirmed Hitler's decision to double-cross his partner. On December 18, he issued military Directive No. 21, headed "Operation Barbarossa," in honor of the medieval German emperor who had won great victories in the East.

The object of Barbarossa was not merely to occupy Russian territory but to destroy the Red Army in huge battles of annihilation along a fantastically large front. Assuming his panzers would advance as rapidly as in France, the *Führer* reckoned that within eight weeks they could capture Leningrad, Moscow, and the Ukraine, putting an end to organized resistance. He decided the campaign could not be "conducted in a knightly fashion" and authorized Gestapo chief Heinrich Himmler to use his secret police independently of the Army in conquered territories. On March 21, 1941, he drafted his infamous Commissar Order: all Soviet commissars who were captured would be shot.

In the original timetable, Barbarossa was to begin in May to insure the conquest of Moscow and Leningrad before the first Russian snows set in. But Mussolini's misfortunes in Greece and the Belgrade coup d'état caused Hitler to postpone the date. The postponement deeply distressed Field Marshal Walther von Brauchitsch, supreme commander of the Eastern Front. Brauchitsch was right. When Nazi divisions began pounding Moscow and Leningrad, the first snows were falling.

German soldiering genius accomplished miracles in preparing this unprecedented offensive. The *Wehrmacht* deployed two hundred and seven divisions, twenty-five of them armored, fleshing out gaps with more than fifty satellite divisions, largely Finnish, Rumanian, and Hungarian. The two-thousand-mile front was divided into three main thrusts under Field Marshal Wilhelm von Leeb, aiming at Leningrad, Field Marshal Fedor von Bock, aiming at Moscow, and Field Marshal Gerd von Rundstedt, aiming across the Ukraine.

At 6:00 A.M., June 22, after initial bombings and barrages had begun, Count Werner von der Schulenburg, Hitler's rather pro-Russian ambassador in Moscow, handed Molotov a note officially declaring war. Pale, tense, silent, the Commissar for Foreign Affairs took the document, spat on it, tore it up, and then rang for Poskrebishev, his secretary. "Show this gentleman out through the back door," he said.

Despite numerous indications of Hitler's decision, Stalin had made no plans to meet an attack. The Soviet regime simply disbelieved all warnings. As a result, the onslaught came with terrible surprise, smashing an incompetently led Red Army that was still engaged in routine border exercises.

The speed of the Nazi advance was impressive on all fronts. Hundreds of Soviet aircraft were destroyed on the ground. Siege guns were trundled up to demolish fortresses of the so-called Stalin Line as they were successively isolated by German panzers. Three Red Army marshals, Kliment Efremovich Voroshilov in the north, Semën Mikhailovich Budënny in the south, and Semën Konstantinovich Timoshenko in the center, faced Leeb, Rundstedt, and Bock. Of the three, only Timoshenko showed any competence.

On the very first day, Brest-Litovsk, key to Soviet central defenses, fell. Confused, cut-off Russian units radioed each other: "We are being fired on. What shall we do?" and received such answers as: "You must be insane. Why is your signal not in code?" On June 27, Minsk fell, and Bock crossed the Berezina, heading for Smolensk. Leeb raced along the Baltic toward Leningrad; Rundstedt paraded into the Ukraine against Budënny's inept cavalry.

When I reached Moscow early in July, after an eleven-day train trip from Ankara, the capital was in a curious daze. Stalin, greatly moved, addressed the nation July 3, calling his startled audience

The Russians, who wore white, quilted
uniforms, could crawl through the snow on
their home front and stay low, camouflaged,
and warm. In contrast, the Germans, still
clad in their dark summer uniforms, were
frequently maimed and frozen to death. The
Nazi offensive on Russia crumbled under
an enemy that Hitler had somehow refused
to heed: the deadly Moscow winter.

119

"brothers and sisters" and "friends" instead of "comrades." Radio sets were commandeered so that only public loudspeakers could announce carefully filtered bulletins. An iron censorship prevented foreign correspondents from transmitting news not culled from the official press.

Moscow itself, basking in the summer sun, had been draped in camouflage. The Bolshoi theater and other buildings easily identified from the air were hung with huge scenic curtains depicting woodland villages. Principal squares were painted to give the wholly unsuccessful impression of rural countryside. When the *Luftwaffe* came over the capital, it was met by thunderous antiaircraft barrages, whose fragments clattered down upon the streets. A few bombs struck the Kremlin compound, and one knocked a corner off the Bolshoi, leaving its pitiful camouflage curtain flapping like a torn dress.

It was not until mid-July that the Nazis met their first serious opposition. At Smolensk heavy fighting developed as Timoshenko threw in trained reserves, and by the time that city fell, three weeks later, a Russian defense line had been established to its east. In late summer, I visited the rolling fields around Yelnya with a Siberian division that had been rushed out of Asia to help pinch off a German sector and stage a brief counterattack. It was comforting to regard this first ground to be retaken from the Germans since September 1, 1939, all cluttered with the wreckage of panzer units, and to hear officers boast: "Now the war will end because the Siberians are here."

But Hitler's plan to encircle and destroy the Red Army had achieved considerable success. There were huge losses all along the front. At Kiev the Germans claimed to capture six hundred thousand Russians. (Even Soviet historians admit to two hundred thousand.) At Smolensk the Germans claimed three hundred forty-eight thousand prisoners. By the end of September Stalin had lost two and a half million men, twenty-two thousand guns, eighteen thousand tanks, and fourteen thousand planes.

Nevertheless, the German advance was slowing down. Russian resistance hardened. Nazi brutality, the ravaging of towns and hamlets, the torture and execution had combined to turn against the invaders a population that in many areas had been inclined at first to accept the enemy as a relief from Stalinist terror. Stalin ordered a scorched-earth policy. Partisan bands were formed from encircled units far to the German rear. And in occupied Europe itself, Communists responded to a Moscow summons to sabotage Brauchitsch's bases and supply lines.

When the Nazi offensive started in June, the U.S.S.R. was incompletely mobilized, with but one hundred and fifty understrength divisions deployed. The Soviets possessed some twenty-one thousand tanks—more than four times the number opposing them—but few were of recent manufacture. The new medium model, T-34, was not thrown against the Germans until Smolensk.

Yet, despite initial disadvantages, the traditional soldiering qualities of the Russian and the traditional Russian strategy of trading space for time slowly rectified the balance. Moreover, manpower was ever plentiful. The Germans began to realize that the Russians could afford to trade lives at a rate of five to one, making up their losses from a population that was three times the size of Germany's—and the Russians were fighting for their homeland. Slowly Soviet Slavs forgot resentments against dictatorship and rallied to Stalin's standard of Patriotic War. A new role was accorded to religion. Privileges and honors that had not existed since the Revolution were returned to officers. Guderian, the German panzer general, recalls meeting a former czarist general at Orel who said: "If only you had come twenty years ago we should have welcomed you with open arms. But now it's too late. We were just beginning to get on our feet and now you arrive and throw us back twenty years so that we will have to start from the beginning all over again. Now we are fighting for Russia and in that cause we are all united."

German losses were both heavy and hard to replace. Halder estimated that by the end of November, 1941, Hitler had forfeited 743,112 men—or 23 per cent of the total originally thrown into the Russian campaign. And as the German advance lost momentum, the Russians managed to assemble quantities of artillery. Since 1936, a new series had been under mass production: guns of 76, 122, and 152 millimeters; tremendous 280-, 305-, and even 406-millimeter howitzers; the famous Katyusha rockets, which rolled up to the line on trucks for the first time on September 12, 1941, at Khandrov, outside Leningrad, and harassed the Germans with their multiple, whistling explosions. The infantry

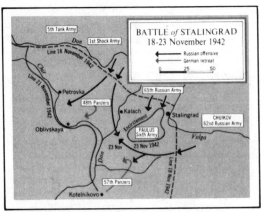

The basic strategy of Hitler's Operation
Barbarossa for the conquest of Russia
was simple: destroy the bulk of the Soviet
Army in western Russia by first cutting
it up with deep thrusts by far-ranging
panzer forces, then following with infantry
and artillery to force surrender of the
isolated pockets of Russia. German Army
Group North, commanded by Field Marshal
Wilhelm von Leeb, drove in the direction of
Leningrad; Army Group Center, under Field
Marshal Fedor von Bock, toward Moscow;
and Field Marshal Gerd von Rundstedt and
his Army Group South toward the Ukraine
and the Caucasus. The map at right shows
how near the *Wehrmacht* came to realizing
these objectives before winter saved the
shattered Soviet forces and almost brought
catastrophe to the Germans. By the next
summer, 1942, Nazi strength, though still
tremendous, had been eroded enough to
limit the German offensive in the south,
as shown on the map, instead of having it
extend along the vast front of the previous
year. Even so, the offensive had Soviet
forces reeling until Hitler uselessly
sacrificed an entire army at Stalingrad
(map above). From that point on, the
fortunes of the *Wehrmacht* deteriorated.

GERMAN OFFENSIVE
22 June 1941 – Nov., 1942

German advance

Northern Line 5 Dec 1941

0   100   200

FINLAND

LAKE ONEGA

LAKE LADOGA

ockholm

Helsinki

Tallinn

ESTONIA

Leningrad

Tikhvin

Riga

LATVIA

Line 9 July 1941

LITHUANIA

Vilna

Volga

Gorki

Line December 1941

Kalinin

Moscow

Grodno

Bialystok

Minsk

Smolensk

UNION OF SOVIET SOCIALIST REPUBLICS

Dnieper

Line 22 June 1941

aw

Brest Litovsk

Pinsk

Gomel

Line November 1942

Orel

Pripet

Saratov

AND

Kursk

Kiev

Lvov

Kharkov

Line November 1942

Don

Uman

Bug

Dnieper

Donets

Stalingrad

Leninsk

Dniester

Odessa

Melitopol

Rostov

Volga

ANTONESCU
Rumanian Army

Sevastopol

SEA OF AZOV

Novorossisk

MANIA

Bucharest

BLACK   SEA

Ordzhonikidze

GARIA

Istanbul

TURKEY

was reequipped with Degtyarev and Goriunov machine guns and Shpagin machine pistols. And the Russians maintained a cavalry force of six hundred thousand men, which, though it took terrible losses, disheartened the Germans by filtering through snowbound forests or suddenly sweeping out of dawn fogs. To support this complex apparatus, on August 25, 1941, Stalin created a "Command of the Rear of the Red Army" to assure logistical support, and an "Army of the Interior" to maintain absolute internal security.

Nevertheless, by October 20, Bock was within forty miles of Moscow. A week earlier, Stalin had decided to evacuate his main ministries and the diplomatic corps to Kuibyshev, a ramshackle provincial town five hundred and fifty miles to the southeast on the Volga, although he himself, with his chief lieutenants, remained in the Kremlin. The evacuees drove to the Kazan railway station through a city consumed by panic. The usual police units had been taken from the streets and rushed into line to plug a gap on the main highway from Vyazma. Families with bundles were hurrying to rail depots. Trucks loaded down with old men, women, children, and deserting bureaucrats were heading eastward. Crowds were looting bakeries and food stores as the usual stern order crumbled into chaos. At the Kazan station, I joined diplomats in seeking to storm the buffet; every inch of the platform and track sidings was littered with huddled families and their pitiful belongings.

Fortunately, the first heavy snow was feathering down, obscuring our evacuation from the *Luftwaffe*. The train was jammed with distinguished passengers: Sir Stafford Cripps, the British ambassador, with his puzzled airedale; Laurence Steinhardt, the American envoy, who joined reporters in a steady poker game; all the diplomatic corps except for a few junior officials left behind as embassy caretakers; famous writers like Ilya Ehrenburg, Aleksei Tolstoi, and Mikhail Sholokhov; Comintern leaders such as Dolores Ibarruri, "La Pasionaria" of the Spanish Civil War. Panayotis Pipinellis, the Greek ambassador, had reached Moscow just in time to join the unhappy voyagers. He dressed himself neatly in frock coat and with impeccable courtesy strode from compartment to compartment, paying his first formal calls.

Boxcars and flatcars moved westward with silent troops and eastward with rusty machinery from Ukrainian and Russian factories, which, with astonishing success, were being reassembled in distant Soviet Asia. Steel production shifted from Mariupol to Magnitogorsk, small arms from Tula to Sverdlovsk, tanks from Kharkov to Chelyabinsk—all east of the Urals. And by November, some two million people had either been shifted from the capital or had somehow managed to flee. Later many were to be ashamed of their desertion.

This was Russia's moment of truth. A Red Army communiqué admitted: "During the night of October 14–15, the position of the Western Front became worse. The German-Fascist troops hurled against our troops large quantities of tanks and motorized infantry, and in one sector broke through our defenses." Actually, Nazi patrols came close enough to see Moscow's Khimke water tower, and the official Soviet history of the war later said: "It was the lowest point reached throughout the war."

From the Kremlin itself, Stalin personally conducted the battle on his doorstep. He dispatched the dogged Timoshenko to take over from Budënny on the southern front, where Rundstedt was now hammering at the gateway to the Caucasus, and replaced him with General Georgi Zhukov, who painstakingly built up his reserves and waited for his ally, "General Winter." Snow alternated with rain, ice with mud, and gradually the Germans bogged down to the west, southeast, and north of Moscow. Hitler's generals pleaded with him to establish a winter line, but he refused, ordering them to press on.

On December 6, Zhukov went over to the offensive. He threw one hundred divisions into a sudden counterassault, and the Nazi lines faltered and dissolved. As Halder was to write: "The myth of the invincibility of the German Army was broken." Droves of Nazi soldiers were taken prisoner and displayed in newspaper photographs wearing women's furs and silk underclothing to supplement their inadequate uniforms against the cold.

In those heroic days outside Moscow, one of the first publicized Soviet war heroes was the gigantic General Andrei Andreyevitch Vlasov, a dramatic and inspiring figure and one of Zhukov's most successful field commanders. Vlasov was later seized by the Germans and promptly switched sides, to become the highest-ranking traitor of World War II. He recruited an army of Russian prisoners and led them for Hitler until May, 1945. General Patton captured him in Czechoslovakia, handed him over to Stalin, and he was hanged.

Snow lay all along the Moscow front, even under birch copses and pine groves. The cold was savage. Everything froze totally and suddenly. Dead horses balanced stiffly on the edge of drifts as ravens pecked their eyes. The silent Russian infantry trudged forward, accompanied by sleighs; guns lumbered up from the rear, and small-arms fire rattled through the woods.

While Moscow was being relieved, Leningrad withstood an extraordinary siege, protected by no less than five thousand gun emplacements. Leeb's soldiers from the southwest and the Finnish Marshal Mannerheim's from the northwest had swiftly approached its suburbs. But although they invested this northern Venice until 1943 and smothered it with shells and bombs, they never managed to penetrate. The suffering of the Leningraders was immense, but they fought and worked with extraordinary grit. When the city was first encircled, it had only a few days' reserve in food. By the middle of that dreadful 1941–42 winter, thirty-five hundred to four thousand people were dying of starvation every day. By official Russian figures, six hundred thirty-two thousand men, women, and children died during the blockade.

Meanwhile, in the Ukraine, Rundstedt was speeding across the Dnieper and isolating huge Soviet formations. Stalin ordered the destruction of his enormous Dnieper dam and, with the same obstinacy so often shown by Hitler, commanded Budënny to hold Kiev. It was too late. German panzers forged a ring of steel around the Ukrainian capital. In a radio appeal, the Soviet dictator exhorted the besieged garrison to hold on. The defenders died in charred clusters around jumbled heaps of gutted tanks, guns, and trucks. When the Kiev area was finally quiet, the Germans claimed they had rounded up some six hundred thousand prisoners. Hitler replaced Rundstedt with Field Marshal Walther von Reichenau, and the latter swiftly overran all the Ukraine. In the Crimea, only Sevastopol remained. After a nine-month siege, Sevastopol finally collapsed the following July, hammered to pieces by air attack, conventional artillery, and a giant siege gun that was called "Dora."

Kharkov, the "Soviet Pittsburgh" on the Donets, was outflanked. Nikita Khrushchev, a Ukrainian commissar at the time, telephoned the Kremlin and protested that the endangered Russian Army should be extricated. Stalin did not personally accept the call, but through Georgi Malenkov he passed on the abrupt message: "Let everything remain as it is." The Nazis proceeded to smother the writhing pocket, and to the south, they thrust into Rostov and the gateway to the Caucasus.

The Germans were able to reestablish a fighting line out of the chaos that resulted from Zhukov's victorious Moscow counteroffensive and the stalwart defense that prevented them from making Leningrad a winter base. Timoshenko recaptured Rostov in the south, and for the duration of the winter, an uneasy stalemate persisted on the lengthy front as both sides regrouped. By this time, it was evident that Hitler would never again be able to muster an offensive along the entire fighting line. A Soviet general assured me the General Staff was preparing for one more German drive—in search of oil for its thirsty war machine. When I was in Washington during April, 1942, a group of intelligence officers, including former United States military attachés in Berlin, Moscow, and Bucharest, asked me for a forecast of the 1942 campaign. I predicted that the Germans would launch one single desperate offensive—in the south; that they would reach Stalingrad and the high Caucasus; that they would then be forced to retreat. The Americans thought I was crazy. They insisted that the Soviet Air Force and Army were already destroyed and without capacity to resist.

Hitler, in Directive No. 45, designated Stalingrad and the Caucasus as the objectives of his 1942 offensive. Halder, his Chief of the General Staff, grumbled that Germany no longer had the power to achieve such ambitious aims and complained that these decisions "were the product of a violent nature following its momentary impulses, which recognized no limits to possibility and which made its wish-dreams the father of its acts." Once, Halder said, when a report was read to the *Führer* of Stalin's reserve strength, "Hitler flew at the man who was reading with clenched fists and foam in the corners of his mouth and forbade him to read any more of such idiotic twaddle."

General Friedrich Paulus, commander of the Sixth Army, was assigned the conquest of Stalingrad. The summer offensive started in July, and Paulus advanced rapidly upon the Volga stronghold. In September Stalin again called upon Zhukov, his ace, and gave

The fighting within Stalingrad was a
fantastic kind of warfare, waged inside
cellars, in sewers, in blasted factories,
behind the walls of demolished buildings.
Every inch of the city was contested,
building by building, floor by floor, room
by room, often in hand-to-hand combat.
Quarter was seldom asked or given, and
in this savage battle surrounded units
commonly fought on until annihilated.

him command of the whole Stalingrad front. The city itself was confided to General Vasili Chuikov, commander of the Sixty-second Army, who had once advised Chiang Kai-shek and who was later to accept Berlin's surrender.

On September 13, a Nazi division broke deep into Stalingrad and, progressing through the bomb-shattered city block by block, room by room, almost reached Chuikov's command post. But Chuikov mined each building on the invaders' path and set up zones of enfilading sniper nests. An unhappy Nazi lieutenant wrote: "The street is no longer measured by metres but by corpses. . . . Stalingrad is no longer a town. By day it is an enormous cloud of burning, blinding smoke; it is a vast furnace lit by the reflection of the flames. And when night arrives, one of those scorching, howling, bleeding nights, the dogs plunge into the Volga and swim desperately to gain the other bank. The nights of Stalingrad are a terror for them. Animals flee this hell; the hardest stones cannot bear it for long; only men endure."

While Chuikov held on, Zhukov brought up massive reinforcements and, on November 19, launched still another counterattack. He hurled six armies into an encircling movement so successful and so shattering that within four days, the enormous Paulus army was trapped. Hitler's generals urged him to order a break-out while there was still a chance. The *Führer* refused. Instead he told Paulus to fight on and promoted him to field marshal, thus adding savor to Paulus's eventual capture by the Russians. The denouement was dreadful and fantastic.

Later, when de Gaulle visited the devastated battlefield on his way to Moscow, he said quietly: "All the same, a formidable people, a very great people. I don't speak of the Russians, I speak of the Germans . . . to have pushed this far." On January 31, 1943, Paulus surrendered with ninety-one thousand emaciated, ragged survivors, all that were left of the three hundred thousand men of his Sixth Army who had first marched confidently into Stalingrad. Only about five thousand ever returned to Germany. The disaster, coming so unbelievably upon the heels of El Alamein, rocked the German people, and an overriding caution set in among the Nazi generals. Field Marshal von Manstein urged widespread withdrawal in the hope of enticing the Russians into traps. But Hitler, fearing the political consequences in an eastern Europe now crawling with guerrillas, spurned such strategy. He summoned his *Wehrmacht* to one final battle of annihilation. Choosing the Kursk salient, north of Kharkov, he built up a new force of five hundred thousand men, including seventeen panzer divisions equipped with the new Tiger tank. On July 4, 1943, this last initiative, what was to be the greatest of all tank battles, began.

The guileful Zhukov, forewarned by Soviet intelligence and familiarity with German strategy, had begun preparing for a Kursk battle as early as April. He laid thick minefields along stretches suitable to Nazi tank advances and built up an immense artillery force of nearly twenty thousand guns and a thousand Katyusha rockets. A Czech deserter tipped off the Russians on the exact date of the German assault, and "Operation Citadel" was shattered by crunching barrages. Then, deliberately choosing his time, Zhukov attacked. He launched the Red Army's first massive summer offensive and put an end, once and for all, to the shibboleth that the Russian soldier was good only when he was on the defensive.

The entire German front began to crumble. Orel, Kharkov, Smolensk, and Kiev were retaken before autumn ended. The first freeze caught the Nazis on the Ukrainian steppe, where infantry units, unable to dig trenches, made lean-tos of corpses roofed with canvas tenting to shelter themselves against the wind. A third Russian winter settled in, grim and hopeless. Hitler, in his East Prussian "Wolf's Lair," cut himself off from his generals and henceforth heeded only the counsel of party fanatics, his physician, and an astrologer. All illusions gone, the *Wehrmacht* began its creaking, tortured withdrawal.

The Russian Army that now headed toward the *Führer's* Fortress Europe was a vastly different army from that which had fallen apart in 1941. It was a strange mixture: an army of quantity, slogging along with antiquated guns behind horse-drawn transport; and an army of quality, spearheaded by magnificent tanks. Huge amounts of matériel had been brought around the Arctic capes by British convoys and out of Iran by the American Persian Gulf Service Command. But useful as these tremendous numbers of trucks, planes, tanks, munitions, and shipments of food proved to be, they were nevertheless still fractional in importance. The U.S.S.R. itself had developed a huge ordnance industry, both around Moscow and in the Siberian reaches, where evacuated machinery was reassembled. From 1942 to 1944, Soviet factories manufactured three hundred and sixty thousand artillery pieces alone. The heavy Stalin-JS tank replaced the old KV-2 and was supplemented by self-propelled guns and howitzers. Four aeronautic designers, Sergei Ilyushin, Alexander Yakovlev, Vladimir Petlyakov, and Semyon Lavochkin, were responsible for the production of improved series of fighters and bombers.

Although in the great encirclement of 1941 and 1942 the Red Army had lost three and one half million men in prisoners alone, by the time of the Kursk counteroffensive, Stalin had built a fresh force of four hundred and nine divisions.

To direct this ponderous array Stalin created hundreds of generals and, ultimately, twenty-nine marshals. Promising officers like Konstantin Rokossovki, who had been purged in 1937 and was in a concentration camp when the invasion came, were forgiven trumped-up offenses and awarded high commands. Even the professionally minded Germans conceded the prowess of the Red Army soldier and the talent of his top commanders. They gave high marks to Konev, who first bloodied their noses at Yelnya, but they reserved their fullest admiration for the short, barrel-chested Zhukov, who came to symbolize Russian military power, which had been held in contempt when World War II began and would be contesting global paramountcy when it ended.

IX

The Politics of World War

Just perfect harmony.

The Anglo-American partnership was as
spirited as this British cartoon, depicting
a chummy F.D.R. and Churchill, suggests.

The politics of World War II were as dazzling and confusing as a pinball game. The West first tended to equate the evil of Stalin's communism with that of Nazism and then discerned in communism sudden Jeffersonian qualities. Hitler worshipped at the altar of the blond baboon; but his closest allies were the dark Italians, and he accorded the Japanese the dubious accolade of "honorary" Aryans. Before Pearl Harbor the United States joined Britain in planning grand military strategy and fought the Germans at sea, all under the banner of neutrality. Russia was first Germany's partner and then its most deadly enemy. Italy changed sides. Roosevelt violated custom to win a third and fourth presidential term; Churchill, having led Britain through its toughest struggle, was voted out of office before its end.

Military convenience took precedence over ideology. Washington successively coddled France's General Giraud and the Vichy Admiral Darlan before begrudgingly accepting de Gaulle. London went to war to preserve Poland's integrity and then, when the conflict ended, agreed to Soviet demands to change Poland's borders. International communism endorsed Hitler until he invaded the U.S.S.R.; then it played the major part in guerrilla resistance to the Nazis. Until 1942, Stalin supported Tito's opponents in Yugoslavia; he consistently favored Chiang Kai-shek over Mao Tse-tung. Britain backed an *émigré* king for Greece and opposed an *émigré* king for Yugoslavia. Japan allied itself to Germany but told Berlin nothing about its plans for attacking Pearl Harbor and honored its nonaggression pact with Stalin even while fighting Hitler's other enemies.

Allied generals squabbled with one another and yet joined in an unprecedented international command. Mussolini's and Hitler's generals squabbled less; but they quit the former and tried to murder the latter. The final showdown in Europe was run on one side from an East Prussian bunker by a madman listening to osteopaths and astrologers, and on the other side by a Combined Chiefs of Staff whose strategy evolved from a series of conferences among chiefs of government.

"It is not so difficult to keep unity in time of war," Stalin acknowledged, "since there is a joint aim to defeat the common enemy, which is clear to everyone. The difficult time will come after the war when diverse interests tend to divide the Allies."

But such interests, though always evident, were deliberately repressed. The principal arguments were about the time and place of a second front: British planners wanted to invade the Balkans and keep Russia out of eastern Europe, while American planners were more interested in simply squashing Hitler swiftly and moving on to the defeat of Japan. The British and Free French were fighting to retain empires that Roosevelt hoped to end. Roosevelt initially foresaw a peace guaranteed by the United States, the U.S.S.R., Britain, and China, although he finally switched to the concept of a global United Nations; Churchill wanted a European balance of power that would include both France and Germany. Roosevelt preferred a direct offensive on the Continent; Churchill favored a flank assault through the Mediterranean. Roosevelt trusted Stalin almost to the end and romanticized Chiang Kai-shek's rotting China. Yet despite all the contradictions and underlying mistrust, the Allied coalition held together.

The reason it held together, General Lord Ismay, Churchill's military shadow, later observed, was perhaps partly because the Axis nations never coordinated their own actions. He wrote: "As we look back on that period we can never be sufficiently thankful that the three Axis powers had from the start pursued their own narrow, selfish ends, and that they had no integrated Plan." There, indeed, lay the crucial difference. The Allies, on the other hand, hammered out their overall strategy at dramatic meetings between Roosevelt and Churchill, Churchill and Stalin, the three together, and, on one occasion, Roosevelt, Churchill, and Chiang. They agreed that Germany must be defeated before Japan, and Stalin promised to help the Western powers in Asia within three months after Hitler's destruction.

Churchill, who was less naïve than Roosevelt, showed much patience in dealing with Stalin. As he later wrote: "I tried my best to build up by frequent personal telegrams the same kind of happy relations which I had developed with President Roosevelt. In this long Moscow series I received many rebuffs and only rarely a kind word. In many cases the telegrams were left unanswered altogether or for many days. The Soviet Government had the impression that they were conferring a great favour on us by fighting in their own country for their own lives. The more they fought, the heavier our debt became. This was not a balanced view."

Twice he flew to Moscow for private Kremlin talks, in August, 1942, and again in October, 1944. The first time he explained

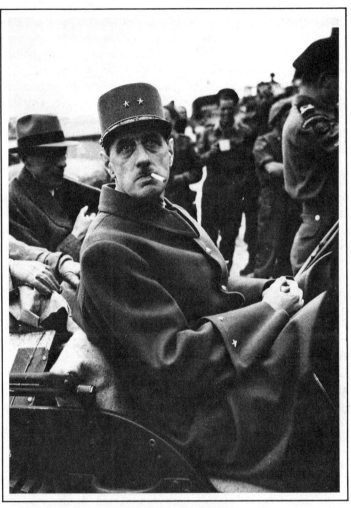

Charles de Gaulle was present at Casablanca
but excluded from every talk that mattered.
No one seemed to know quite what to do
with him. With the fall of France in June,
1940, de Gaulle established a base in London
from which he led the Free French with his
incomparable charisma. He lived, literally
and ironically, it seems, his own personal
philosophy: "Authority requires prestige,
and prestige requires remoteness."

why an Allied landing in France was being delayed in favor of the North African invasion. He was rewarded with a series of insults, including a Stalin retort that the British were cowards. The second time, Churchill and Stalin divided the Balkans into spheres of influence—theoretically for the war period only. Churchill also acknowledged realities in Poland by persuading some leading Polish *émigrés* to accept the Curzon Line. This deal was kept quiet until after the United States elections in November, 1944, in order not to embarrass Roosevelt with Polish-American and other Catholic voters.

Roosevelt often deliberately played up to Stalin and sought to conciliate the Soviet dictator. At the Teheran Conference in 1943 and again at Yalta in 1945, the President strongly opposed the old-fashioned colonial system on which the British Empire was founded, even once suggesting that Britain should abandon Hong Kong. Churchill was sometimes hurt and angered, but Stalin remained unmoved. He coldly pushed Soviet interests and ignored, both in Russia and eastern Europe, all promises of political liberty to which he had agreed.

The first effort to bring together Roosevelt, Churchill, and Stalin was made in early December, 1942, when the time had come to discuss what moves should follow the conquest of North Africa. Roosevelt and Churchill invited Stalin to meet them at Casablanca, on Morocco's Atlantic coast; but the Soviet Premier, although he professed to welcome the idea, said he could not leave Russia "even for a day, as it is just now that important military operations of our military campaign are developing." He also reminded Western leaders of their "promise" to establish a "second front in Western Europe in the spring of 1943."

Nonetheless, Roosevelt and Churchill went to Casablanca along with their top military planners. There they reluctantly concluded that a cross-Channel assault, then code-named "Roundup," was out of the question in 1943, but they also agreed that victory in Africa should be succeeded as quickly as possible by a drive into what Churchill called "the soft under-belly" of Hitler's Europe. Sicily was to be the target and July the date.

Although France as an immediate operational theater was relegated to the background at the Casablanca discussions, politically it was a central and disagreeable theme. On January 22, General de Gaulle was flown to Morocco. His disgruntled mood did not improve when he found himself guarded by American soldiers on what he considered French soil. General Henri Honoré

Giraud, who had escaped from a Nazi prison and was at that time de Gaulle's principal rival, was already at Casablanca. Roosevelt later insisted: "My job was to produce the bride in the person of General Giraud while Churchill was to bring in General de Gaulle to play the role of bridegroom in a shotgun wedding." Roosevelt heartily disliked de Gaulle, who, the President thought, saw himself as a new Joan of Arc, "with whom it is said one of his ancestors served as a faithful adherent." "Yes," Churchill is said to have replied, "but my bishops won't let me burn him!" Churchill admonished the General: "You claim to be France! I do not recognize you as France. . . ." "Then why," de Gaulle interrupted, "and with what rights are you dealing with me concerning her worldwide interests?"

De Gaulle wrote of this tense encounter: "I was starting from scratch. In France, no following and no reputation. Abroad, neither credit nor standing. But this very destitution showed me my line of conduct. It was by adopting without compromise the cause of the national recovery that I could acquire authority. At this moment, the worst in her history, it was for me to assume the burden of France."

At the close of the Casablanca meeting, Roosevelt and Churchill mischievously contrived to have de Gaulle and Giraud sit with them at a press conference at noon on Sunday, January 24. Churchill later confessed: "We forced them to shake hands in public before all the reporters and photographers. They did so, and the pictures of this event cannot be viewed even in the setting of these tragic times without a laugh." When pondering de Gaulle's subsequent actions, one wonders who laughed last. After their handshake, which they repeated for the benefit of photographers, the two French generals retired while the President and the Prime Minister talked to the press.

Roosevelt, discussing the conference, said: "Peace can come to the world only by the total elimination of German and Japanese war power. . . . The elimination of German, Japanese, and Italian war power means the *unconditional surrender* [my italics] of Germany, Italy and Japan. . . . " The British, particularly Churchill and his R.A.F. commanders, disliked the phrase. Churchill said afterward: "I would not myself have used these words." He felt that the absolute and categorical expression could only stiffen enemy resolve.

In late 1943, a second series of conferences was held. From

On the afternoon of Sunday, January 24,
1943, Roosevelt and Churchill sat down in
the Casablanca sunshine and held a press
conference, during which F.D.R. tossed
off the ominous phrase "unconditional
surrender." The day before, the Combined
Chiefs of Staff, after eleven days of
deliberation, had come to an agreement
on how the war should be run.

November 22 to 26, Roosevelt and Churchill met with Chiang Kai-shek in Cairo, where a chain of villas near the pyramids and Mena House Hotel was requisitioned for them and isolated behind barbed wire. The talk centered on Far Eastern problems, and it was agreed to strip Japan of all her twentieth-century conquests, starting with Korea, Formosa, and Manchuria. The atmosphere was not happy. General "Vinegar Joe" Stilwell used the occasion to lobby savagely against Chiang. Chiang himself fought back, extracting concessions from Roosevelt, while his beautiful Wellesley-educated wife occupied herself with shopping tours and with casting poisonous conversational darts while attending the meeting's numerous social gatherings.

The upshot of the Cairo Conference was that Japan was doomed to lose even its oldest colonies, and flabby China was to have Great Power status in the postwar world. The negotiations were held with maximum secrecy, and little was made public.

Roosevelt first met Stalin at the subsequent Teheran meeting, the first Big Three conference, which lasted from November 28 to December 1, 1943, and at which the American President unexpectedly became the Soviet dictator's house guest. Concerned that enemy agents might be active in the city, Stalin invited Roosevelt to live in the Soviet embassy compound, which, the American Secret Service agreed, was more easily protected than that of the United States. Special precautions also were taken at the nearby British compound where Churchill and his party were staying.

Roosevelt, who had looked forward to meeting the Communist boss, reported afterward to Congress that he "got along fine" with his host. Ismay rather less exuberantly recollected: "It is doubtful that many of those who listened to the discussion grasped the significance of Stalin's determination to keep Anglo-American forces as far as possible away from the Balkans. It was not until later that we realized that his ambitions were just as imperialistic as those of the czars, whose power and property he now enjoyed, but that he was capable of looking much further ahead than they had ever been."

That was an extraordinary confrontation, held in the capital of an ancient empire whose shah was a pawn in the hands of three guests whose armies occupied the country. There were the tall, almost gigantic American in a wheelchair, with his beautiful, strong features, graven by pain and humor, and his easygoing, affable manner; the lumpy, infinitely polite, but obstinate Englishman who reflected his compound lineage of dukes, millionaires, and generals as he fought to preserve a crumbling empire; and the short, almost frail Russian from Georgia, who had been a religious seminarian and a bank robber and who was the toughest of the three. Stalin spoke mildly and displayed unexpected charm. He listened to Roosevelt's sallies at Churchill's expense with little perceptible humor, accepted much, and gave little.

The two most important decisions at Teheran were that the Anglo-American invasion across the Channel (now known as Overlord) would be launched in June of 1944, supported by a landing from Italy on the south coast of France and a stepped-up Russian offensive in the east; and that once Germany was destroyed, Russia would enter the war against Japan. Further discussions centered on eastern Europe. The three agreed henceforth to support Tito's Communist partisans and decided that parts of eastern Poland would be ceded to Moscow. Stalin opposed suggestions that Turkey be brought into the war and Churchill's wish to invade the Balkans.

France featured Teheran as a disagreeable footnote. On his way to the conference, Roosevelt told his Joint Chiefs of Staff that "France would certainly not again become a first class power for at least 25 years," and that Britain was supporting the French in order to use their future strength. Roosevelt also adduced the strange theory that no Frenchman over forty should be allowed to hold office in postwar France. He agreed with Stalin that "the French must pay for their criminal collaboration with Germany." All this, needless to say, helped complicate Franco-American relations a generation afterward.

While the Great Power leaders were meeting in Casablanca, Cairo, and Teheran, a contest was taking place for influence in the enormously rich Middle Eastern petroleum fields. Stalin was not a prominent figure in the intra-allied oil competition. He had made an unsuccessful effort to move into that area back in the days when he was courting Hitler. On November 26, 1940, he had virtually offered to join the Axis in exchange for dominance of the Persian Gulf region, but Hitler had by then resolved on Barbarossa. Less than a year later, on August 25, 1941, Soviet and British troops moved into Iran to end German intrigues with the shah. However, the southern oil fields fell within the British occupation zone. And at that time, the Russians were more preoccupied with German efforts to capture Soviet oil wells located around Grozny and the Apsheron Peninsula.

The British possessed extensive petroleum fields in the Arab provinces of the former Ottoman Empire, but in Saudi Arabia, a potentially huge development had been started by a United States company, California Arabian Standard Oil Company (later Aramco), which had been granted a concession in 1933 by King Ibn Saud. Although Washington had opened diplomatic relations with Ibn Saud to insure adequate reserves for our Navy and Air Corps, Aramco rejected a proposal by Interior Secretary Harold Ickes that the United States Government become a shareholder in the operation. As a result, Washington was put in the invidious position of protecting private companies without governmental profit. Nevertheless, rapid extension of American petroleum holdings for the first time engendered an active State Department involvement in the Middle East.

Oil was but one aspect of wartime economic competition. Hitler shaped his 1942 Russian strategy around his petroleum needs, but his agents were also continually engaged in a search for other raw materials that were required for new weapons systems: hard metals needed for jet engines and missiles; rare minerals available only in neutral lands such as Sweden, Portugal, and Turkey. The income of those countries zoomed as Axis purchasers competed with Allied preemptive buying missions for chromium, wolfram, and cinnabar.

There was global competition, too, for what may have been as important as oil, even in mechanized modern warfare: public opinion. Radio by this time had become a major weapon. Stalin, Roosevelt, and Churchill, Hitler and Mussolini, were all using it with powerful effect. The Axis found a pitiful chorus of traitors ready to echo its cause on the airwaves: Axis Sally, Lord Haw Haw, Jane Anderson, Fred Kaltenabach, and Otto Koischwitz. Broadcasts were supplemented by leaflets, fired by artillery or dropped from bombers, that counseled soldiers to desert. The Russians added a grim note by trussing up the corpses of frozen Germans and dropping them from aircraft behind the Nazi lines. Nazi brochures asked GIs in Italy: "Who is cashing in on the huge war profits at home while Americans shed their blood over here?" Tokyo Rose broadcast to United States troops in the Pacific: "The girl back home is drinking with some 4-F who's rolling in easy money." The Americans distributed photographs of well-clad Axis prisoners eating enormous meals, captioned: "Better Free than a Prisoner of War: Better a Prisoner of War than Dead."

The British Political Warfare Executive (PWE) and the American Office of War Information (OWI) pooled their efforts to "reduce the cost of the physical battle" and undermine enemy morale. As the tide of conflict turned, the two organizations laid increasing stress on the terror that continued war would bring to Germany and Japan, and they dropped pictures of bomb-shattered cities on front-line troops. Code messages directed to guerrilla organizations and sabotage groups were mixed with skillfully camouflaged propaganda broadcasts that seemed to originate inside occupied territory.

At the same time, the classical wartime use of spies and saboteurs was rendered far more effective by employing aircraft and submarines to deliver them. Both sides produced audacious special agents, trained in silent killing and equipped with gold coins, counterfeit notes, booby-trap devices, portable communications systems, and light weapons. Yugoslavia, Greece, Albania, northern Italy, and most of France gradually filled up with teams of Englishmen and Americans who fought beside local partisans and transmitted detailed information on enemy dispositions to air strike forces and commando assault groups abroad. Patrick Leigh Fermor, a young British officer, kidnapped the German commander in Crete and brought him off safely to Cairo. The American OSS (Office of Strategic Services) had nearly thirty thousand persons on its roster around the world by the time peace came. One OSS agent planted a microphone in the *Luftwaffe*'s Paris headquarters. Allen Dulles, in charge of OSS operations from Switzerland and later head of the CIA, managed to penetrate the *Abwehr* (the German Intelligence Bureau) of Admiral Wilhelm Canaris, an anti-Hitler officer garroted after the 1944 attempt on the *Führer*'s life.

On the German side, Nazi killers spread terror from Teheran to the Ardennes. And German spies were dropped in England, shipped by yacht to South Africa, landed by submarine in the United States. The FBI rounded up thirty-one Nazi agents on August 1, 1941. The following year, eight German saboteurs brought by U-boat to Long Island and the Florida coast were arrested and six of them executed.

Perhaps the most fascinating espionage tale of World War II was that of Elyesa Bazna, an Albanian citizen of Turkey and valet to the British ambassador in Ankara, Sir Hughe Knatchbull-Hugessen. He regularly opened Hugessen's safe and photographed top-secret papers, selling them for sterling to the German embassy. His activities, inspired primarily by avarice, were so successful

Russia, the country that American military
experts had once figured Hitler could crush
in three months, had become a gigantic world
power; and it was right under the thumb of
one man, Joseph Stalin. Despotic, maniacally
driven, steeled by an unfaltering confidence
and an impenetrable faith, Stalin was fueled
by ambitions that reached far beyond the
conquest and suppression of Nazi Germany.

that he was given the code name Cicero by Berlin and offered enormous sums as encouragement. However, the Nazis could not believe their own good fortune and not only mistrusted much of Cicero's information but paid him in counterfeit money. The Royal Navy commander in charge of British intelligence in Turkey later told me that the incident demonstrated criminal negligence. Hugessen was made envoy to Belgium after the war.

Although immensely valuable information on operational plans was supplied by agents like Cicero, the richest target for espionage was in the realm of secret weapons. A combination of spy reports and expert interpretation of aerial photographs provided the Allies with critically important data about German V-weapons, missiles, and robot aircraft, and enabled them to bomb the experimental rocket center at Peenemünde. Allied and Axis scientists, who had shared a common fund of atomic knowledge before the war, kept watch on each other's subsequent efforts through intelligence reports.

Never were new weapons of such vital importance as during World War II. Had Hitler been able to wed a nuclear warhead to his missiles, he could have achieved at least a stalemate. Had the United States not possessed atomic bombs, hundreds of thousands of American lives might have been lost in the assault on Japan's home islands. The scientists on both sides knew that they probably held the key to success or failure, and this was particularly true of nuclear physicists.

In January, 1939, the German Otto Hahn and his associates had achieved the first stage of nuclear fission, and French and American physicists were seeking to emulate his experiment as the war clouds gathered. Albert Einstein, fearful that the Nazis might develop a nuclear warhead, wrote to President Roosevelt on August 2, 1939, to warn him: "A single bomb of this type, carried by boat and exploded in a port, might very well destroy the whole port, together with some of the surrounding territory." Roosevelt was sufficiently impressed to appoint an Advisory Committee on Uranium that October. The committee reported that the kind of bomb mentioned by Einstein was "a possibility," and Western scientists began to censor their reports.

The Nazi victories of 1940 disrupted Allied scientific endeavors. French physicists, under Frédéric Joliot-Curie, had been conducting atomic experiments with heavy water that was manufactured in quantity only at Rjukan, Norway. While the Battle of France was still being fought, Joliot-Curie sent one of his principal aides, Hans von Halban, to England with the French stock of heavy water. Anglo-French scientists at Cambridge then managed to achieve a chain reaction. Their work was later coordinated with that of American colleagues.

In May of 1941, the United States Government created an Office of Scientific Research and Development under Dr. Vannevar Bush, and thirteen months later, President Roosevelt made the decision to try to manufacture an atomic bomb. Two months afterward, an organization called the Manhattan Engineer District was established under General Leslie R. Groves. On December 2, 1942, Enrico Fermi achieved a controlled chain reaction in an atomic pile at Chicago that prompted the famous message from Nobel-prize-winning physicist Arthur Compton to James B. Conant: "The Italian Navigator has just landed in the New World. The Natives are friendly."

Allied intelligence had, however, learned disquieting news. The Nazis, after occupying Norway, had ordered the factory at Rjukan to produce three thousand pounds of heavy water a year, and in 1942, this target was raised to ten thousand pounds. Norwegian underground agents reported that the heavy water was being shipped to the Kaiser Wilhelm Institute for nuclear research. For this reason, Rjukan was repeatedly attacked by Allied bombers, commandos, and saboteurs until its output came to a standstill. The Nazis decided to move the entire store of heavy water to Germany, but the transport was sunk by a Norwegian saboteur's time bomb.

Nevertheless, German physicists, led by Werner Heisenberg, came startlingly close to developing an atomic weapon. They might well have succeeded had Hitler not cut back nuclear research in order to accelerate his V-weapon program. As a result, German scientists, including Wernher von Braun, did manage to achieve brilliant success in rocket projectiles, manufacturing the V-1's and V-2's that caused much damage to London and Antwerp in 1944 and 1945. But they lacked the totally destructive warhead that might have staved off defeat. The conflict in Europe ended before any nuclear device had been successfully exploded. Roosevelt was dead, Churchill was out of office, Mussolini had been shot, and Hitler had committed suicide before the Atomic Age began.

X

Counterattack in the Pacific

Riflemen of the British-Indian Fourteenth
Army move past a Burmese pagoda. The
Allied offensive yielded them some of
the fiercest jungle fighting of the war.

In the summer of 1942, the eastern boundary of the Japanese Empire ran from the Aleutians in the North Pacific down past Wake Island in the Central Pacific to the Gilberts on the equator; its western boundary ran from the Manchurian-Soviet border through eastern China and Burma to India; on the south it took in Sumatra, Java, Timor, half of New Guinea, and all of the Solomons. But by the summer of 1942, Japan's time of swift and furious expansion was about over. The Japanese never felt strong enough to attack Russia; they could have pushed on into India without much trouble, but chose to hold off; and the Battle of Midway had already finished any hopes they had of destroying the American Pacific Fleet and driving farther east. There was, however, one front left for them where the prospects for conquest still looked promising. If they could drive across the Owen Stanley Mountains on New Guinea and take Port Moresby on that island's southern coast, and if they could set up airfields on the southern Solomons, they would have bases almost on top of Australia and the supply lines from the United States.

Australia was the one place where the Allies could organize for a counterattack, and the buildup there under MacArthur was moving fast. Australian units in the Middle East had been called home. New units in Australia and New Zealand were being raised. And the United States Navy was moving American planes, guns and troops in impressive numbers across the Pacific. Germany may have been the priority target according to official American strategy, but in the first half of 1942, about four times as many men were being sent to the Pacific as to Europe.

So when it was discovered that the Japanese were constructing an air base on Guadalcanal, one of the southernmost of the Solomon Islands, and that the lifeline to Australia might soon be cut by land-based bombers, a major amphibious assault already agreed on in Washington was rushed into action. At dawn on the seventh of August, exactly eight months after Pearl Harbor, the first big Allied invasion armada of the war appeared off the coast of Guadalcanal and its steaming little satellites, Tulagi, Florida Island, and Gavutu. After an intensive three-hour bombardment, combat groups of the 1st Marines went ashore. Although there was sharp fighting on the offshore islets, the initial Guadalcanal landing was unopposed. The Marines, commanded by Major

As this map shows, the scale of the Pacific
war was enormous, the strategy essentially
simple. Two great thrusts westward, one
starting at Guadalcanal (lower right), the
other at the Gilbert and Marshall islands
(center right), would, if all went well,
converge on the Philippines. Islands along
the way would be taken one after the
other, unless, as was the case with Rabaul
and Truk, they could be merely bypassed.

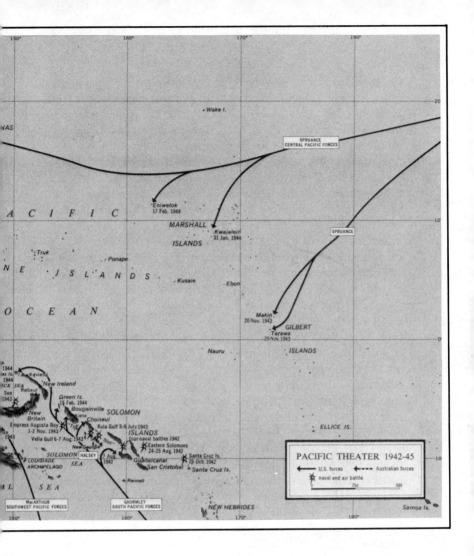

PACIFIC THEATER 1942-45

← U.S. forces   ←---- Australian forces

✶ naval and air battle   0   250   500

Wake I.

SPRUANCE
CENTRAL PACIFIC FORCES

Eniwetok
17 Feb. 1944

MARSHALL

Kwajalein
31 Jan. 1944

ISLANDS

SPRUANCE

Truk   Ponape

ISLANDS

Kusaie   Ebon

OCEAN

Makin
20 Nov. 1943

GILBERT

Tarawa
20 Nov. 1943

Nauru   ISLANDS

ELLICE IS.

Kavieng
New Ireland

Green Is.
15 Feb. 1944

Bougainville   SOLOMON
Choiseul
Kula Gulf 5-6 July 1943

New
Britain
Empress Augusta Bay
1-2 Nov. 1943

Vella Gulf 6-7 Aug. 1943
New Georgia   ISLANDS
four naval battles 1942

Eastern Solomons
24-25 Aug. 1942

SOLOMON   HALSEY
SEA   Aug.
1942

Guadalcanal
San Cristobal

Santa Cruz Is.
26 Oct. 1942

Santa Cruz Is.

LOUISIADE
ARCHIPELAGO

Rennell

SEA

NEW HEBRIDES

Samoa Is.

MacARTHUR
SOUTHWEST PACIFIC FORCES

GHORMLEY
SOUTH PACIFIC FORCES

PACIFIC

ISLANDS

150°   160°   170°   180°

General Alexander A. Vandegrift, swiftly captured their main objective, the still unfinished airstrip, and renamed it Henderson Field. But the calm was deceptive. Before it had ended, the campaign would include six separate naval encounters and a bloody jungle fight that would drag on for nearly eight months.

Two days after the landings, a Japanese naval task force struck back fiercely against American ships off Guadalcanal. In what became known as the Battle of Savo Island, the Japanese sank one Australian and three American cruisers. But then, to the astonishment of the beleaguered Allies, the enemy commander called off the attack and disappeared without touching a cluster of defenseless transports loaded down with reinforcements.

Throughout August and September, the beachhead was built up until some seventeen thousand Marines occupied a seven-by-four mile strip, including Henderson Field. The Japanese decided that Guadalcanal had to be cleared and sent shiploads of reinforcements from Rabaul down the waters between the adjacent islands, a passage the Americans called "the Slot." Japanese cruisers and destroyers hammered at the Marines on the island and at American and Australian convoys trying to supply them.

In mid-October the Japanese moved a task force that included four carriers north of Guadalcanal. On the night of the twenty-sixth, the Battle of the Santa Cruz Islands began when two United States carrier forces, led by the *Hornet* and the *Enterprise* and commanded by Admiral Thomas Kinkaid, went to meet them. The battle cost the Japanese two destroyers sunk and and several heavier units damaged, including two carriers and two battleships. But it also cost the United States the *Hornet*, which was sunk by Japanese destroyers after it had been badly damaged by dive bombers.

Finally, on the night of November 13, the Imperial Fleet staged a dramatic sortie. This, the most furious sea encounter of the Solomons, became known as the Naval Battle of Guadalcanal. Led by two battleships, a Japanese force came down "the Slot" to land more troops and delivered a heavy shelling attack on a much smaller American task force. All night there was a tremendous mix-up, with the smaller, more maneuverable American ships pressing the attack. Ships sometimes drew so close that they had trouble depressing their guns. The Americans lost two cruisers sunk and badly damaged, which they could ill afford; but the Japanese lost a battleship. The following night, a second Japanese flotilla was located by planes from the *Enterprise* and was heavily punished. Bombers from Henderson Field took off in daylight and sank seven and damaged four of eleven Japanese transports ferrying reinforcements. On the night of November 14–15, the Japanese mustered their remaining naval strength, led by a battleship and four cruisers, in an effort to cut off the beachhead. At this moment an American flotilla commanded by Admiral Willis A. Lee roared up Ironbottom Sound, so named for the number of ships already rusting beneath its greasy surface. Lee sank another Imperial battleship and damaged two more cruisers, repelling Japanese efforts to build up their land forces. By dawn of the fifteenth, it was clear that the attempt had failed.

The land campaign, which lasted until February, was the first Marine experience in that particular kind of jungle warfare with which they were to become so intimately acquainted during the next three years. They had to learn how to hack their way through tangles of roots, always on the lookout for snipers lashed to tree branches or hidden in the underbrush. They became familiar with malarial mosquitoes, scorpions, and snakes, and accustomed to distinguishing the cries of animals from those of enemy sentries. They fought their way forward through intense heat and the foul slime of decomposing vegetation, blasting the Japanese from jungle strongpoints and hillside caves. Progess at first was painfully slow and nerve-racking. However, once it was clear that the Imperial Fleet had been driven off and that the flow of enemy reinforcements was dammed, the jungle advance gathered momentum. Finally, in the first week of February, the Japanese managed to bring destroyers in at night and evacuate about twelve thousand troops at Cape Esperance, on the island's northwestern tip. By the ninth, not a single living enemy was left on Guadalcanal. The Japanese had suffered their first land defeat of the war, and the first American offensive was a success.

When MacArthur arrived in Australia from Bataan in March, 1942, he found scant forces there for the defensive action needed if the Japanese were to be stopped in their surge southward. Even so, he decided that the best way to protect Australia was to throw as much strength as he could into New Guinea, in order to hold the Japanese on the far side of the Owen Stanley Mountains

Marines storm a heavily fortified Japanese
bomb shelter on Tarawa. In the battle for
the Gilbert Islands, Admiral Nimitz ordered
a bipartite attack on Makin and Tarawa for
November 20, 1943. A weak garrison, Makin
succumbed within four days. On bombarded
Tarawa, however, one-third of the Marines
were hit just upon going ashore. Despite a
tenacious resistance that included suicidal
counterattacks, the Japanese finally fell.

and secure the vital Australian base at Port Moresby. The first Japanese try at taking Port Moresby resulted in the inconclusive Battle of the Coral Sea in May, 1942.

Then, on July 21, the Japanese landed at Buna, on the north coast, and proceeded to do what no one among the Allied strategists had thought possible; they crossed the Owen Stanleys and drove on Port Moresby. By mid-September, at the time when the Allied campaign on Guadalcanal was looking very doubtful indeed, the Japanese were within thirty miles of Port Moresby. But MacArthur rushed in troops and planes, and in the next ten months the Allies battled the Japanese back over the mountains, took Buna, and began the long drive up the northern coast of New Guinea that was to be one side of a giant pincers movement that would eventually isolate Rabaul, Japan's Gibralter of the South Pacific.

MacArthur had stopped the Japanese advance in New Guinea. The Japanese now tried to save their New Guinea forces by reinforcing the garrisons at Lae and Salamaua. On March 1, 1943, United States reconnaissance planes spotted a powerful Imperial convoy carrying seven thousand troops and trying, under cover of bad weather, to make from Rabaul through the Bismarck Sea to Lae, on New Guinea's northeastern coast. Two days later, on March 3, in the major action of the three-day Battle of the Bismarck Sea, Major General George C. Kenney's Fifth Air Force, operating from Papua, smashed the convoy and Japanese plans for holding New Guinea. By the time they finished, they had sunk or damaged most of the ten warships and twelve transports in the formation, drowning all save a handful of the reinforcements. The Japanese lost one hundred and two aircraft. Kenney's B-17's and B-25's had given, as Churchill put it, "a striking testimony to the proper use of air power."

Thus, at last, Tokyo found its dynamism checked at its outermost fringes. Thrust back from Guadalcanal and New Guinea, it withdrew from the borders of India and the sea around Ceylon when those crucial areas lay open for the taking; and across the mainland Asian battlefront, Japan's energies continued to be drained in a brutal war with China that produced few, if any, definitive results.

By mid-summer of 1943, MacArthur had four American divisions and six Australian divisions supported by Admiral William

F. Halsey's South Pacific Fleet. Nimitz had nine U.S. Army and Marine divisions in the Central Pacific. With these relatively small forces, they stepped up the counterattack against strong Japanese dispositions in heavily fortified bases. They moved up the Solomons and New Guinea and inward across the little-known, savage Gilberts, Marshalls, and Marianas. The two great American captains, MacArthur and Nimitz, who had spent a lifetime in services with wholly different traditional and tactical concepts, perfected a novel kind of island-hopping warfare, the goal of which was to outflank and bypass enemy strongpoints wherever it proved to be possible, leaving isolated garrisons far to the rear of the actual fighting front.

There was something fatefully repetitious about that twin advance by the forces of the arrogant, jauntily capped MacArthur, and of the deeply honest Nimitz, with his clear blue eyes and modest, craggy face. Island after island, the story was nearly always the same: Japanese troops holed up in their elaborate bunkers, listening to distant radio broadcasts, dreaming of their dainty, pastel-kimonoed wives, waiting for the inevitable storm of fire and death from offshore. Outside, the clear Pacific and the endless rhythm of the surf. And all the while, lumbering through swells, the grey ships filled with sweating Marines; no smoking on the blacked-out decks; the dull thud of engines; the rattling of planes being readied by their mechanics; the creaking of davits and the hum of ammunition lifts in the quiet predawn. And then, the sudden and terrible explosion of light and sound, turning paradise to fury. When the last bomb and shell had fallen and the last machine-gun barrel cooled, swarms of Seabees came with their monstrous machinery to sweep away the mess and carve still another base for the inexorable advance. Or—sometimes —there was simply quiet again.

All the time that MacArthur's forces were pressing along the northern coast of New Guinea, the Marines and the Army started up the Solomon Islands "ladder": the Russell Islands (February, 1943), New Georgia (June), Vella Lavella (August), Choiseul and the Treasury Islands (October), and finally, Bougainville (in November), the biggest island of the chain. All the while the Air Corps and carrier-based dive bombers pounded away at Rabaul.

Within little more than a year, MacArthur's effective and economical strategy had reached far up the Southwest Pacific archipelagoes and severed some one hundred and thirty-five thousand Japanese from all prospect of rescue. Simultaneously, Nimitz guided Spruance's Fifth Fleet westward, encompassing the Gilberts, the Marshalls, the Carolines, and the Marianas, ravaging enemy ships and garrisons with the power of their carrier planes, and asserting a freedom of maneuver that seemed unimaginable less than two years after Pearl Harbor had crippled the U.S. Navy.

Makin and Tarawa in the Gilberts, where the Central and South Pacific commands met, were now assailed by Nimitz. On November 20, his carriers started a heavy bombardment of Makin. A few days later, the island was overwhelmed in a short, sharp series of amphibious assaults marked by a fanatical defense by a garrison well fortified with rice wine. Tarawa, an atoll of some two dozen islets linked by coral reefs, was a more difficult objective. Tokyo had boasted that it could not be taken by assault. The principal strongpoint at Betio, held by three thousand crack Imperial Marines, comprised hundreds of connected pillboxes made of concrete and coral work, reinforced with steel beams and coconut logs. These positions were intensely shelled and bombed by the Americans; nevertheless, when the Marines waded ashore, they were met by withering fire.

The battle was one of the bloodiest fights of the whole Pacific campaign. American ships maintained a steady artillery barrage as landing barges discharged troops and supplies and Marines stormed each bastion with flame throwers and grenades. Colonel David Shoup, commander of the 2nd Marine Regiment, reported to the flagship standing offshore: "Our casualties heavy. Enemy casualties unknown. Situation: we are winning." Four days later, his optimism proved warranted: the Americans had won. But they paid a price of eleven hundred lives.

Promptly the ingenious Seabee's set to work constructing a base for an attack on the Marshalls to the north. There the main target was Kwajalein, largest atoll in the world, sixty-six miles long and eighteen miles wide. This time Nimitz took no chances before sending his men ashore; his ships and planes dropped fifteen thousand tons of explosives on Kwajalein before the first landing craft touched ground. The atoll was a mass of dust-covered rubble when the invasion began, but the Japanese, who were for the first time defending a piece of prewar Imperial territory, fought

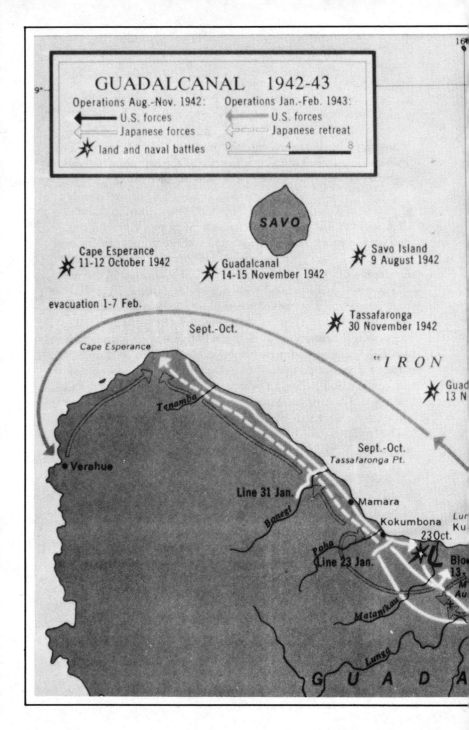

GUADALCANAL 1942-43

Operations Aug.-Nov. 1942:
→ U.S. forces
⇐ Japanese forces
✳ land and naval battles

Operations Jan.-Feb. 1943:
⇐ U.S. forces
⇐ Japanese retreat

0 — 4 — 8

9°

16°

SAVO

✳ Cape Esperance
11-12 October 1942

✳ Guadalcanal
14-15 November 1942

✳ Savo Island
9 August 1942

evacuation 1-7 Feb.

Sept.-Oct.

Cape Esperance

Tenamba

● Verahue

✳ Tassafaronga
30 November 1942

"IRON

✳ Guad
13 N

Sept.-Oct.
Tassafaronga Pt.

Line 31 Jan.

Banegi

Poha

Line 23 Jan.

● Mamara

Kokumbona

Lur
Ku
230ct.

Blo
13
M
Au

Matanikau

Lunga

G U A D A

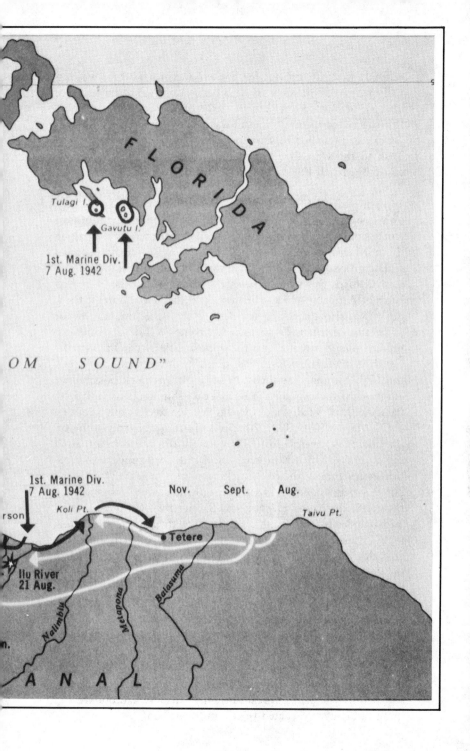

FLORIDA

Tulagi I.
Gavutu I.
1st. Marine Div.
7 Aug. 1942

OM   SOUND"

1st. Marine Div.
7 Aug. 1942

Nov.   Sept.   Aug.

rson   Koli Pt.
Taivu Pt.

Tetere

Ilu River
21 Aug.

Nalimbiu   Metapona   Balasuna

A N A L

savagely from the debris. Again the American advance was initially painstakingly slow, as each fortication had to be reduced, blasted, or burned out. But by early 1944, Nimitz's task forces had succeeded in mastering all the Gilberts and Marshalls, and his carrier raids had so shattered the great Carolines air base of Truk to the west that its garrison of fifty thousand could be easily bypassed. For the rest of the war, Truk lay useless.

While the new technique of amphibious fighting was proceeding in the tropical Pacific, an odd, militarily unimportant but politically and emotionally vital campaign took place along the northeastern edge of the Japanese empire, in the Aleutian sealing grounds. In 1942, when Yamamoto led his fleet to Midway, a small force was simultaneously sent to occupy the barren islands of Attu and Kiska. The move was, in fact, a strategic feint, but it was also a check to any designs the Allies might have for using the Aleutians as an invasion route to Tokyo. American public opinion saw it as just the opposite; Alaska and the Pacific Northwest were now, it seemed, seriously threatened. The American high command wished to choke off any such possibilities and to clear the way for the Lend-Lease shipments to the Soviet Pacific port of Vladivostok. It was decided to eject the Japanese.

On May 11, 1943, U.S. 7th Division troops began landing on mountainous, treeless Attu. They fought for eighteen days amid fog and rain, which hampered aerial and naval support and imprisoned armor in the cold, sucking mud. On May 29, the desperate Japanese defenders staged a suicide charge. From a ridge between Chichagof Harbor and Sarana Bay, Colonel Yasuyo Yamasaki led his surviving forces down on the Americans screaming: "Japanese drink blood like wine." Those who were not butchered along the slopes held hand grenades to their bellies and blew out their intestines. Among the letters found in the pockets of the dead, one said: "I will become a deity with a smile in this heavy fog. I am only waiting for the day of death."

The liberation of Kiska three months later was a different story. A large force, including five thousand Canadians, nervously crept about the island for five days looking for the enemy, sometimes shooting at each other among exploding booby traps. At the end the astonishing discovery was made that, prior to the landings, shielded by the dank, boreal mist, the Japanese had quietly and quite brilliantly evacuated their entire garrison.

Though command arrangements for the war against Japan were often enormously complicated, the overall idea was simply that the United States had the responsibility for the entire "Pacific area," while Britain took charge of South Asia and the Middle East. But even so, China had to be accorded a special position, as it was regarded as a region of special American interest. Chiang Kai-shek was recognized as supreme commander, but his chief of staff was an American general, Stilwell. Stilwell also commanded United States forces in what become the China-Burma-India theater and thus had the dubious distinction of being simultaneously responsible to Washington, to Chiang, and to the British commander in India. Stilwell was not ideally suited to the task. He was brave and aggressive but almost totally without tact. He quarreled with the British and denounced Chiang for his "stupid, gutless command."

Chiang, on the other had, thanks to circumstance, geography, and Roosevelt's personal prejudice, was accorded considerable influence and played his cards shrewdly. He gave more thought to his postwar problems and the inevitable power struggle with the Communists than to the war itself. He banked on the traditional sympathy of the American people, whose commercial and missionary interests in China dated back for generations, on the American vision of a postwar China that could act as a balance to Japan, and on the fact of China's vast geography and population.

Washington was as adamant in its support of Chiang in Asia as in its opposition to de Gaulle in Europe; and oddly enough, although Mao Tse-tung's Communist armies, based around Sian, were at times fighting Chiang as well as the Japanese, Stalin endorsed Roosevelt's backing of the Generalissimo. Churchill, however, later on reported: "I have found the extraordinary significance of China in American minds, even at the top, strangely out of proportion. I was conscious of a standard of values which accorded China almost an equal fighting power with the British Empire, and rated the Chinese armies as a factor to be mentioned in the same breath as the armies of Russia. I told the President how much I felt American opinion overestimated the contributions which China could make to the general war. He differed strongly. There were five hundred million people in China. What would happen if this enormous population developed in the same way as Japan had done in the last century and got a hold

Having finally defeated the savagely
determined Japanese forces at Guadalcanal,
the triumphant Marines set up housekeeping
and established a rest and retraining
center. Here, under huge coconut trees,
four men of the 3rd Marines stroll the
main street of their division headquarters
after a typical South Seas "shower."

of modern weapons? I replied I was speaking of the present war, which was quite enough to go on with for the time being." The "enormous population" did indeed, subsequently get "hold of modern weapons," but it was not that China envisioned by Roosevelt.

During the war, Chiang reigned supreme in Allied calculations, and Chiang insisted that Burma should be the scene of the initial mainland offensive against the Japanese. He opposed operations in the north, where his own divisions would have to provide needed manpower. Instead, he argued: "Burma is the key to the whole campaign in Asia. After the enemy has been cleared out of Burma, his next stand would be in North China and, finally, in Manchuria." Churchill was unenthusiastic, agreeing with the American admirals King and Nimitz, who wished to force an ultimate decision by sea power. But by appealing for an extension of the supply route across Burma in order to sustain Chinese morale, Chiang gained Roosevelt's backing.

A Southeast Asia Command was created under the English king's cousin, Lord Louis Mountbatten, and was charged with conducting a war of which Mountbatten's own government did not heartily approve. The command depended upon an American military system that sought different objectives, and upon a Chinese government that was fighting almost a private war for purposes largely its own. The Casablanca Conference of January, 1943, nevertheless agreed on a Burma campaign that, from its very genesis, was marked by quarrels and discord. Churchill complained to his Chiefs of Staff: "Going into the swampy jungles to fight the Japanese is like going into the water to fight a shark." Mountbatten viewed Burma as a subsidiary objective. Stilwell favored a Burmese drive—but only in the north, where he wished Chiang would do some serious fighting. Major General Claire Chennault, by now commanding the U.S. Fourteenth Air Force in China, agreed with Chiang that divisions were less important than aircraft but wanted the Japanese to be bombed out of Burma. No one was satisfied. Stilwell and Chennault carried their acrimonious debate right to the Trident Conference in Washington in May, 1943. The irascible Stilwell shouted: "It's the ground soldier slogging through the mud and fighting in the trenches who will win the war." Chennault hollered back: "But God damn it, Stilwell, there aren't any men in the trenches."

The Allied carpenters, however, managed to fashion an operation, one of the goals of which was to increase to ten thousand tons a month the capacity of the Air Transport supply system over the Burmese Hump to China. Their new plan assigned to Mountbatten and Stilwell the task of investing northern and central Burma. A specially trained American infantry combat team known as the Galahad Force, commanded by Brigadier General Frank D. Merrill, was ordered to join the Chinese 22nd and 39th divisions coming down the Hukwang Valley.

Aware of Allied preparations, the Japanese initiated their own offensive during the 1943–44 winter. They attempted to capture the Indian province of Assam and to sever the link to China via the Hump and the Ledo Road, which was being built across north Burma from India to hook up with the old Burma Road into China. British and Indian airborne troops were able to check and finally reverse this short-lived invasion. Then, with the British driving along the Bay of Bengal in the south and the Chinese and Merrill advancing on Myitkyina in the north, the Japanese were forced gradually backward. Major General Orde Wingate, the English disciplinarian who had already earned fame in Ethiopia, dropped on the Japanese rear with his long-range penetration groups.

Wingate's Chindits (a mispronunciation of Chinthe, the Burmese word for lion) and Merrill's Marauders fought remarkably well, outdoing the Japanese in a type of jungle combat the latter had originated. Throughout the end of 1943, when the Japanese tried again to move on India, Wingate's commandos kept the invaders off balance, severing their communications lines. They were supplied exclusively from the air and managed to build a landing strip far behind enemy lines. Merrill, for his part, persuaded a tribe of dark, belligerent north Burmese, called Kachins, to join him in fighting the Japanese. American OSS representatives formed a Kachin unit called Detachment 101 and managed to kill 5,447 Japanese, with a loss of only fifteen Americans and seventy Kachins. Despite divergent national political ambitions and despite rivalries and jealousies among strategists and commanders at the top, Allied field action in Burma was remarkably effective. Wingate, unfortunately, was killed on March 24, 1944, in a plane crash. Churchill called him "a man of genius who might well have become also a man of destiny." He was only forty-one.

The campaign against Japan covered flabbergasting distances; its scope was enormous; and Allied interests were so disparate and contradictory that it was difficult to coordinate strategic plans. The critically important Soviet-Manchurian frontier remained quiescent until weeks after the Nazi surrender in Europe, as it was in the interests of both Russia and Japan to honor their nonaggression pact. Native nationalism in colonial Indochina, Malaya, Indonesia, Burma, and India initially favored the Japanese. Subsequently, however, the invaders' barbarity turned these populations against them, much as Ukrainian nationalists changed their attitude toward the Germans once they got acquainted with the facts of life under the Nazis. China's principal use to the Allies was as an enormous bog that sucked up Japanese armies. The real road to Tokyo would be by sea, and at the close of 1943, there was still plenty of road to travel.

XI

Italy

American tanks of the Fifth Army pass
the ancient Colosseum as they begin to
occupy Rome on June 4, 1944.

The Italian campaign of 1944–45 was a serious strategic error, in my opinion. It was of course both logical and necessary to eliminate Hitler's principal partner in the European war and to gain southern Italy's port facilities and air bases, from which every corner of *Festung Europa* could be bombed. But it was folly to keep on driving up the narrow, mountainous peninsula, where geography favored defense and greatly handicapped any heavily mechanized ground advance.

The argument that the painful Italian thrust pinned down German divisions that otherwise would have been free to fight elsewhere is, I believe, fallacious. Had the Allies been content to hold a river line from the Garigliano across to the Sangro, a line they had reached by mid-January, 1944, they could have mustered from Naples the expedition for their landing in southern France and would have retained the vital air bases at Foggia.

Such a strategy still would have required the Germans to maintain large troop concentrations in Italy, in order to prop up Mussolini's regime in the north and to guard against amphibious end-runs such as that at Anzio. Italy was wide open to naval assaults and landings, a possibility the Nazis were forced to guard against continually.

Churchill always wanted to cross the Adriatic and, with the help of Greek, Yugoslav, and Albanian guerrillas, march up the Balkans and into the Danube Valley. But the United States turned a deaf ear to his proposals, and one ultimate result of the decision to press the Italian campaign was Churchill's subsequent deal with Stalin, dividing the Balkan countries into wartime spheres of influence that lasted on into peace, with only Greece being accorded a dominant Western bias.

The basic decision to attack at Sicily was reached at the Casablanca Conference in January, 1943. That same month, General Mark Clark had activated the U.S. Fifth Army in northern Morocco, while General Alphonse Juin, French commander in North Africa, was forming an expeditionary corps of Moroccans, Algerians, and French nationals. (Clark was later to say of them, "A more gallant fighting organization never existed.")

The forces of Clark and Juin were held in reserve for the invasion of mainland Italy. But on July 5, the U.S. Seventh Army under Patton embarked from Oran, Algiers, and Bizerte for Sicily, in an armada commanded by Vice Admiral H. Kent Hewitt. Simultaneously, Montgomery's British Eighth Army sailed from Tripoli, Benghazi, Alexandria, Port Said, and distant Haifa and Beirut. There were nearly three thousand landing craft and warships, one hundred and sixty thousand troops, fourteen thousand vehicles, six hundred tanks, and eighteen hundred artillery pieces. Britain undertook to supply 80 per cent of the naval cover and 45 per cent of the air cover required; the rest was assumed by the United States.

For weeks, enemy defenses had been softened up by continued bombing of Sicily, southern Italy, Sardinia, and the little cluster of offshore islands that included strongly fortified Pantelleria. Eisenhower had decided to invade Pantelleria as a first step, but on June 11, it had surrendered without a fight after heavy aerial bombardment. The only Allied casualty was a private bitten by a mule. Sicily itself was a far tougher nut: barren, mountainous, and held by three hundred thousand Italian and German soldiers under Field Marshal Alfred Kesselring. Kesselring thought that if Sicily would be Eisenhower's next target, the landing must come on the southwest coast, opposite Tunisia, or on the north coast, close to Messina, the escape route to the mainland.

Just to keep Kesselring confused, the Allies spread rumors of an impending attack on Greece or Sardinia. British intelligence dressed a corpse in a Royal Marines uniform, adorned it with false credentials and "secret" documents indicating that the real assault would come in Greece, and floated the body ashore in Spain. The Spanish authorities immediately handed the faked papers on to Nazi intelligence. This ingenious deception was accompanied by a publicized trip to the Middle East by an actor who looked astonishingly like Montgomery and was dressed in the General's uniform.

On the afternoon of July 9, the invasion armada converged south of Malta, in the midst of heavy seas and thirty-five-mile-an-hour winds. The gale kept blowing as night fell, and the landing faced disaster. But by dawn of the tenth, both gusts and waves subsided. The landing craft pitched through the breakers and began discharging men and machines, including an ingenious new amphibious load-carrier known as DUKW, on Sicily's south coast. Despite the fact that a large number of British airborne troops were drowned when their gliders were prematurely released into the sea, Eisenhower, was able to report before noon: "The success of the landings is already assured." Thanks in part to foul weather, the initial lodgment had come as a tactical surprise. Although some German panzers struck back sharply, most of the Italian defenders offered only token resistance. They surrendered in droves, or, wearing civilian clothes, vanished into the hills. The Sicilians themselves greeted the invaders joyfully, handing out fruit, flowers, and wine.

Montgomery's Eighth Army slashed up the east coast, swiftly taking ancient Syracuse, and entered the malaria-infested Catanian plain. There, meeting stiff German resistance, the British commander cautiously halted to bring up his main strength—a decision that inspired American complaints. Patton's Seventh Army landed at Gela and Licata in the south and proceeded, according to Patton's theory of war, to "go like Hell." Within two weeks he would drive all the way to Palermo on the northern coast of Sicily, slicing the island in half. On July 20, he was ordered to head for Messina. The Germans withdrew slowly toward the northeast, fighting a dogged defense until mid-August, when sixty thousand of them managed to escape to the toe of Italy across the narrow Strait of Messina. This was a considerable achievement; nevertheless, by the time the American forces took Messina on August 17, the Axis had lost 135,000 prisoners and 32,000 dead or wounded. Allied casualties came to a total of 31,158.

The Allies, whose intelligence from Italy was both accurate and extensive, had prepared the political and psychological machinery to benefit from the collapse of Sicily. On July 17, United States and British aircraft had begun dropping over Rome and other cities leaflets signed by Roosevelt and Churchill: "Mussolini carried you into this war as the satellite of a brutal destroyer of peoples and liberties. Mussolini plunged you into a war which he thought Hitler had already won. In spite of Italy's great vulnerability to attack by air and sea, your Fascist leaders sent your sons, your ships, your air forces, to distant battlefields to aid Germany in her attempt to conquer England, Russia, and the world. . . . The time has now come for you, the Italian people, to consult your own self-respect and your own interests and your own desire for a restoration of national dignity, security, and

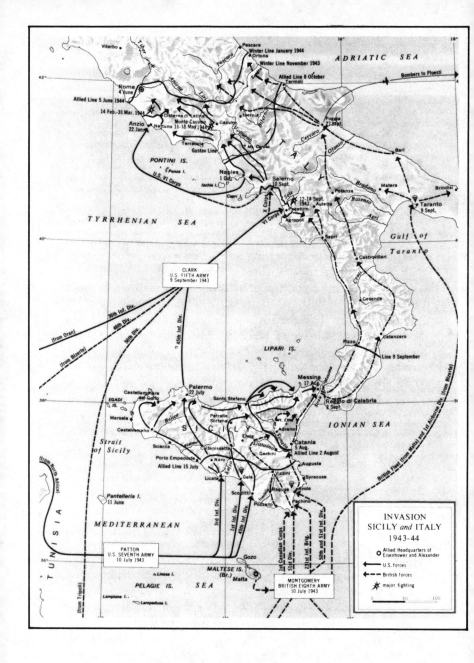

INVASION
SICILY *and* ITALY
1943-44

◎ Allied Headquarters of
   Eisenhower and Alexander
→ U.S. forces
⇢ British forces
✦ major fighting

0   50   100

CLARK
U.S. FIFTH ARMY
9 September 1943

PATTON
U.S. SEVENTH ARMY
10 July 1943

MONTGOMERY
BRITISH EIGHTH ARMY
10 July 1943

168

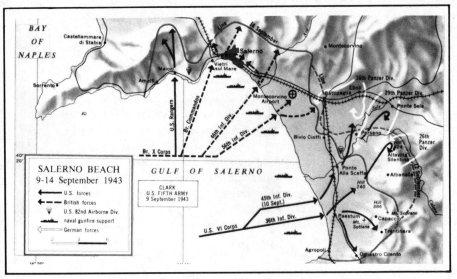

The Allied invasion of Sicily in July, 1943, was to be a campaign of limited objectives, aimed at freeing Mediterranean shipping from Axis harassment, diverting German strength from the Russian front, and increasing the pressure on Italy to desert Hitler. It was also hoped that Messina, on Sicily's northeast coast, could be seized fast enough to seal off the third of a million Axis troops on the island before they could escape across the two-mile-wide strait to the mainland. Churchill, however, saw the invasion as a preliminary to an attack on Italy, the "soft underbelly" of Europe, and his view finally prevailed. But as Samuel Eliot Morison later wrote, "the underbelly proved to be boned with the Apennines, plated with the hard scales of Kesselring's armor, and shadowed by the wings of the Luftwaffe." From Salerno to Anzio to Cassino, "sunny Italy" would provide some of the hardest fighting of the war. Muddy plains, snow-choked mountains, and the freezing cold of an exceptionally severe Italian winter proved to be among the most effective collaborators that the soldiers of the Third Reich ever had.

peace. The time has come for you to decide whether Italians shall die for Mussolini and Hitler—or live for Italy, and for civilization."

Mussolini's control had started to crumble long before the Sicilian landing. As Allied air power had smashed Italian cities and communications, national morale faded; the food situation worsened; strikes and riots broke out in industrial centers. Mussolini's secret police advised him that many ardent Fascists were now conspiring against him: Count Dino Grandi; Marshal Pietro Badoglio, the conqueror of Ethiopia; General Vittorio Ambrosio, Chief of the General Staff.

On July 19, as the British and Americans were smashing across Sicily, Mussolini conferred with Hitler at a villa near Rimini. The *Fürer* counseled: "Sicily must be made into a Stalingrad. . . . We must hold out until winter, when new secret weapons will be ready for use against England." But he offered no further reinforcements for the collapsing Italian Army, and the dialogue was punctuated by the bleak news that seven hundred Allied aircraft had bombed Rome.

Five days later, the *Duce* summoned the Fascist Grand Council to the Palazzo Venezia for its first meeting since 1939. In a passionate two-hour speech he sought to arouse his weary, blackshirted collaborators. But he failed. Grandi had the audacity to introduce a resolution demanding that Mussolini relinquish to King Victor Emmanuel the command of the armed forces. Nineteen of the Fascists supported this motion; seven opposed, and two abstained. Mussolini strode out of the room aware that his game was up.

The council ended in the early morning hours of Sunday, July 25. Later that day, the angry *Duce* called on Victor Emmanuel, who informed him that he was no longer head of the Government. "The soldiers don't want to fight any more," said the hapless little king. "At this moment you are the most hated man in Italy." When he left the palace, Mussolini was arrested by *carabinieri*, shoved into an ambulance, and smuggled off to internment on the island of Ponza. The king took command of his dissolving military forces and instructed Badoglio to form a new cabinet. The Italian people demonstrated with ferocious joy.

The Allies, although their agents had established contact with anti-Fascist elements at various levels, proved inept and slow-moving at this critical moment. For five weeks they bickered

On July 22, 1943, just twelve days after
the initial Allied landings on Sicily,
tanks of the Seventh Army rolled into
Palermo. Patton's men were warmly welcomed
by the capital's jubilant residents, who
waved flags, applauded, and shouted "Long
live America" and "Down with Mussolini."

over surrender negotiations. Then, on August 19, General Giuseppe Castellano met American and British military representatives in Lisbon. He made a rather startling offer to switch sides and join the Allies against Germany. Terms accepting this proposal were finally negotiated, approved by the king, and communicated to Eisenhower's headquarters on the first of September. It was planned that they should be announced by Badoglio over the radio on September 8, to coincide with the intended Allied landing that same night on the mainland at Salerno.

Eisenhower drafted an emergency plan for a daring parachute landing on Rome and, on September 7, sent General Maxwell Taylor on a secret visit to the Italian capital to estimate German military strength and how much support the Allies might expect from the Italians. But the venture was dropped. On September 8, at eight o'clock in the evening, Badoglio announced on the radio that the nation was giving up its fight.

Both the *Gestapo* and the *Abwehr* (the intelligence bureau of the German high command) had had advance information of the conspiracy to overthrow Mussolini and had kept abreast of Italy's dealings with the Allies. While the envoys of Eisenhower and Badoglio were negotiating, Hitler had rushed crack units to Kesselring's aid. When the mainland invasion finally came, it was heavily and effectively opposed.

The first lodgment on the Italian peninsula was made by Montgomery's Eight Army, which on September 3 crossed the Strait of Messina under heavy artillery and air cover and raced northward through Calabria. Six days later, Mark Clark's U.S. Fifth Army disembarked on the sandy beaches along the Gulf of Salerno. Montgomery had a relatively easy time. As his veteran troops fanned northward and eastward, they were joined by six thousand men of the First British Airborne Division, which seized the naval base of Taranto on September 9 and then swept up to the Adriatic port of Bari.

Clark's forces, however, ran into difficulty from the start. They were landed by night without benefit of preliminary shelling, in the hope of achieving surprise. It was believed that by entering Italy as far north as Salerno, they could quickly take nearby Naples. But the German coastal defenses were inviolate. Furthermore, the GIs, having just heard the announcement of Italy's surrender, expected an easy landing. Instead they were met by heavy artillery and tank fire. They found themselves compressed into a small beachhead that extended less than five miles inland. Many assault boats were unable to reach their designated targets. Paratroopers sent to back them up suffered heavy losses en route. German loudspeakers meanwhile kept roaring in English: "Come on in and give up. You're covered." The invasion fleet suffered from confused communications and had trouble discharging heavy weapons. Four days after the landings, Kesselring staged a massive counterattack that almost split the Fifth Army in two. Berlin radio began hailing the prospect of "another Dunkirk."

At this crucial point, from bases in Sicily and North Africa, the U.S. Strategic Air Force began bombing the hills surrounding Salerno, and Montgomery was ordered to speed up his advance in order to relieve the pressure on his beleaguered allies. Clark organized everyone into fighting units: truck drivers, mechanics, and even a regimental band, which defended a hill thenceforth called Piccolo Peak. The Germans began to waver and finally, on September 15, to withdraw to Naples. Clark seized the initiative. Within a month he had unloaded one hundred and thirty-five thousand troops, thirty thousand vehicles, and one hundred thousand tons of supplies to nourish a northward drive. At the same time, Fighting French troops, aided by local guerrillas, captured Corsica, and the Germans abandoned Sardinia. The bulk of the Italian fleet sailed into Malta for internment.

Italy had by now become a battleground in which the Italians themselves figured only as doleful victims. Badoglio's and the king's scheme to switch sides and thus avoid disaster had backfired. In 1940 Mussolini had said: "If the Germans ever get here they will never go home." He was right. Hitler left Kesselring to fight the campaign in the south, sent Rommel to organize northern Italian defenses, and took ruthlessly effective control of all the area not already in Allied hands.

Badoglio and the royal family had fled Rome in a panic on September 9, and had reconstituted the semblance of a government in Brindisi, far to the south. A week later, Badoglio, the old Fascist, summoned his countrymen "to fight the Germans in every way, everywhere, and all the time." On October 13, Victor Emmanuel formally declared war on Germany. Italy was recognized by the Allies as a "co-belligerent." She was promised that her punishment would be lessened according to the degree of success with which she worked her miserable passage.

Close to the landing beaches at Paestum,
the ancient Greek Temple of Neptune was
appropriated for an American Army field
headquarters. Italy seemed a far "more
civilized" place, as one GI put it, to
fight a war than North Africa had been.
Although the troops had little time to
dwell on it, Italy overflowed with a way
of life and a heritage that struck at the
heart of why the Allies were fighting.

The German answer to betrayal, facilitated by five weeks' delay in surrender parleys, was formidable. Nazi military headquarters ordered immediate disarming of all Italian troops. Within an hour of Badoglio's announcement of an armistice, Nazi patrols took over from Salerno to Nice and the Brenner Pass. Italy's Fourth Army on the French border was disbanded. Rommel seized Trieste and the routes to Yugoslavia, thus completing the isolation of thirty-two Italian divisions. Most of these capitulated. It has been estimated that Germany took six hundred and forty thousand Italian prisoners on the peninsula and on the Balkans; the majority were shipped to Nazi internment camps, where some thirty thousand died. Rome capitulated to a threat of *Luftwaffe* bombs, and on September 11, Kesselring proclaimed Italy a war theater under German control. The Nazis seized Italy's gold reserves and began immediate persecution of those Jews who had managed to survive Mussolini's half-hearted restrictions.

While the great mass of Italian soldiers deserted or yielded without a struggle, there were two divisions in southwest Yugoslavia that joined Tito as a "Garibaldi Partisan Division." In France, Albania, and Greece, many Italians linked up with local guerrillas. In northern Italy, partisans achieved a splendid record fighting the Nazis. Nevertheless, such determination was rare. Only seven of Italy's sixty-one divisions became available to the Allies, and the morale of these troops was poor, although some forty-eight thousand did take part in the final 1945 drive against the Germans.

Mussolini himself had one more great adventure in store. From Ponza he was removed to a small mountain resort in the Abruzzi, from which Hitler swore to save him. In mid-September, 1943, Otto Skorzeny, the remarkable Nazi commando leader, overran the resort with glider troops and kidnapped the *Duce* in a light airplane. He was thenceforth set up as the puppet head of a Fascist republic in the north, proclaiming: "I, Mussolini, resume supreme direction of Fascism in Italy." History has paid scant attention to the episode.

Meanwhile, the Fifth Army of General Clark, a tall, hawknosed, fearless, ambitious, and incredibly vain commander, had successfully passed its test at Salerno and now drove on Naples, the most important single prize in south Italy. The Germans, fighting a skilled defense, did not bother to defend the city but, taking vengeance for Italy's defection, smashed it and withdrew northward. When the Americans and British entered Naples early on the morning of October 1, they found that the port and every-thing within three hundred yards of it had been destroyed by the Nazis. The population was half-starved, frightened by looters, and bullied by criminals released from prison by the departing Germans. The grand old university had been deliberately wrecked; hospitals had been looted; and a number of hostages had been taken off. The citizens of Naples gave their Allied conquerors a wild welcome. American engineers set to work on the wreckage and soon had the harbor and neighboring airfields in operation.

To the northeast, Montgomery's Eighth Army had succeeded, against relatively slight opposition, in achieving its initial objec-tives. The extensive network of airfields at Foggia began fur-nishing fighter cover to advancing Allied troops as well as dispatching bombers over Austria and the Balkans. But Kesselring, with his fine eye for terrain, established a new position to frus-trate Clark on the north bank of the Volturno River, where Gari-baldi had won a significant victory in 1860. There began the slow hacking campaign in which, pushing between rock ridges and along muddy valleys through Italy's worst winter in decades, the Allies inched toward Rome and Tuscany.

To pursue this ill-conceived strategy, the Allies installed an-other team of commanders. Eisenhower had been recalled to En-gland to prepare for the Normandy invasion. With him he took his most renowned generals: Montgomery, Bradley, and Patton. Sir Harold Alexander, who had, with minimal fanfare, super-vised Montgomery's operations from the Nile to Tunisia, was left behind as commander in Italy. Under him were Clark and the calm, little-known Sir Oliver Leese, who head the British Eighth Army on the Adriatic. General Ira Eaker, a tough, poker-faced American, took over the Allied Mediterranean air forces. General Sir Henry "Jumbo" Wilson, whose affable demeanor and swollen shape masked a far greater talent for generalship than history remembers, was given ultimate responsibility for the theater.

Hitler likewise reordered his command. He sent Rommel to France and left Italy to Kesselring, ordering him to hold "at all costs for the sake of the political consequences which would fol-low a completely successful defense. The *Führer* expects the bitterest struggle for every yard."

Kesselring did what he was told. Clark was slowed up on the

The tomb and cell of Saint Benedict, the
founder of Monte Cassino, remained intact
amidst the ruins of the rest of the abbey.
Rebuilt in the fourteenth century on the
site of the monastery founded in 529, Monte
Cassino was pulverized by five hundred tons
of Allied bombs on Valentine's Day, 1944.
The abbot and a few priests remained in a
subterranean chapel throughout the bombing.

Volturno and at successive hilltop villages, but the Allies hoped to outflank the Germans by amphibious tactics. On January 22, 1944, they swept by sea round the right flank of the Germans' Gustav Line and landed two divisions thirty-three miles south of Rome, at the pleasant resort towns of Anzio and Nettuno.

Anzio came close to being a disaster. The initial landing went well, but it was not exploited, and the surprised Germans had ample time to mass troops and artillery around the beachhead's perimeter. Their eventual counterattacks almost succeeded in wiping out the beachhead. The purpose of the landing—to relieve pressure from the main drive along the road to Rome—failed. Churchill, who had endorsed the project, admitted: "The story of Anzio was a story of high opportunity and shattered hopes, of skillful inception on our part and swift recovery by the enemy, of valor shared by both."

The failure at Anzio threw the main weight of the campaign back on the positions around the town of Cassino, hinge of Kesselring's Gustav Line. Apart from its magnificent position along the Liri and Rapido rivers, giving it domination of the narrow valley leading up toward Rome, Cassino was marked by a monastery built on the massif above it by St. Benedict in the sixth century. The historic Abbey of Monte Cassino had been successively ravaged by conquerors and an earthquake in the Middle Ages. It was now to be destroyed again.

From the heights around the abbey, German eighty-eights were picking off Allied armor, while mortars and *nebelwerfers*, dubbed "screaming meemies" by the Americans, were plastering the advancing infantry. The Allied command concluded that the advantages posed by the monastery could no longer be ignored. There was a suspicion that Nazi outposts actually had been established within the abbey—although this was later disproved. At any rate, a conclave of generals resolved that the fortress sanctuary must be destroyed. Leaflets were dropped over enemy lines saying: "Against our will we are now obliged to direct our weapons against the Monastery itself. We warn you so that you may now save yourselves. Leave the Monastery at once." And on February 15, the vast abbey was bombed by two hundred and fifty-four planes. Only the cell and tomb of St. Benedict escaped damage.

The attack on this holy shrine achieved nothing but a worldwide wave of protest, which was carefully fanned by German propaganda. The Nazi defenders moved into the ruins and set up impregnable positions amid the shattered masonry. The town of Cassino itself was hit again and again by Allied guns and aircraft. One raid, in which I participated as an observer, involved more aircraft than had yet been used on any operation; the entire town was obliterated in a cloud of flame, smoke, and shattered stone. Yet despite the attacks, when Allied patrols sought to enter Cassino, they were promptly driven back by the expert German First Parachute Division.

That was a winter of deep discontent for Alexander's armies, which included Americans, British, Canadians, French, New Zealanders, South Africans, Poles, Indians, Brazilians, Greeks, Moroccans, Algerians, Senegalese, a brigade of Palestinian Jews, and a handful of royalist Italians. The mud was like glue at midday and like iron in the freezing nights. Cold winds and snow swept the jagged crags. Dead GIs lay in the cratered valley they called Purple Heart, their throats eaten out by scavenger dogs. Trench foot and frostbite were common. A brave batallion of Japanese Americans from Hawaii suffered heavily from the cold; few sights were more pathetic than their tiny cast-off shoes on the monastery slopes. A force of Nepalese Gurkha was cut off for days on an outpost below the abbey. Each day, in this battle in a bowl, American fighter-bombers dropped gaily-colored parachutes with canisters of ammunition, food, and water to the isolated hillmen, who scrambled to secure them amid withering machine-gun fire. Among the most disheartening sights of all was Vesuvius far to the south of the battle lines. The volcano exploded in a sudden eruption that cast an ashen cloud far exceeding anything the Allies, with all their aircraft and artillery, could produce at Cassino.

At last, on May 14, 1944, after a reordering of forces, the Allied command began a new offensive, moving the Fifth and Eighth armies across the Garigliano and Rapido rivers and breaking Kesselring's Gustav Line after a week of difficult assault. The Polish troops of General Anders, reassembled from prisoner-of-war camps in Russia and allowed to join the British in the Middle East, were given the honor of capturing the abbey. Their role is still marked by a cemetery filled with Polish names.

An American private receives a grateful
kiss from a woman as the Allies occupy
Rome. At the beginning of the Italian
campaign, leaflets signed by Roosevelt
and Churchill were dropped over Italy:
". . . The time has now come for you, the
Italian people . . . to decide whether Italians
shall die for Mussolini and Hitler—or live
for Italy, and for civilization."

Once again the Germans began a difficult but orderly withdrawal. The Fifth Army thrust out from its separated Cassino and Anzio positions, entering Rome at last on June 4, 1944, and marching through the Piazza Venezia. Clark, who rode into Rome with the vanguard on June 5, recalls: "There were gay crowds in the streets, many of of them waving flags, as our infantry marched through the capital. Flowers were stuck in the muzzles of the soldiers' rifles and of guns on the tanks. Many Romans seemed to be on the verge of hysteria in their enthusiasm for the American troops. . . . It was on this day that a doughboy made the classic remark of the Italian campaign, when he took a long look at the ruins of the Colosseum, whistled softly, and said, 'Gee, I didn't know our bombers had done *that* much damage in Rome.'"

The fall of Rome marked the beginning of the last phase of the European war. Two days later, Eisenhower's forces landed in Normandy and burst through the front door of the *Führer*'s Fortress Europe.

XII

Over Here

"Th' hell this ain't th' most important hole in th' world. I'm in it."

Bill Mauldin's cartoons brought to life the war's best-known knights in shining armor, Willy and Joe.

When American troops went into action in North Africa and Italy, their abilities were assayed with considerable curiosity by their more experienced allies and enemies. Britain's Chief of Staff, Sir Alan Brooke, decided: "The Americans had a lot to learn. . . . But in the art of war . . . when they once got down to it they were determined to make a success of it." Field Marshal Rommel reflected afterward: "What was really amazing was the speed with which the Americans adapted themselves to modern warfare. They were assisted in this by their tremendous practical and material sense and by their lack of all understanding for tradition and useless theories." He concluded: "Starting from scratch an army has been created in the very minimum of time, which, in equipment, armament and organization of all arms, surpasses anything the world has yet seen."

The fact was that the U.S. Armed Forces were built, to use Rommel's phrase, "in a minimum of time," out of whatever the draft boards were able to send along. Those whom Alan Brooke saw as "determined to make a success of it" were the standard U.S. Government Issues, the very nonmilitary male civilian Americans, the GIs. In the early years of the war, the Navy and the Marine Corps were fleshed out with volunteers only. But the American soldier was in uniform because he had no other choice. He had to be taught how to fight, and once taught, he had no great desire to fight; but, at the same time he had no doubt that he would win.

This average American soldier of World War II was taller and heavier than his father who had fought in World War I. When he went off to serve his country, he had had some high school education; he knew how to drive a car, how to swim, how to do the jitterbug or the Big Apple or the Lindy. He usually came from a city or big town. Chances were he had never fired a rifle; he spoke no other language than his own; and as yet he had not learned how to shoot craps. Once in the hands of the Army, he was given a remarkably fast haircut at no charge, then punctured with inoculations, garbed in a floppy olive-drab outfit called "fatigues," and put under the tutelage of a hard-cussing buck sergeant who barked weird commands and soon had him throwing out his chest and talking in a jargon that he would remember for the rest of his life.

In the world of the U.S. armed forces,
camaraderie could not get any thicker,
as shown in this photograph of soldiers
en route from England to Africa. At least
half the business of soldiering with the
United States Army meant standing in
line, or so it seemed. The other half was
being shipped, bussed, trucked, or trained
here and there for days on end.

One of the best descriptions of this process was written by a draftee from North Carolina named Marion Hargrove. In his best-selling book on life at Fort Bragg, *See Here, Private Hargrove,* he included an anonymous letter that was going the rounds of his company:

"Dear, unfortunate civilian friend: I am very enthusiastic about Army life. We lie around in bed every morning until at least six o'clock. This, of course, gives us plenty of time to get washed and dressed and make the bunks, etc., by 6:10. At 6:15 we stand outside and shiver while some (deleted) blows a bugle. After we are reasonably chilled, we grope our way through the darkness to the mess hall. Here we have a hearty breakfast consisting of an unidentified liquid and a choice of white or rye crusts.

"After gorging ourselves with this delicious repast, we waddle our way back to the barracks. We have nothing to do until 7:30 so we just sit around and scrub toilets, mop the floors, wash windows and pick up all the match sticks and cigarette butts within a radius of 2,000 feet of the barracks.

"Soon the sergeant comes in and says, 'Come out in the sunshine, kiddies!' So we go out and bask in the wonderful North Carolina sunshine—of course, we stand knee-deep in the wonderful North Carolina sand. To limber up, we do a few simple calisthenics, such as touching your toes with both feet off the ground and grabbing yourself by the hair and holding yourself at arm's length.

"At eight o'clock we put on our light packs and go for a tramp in the hills. The light pack includes gun, bayonet, canteen, fork, knife, spoon, meat cans, cup, shaving kit, pup tent, raincoat, cartridge belt, first aid kit, fire extinguisher, tent pins, rope, tent pole, hand ax, small spade, and a few other negligible items. Carrying my light pack, I weigh 217 1/2 pounds. I weighed 131 pounds when I left home, so you can see how easy it is to gain weight in the Army."

As Hargrove himself pointed out, the only weak spot in the letter was the part about breakfast. As a matter of fact, U.S. Army meals, even at the front, were, for the most part, pretty good. "A" rations, served in areas where food could be preserved under refrigeration, were excellent. The combat rations "C" and "K," though still recalled with horror by millions of American men, were superior to those provided by other armies. The "C" ration included ten different meat compounds (the most celebrated of them being the ubiquitous Spam), stews, spaghetti, vegetables, dehydrated eggs,and potatoes. The "K" comprised ingenious compounds that, if nothing else, were nourishing. Also among the combat food was the famous "D" bar, which was hard as a rock and took about half an hour to gnaw through. The main trouble with the diet was that it was monotonous. Men wrote home desperately for anything spicy, anything that had flavor. The greatest gifts for "the boys overseas" were fruitcakes, jam, and salami.

As the immense machinery for turning civilians into soldiers picked up speed and units became ready to head for the Pacific, Africa, and England, the War and Navy Departments thoughtfully issued them pocket guidebooks with tips on how to get along overseas. Those who were bound for Britain were advised: "The British don't know how to make a good cup of coffee. You don't know how to make a good cup of tea—It's an even swap"; and a special glossary explained that in England, dust bin means ash can, lift is elevator, first floor is second floor, flicks are movies, and a dickey is a rumble seat. Soldiers embarking for North Africa were cautioned that Muhammadans were not "heathens," and that when indulging in a local meal, "it is advisable not to drink much liquid after eating *kuskus* as the grain is only partly cooked and bloating will result." They were also admonished: "If you enter a bakery, leave your shoes at the door. . . . Never try to remove the veil [from a Moslem woman]. This is most important. Serious injury if not death at the hands of Moslem men may result. . . ."

Once overseas, the GI was kept in touch with relatives and friends at home by V-mail—little letters that could reach even the most outlandish destination in about ten days—and by miniature overseas editions of magazines and books. He was looked after by the Red Cross, which, along with collecting blood plasma, making bandages, and recruiting nurses, set up "clubmobiles" where girls served coffee and doughnuts. The U.S.O. put on dances and stage shows for him, and sent such Hollywood celebrities as Joe E. Brown, Bing Crosby, Bob Hope, Jo Stafford, and Frances Langford to far-flung desert and jungle sites and to the Aleutian Islands. They gave the lonely GI a laugh or the rare chance to let fly with a wolf call. Bob Hope endeared himself to hundreds of wounded men by coming up to their beds and saying: "Hi. Did you see my show tonight or were you already sick?"

American soldiers in Sicily wait in line for chow. Monotony permeated the days of inactive troops to the point that even the smallest pleasures became memorable events: the first taste of fresh vegetables after months at sea, a cold beer, an after-dinner movie in the rain, even advertisements for soap and whiskey and white shirts. Best of all was mail from home; there was never quite enough of that.

To keep the American soldier fit and fighting, an array of new drugs and preventive medicines was developed. Special clothing—jackets, boots, headgear—were devised to protect him against extremes of temperature and terrain. To keep him out of trouble, especially when he went on leave, a police force was set up; its white belts, gloves, leggings, helmet liners, and "MP" armbands became well-known symbols around the world. And to advise "the folks back home" on the latest doings, a force of some seven hundred correspondents was mustered by American newspapers, magazines, and radio stations. During 1944 alone, they sent back some two hundred million words from the battlefronts. (The Normandy landings alone were reported by some four hundred and fifty correspondents.) They traveled by landing craft, tank, truck, jeep, mule, and foot through Italy, France, Germany, and, island by island, across the Pacific. They wrote about the men who were making the decisions that affected the GI's life—Eisenhower, Bradley, Patton, Arnold, and Spaatz in Europe; MacArthur, Nimitz, Halsey, Smith, Vandegrift in the Pacific. For millions of mothers and fathers, wives and sweethearts, knowing just who these commanders were was vitally important.

But the man about whom the most was written was, inevitably, the man who was himself commanded, who did the bulk of the fighting even in an age of mechanized war: the nearly always uncomfortable, unromantic, anonymous infantryman, the GI. Various correspondents evaluated his professional skills. A *New York Times* reporter, for example, wrote:

"The Americans were not as good campaigners—as differentiated as fighters—as the British. Nor would they adopt the attitude that war is a natural part of life, held by the French soldiers. . . . They were unhappy in defensive fighting, at their best in a big push forward. The only emotion they would show was a deep pride in their combat team or division, a burning desire to see that it 'did the job.'

"In action the American attacked silently, not singing as did the British or shouting as did the French. . . . There were German prisoners who testified to the fear of these silent soldiers moving remorselessly forward that grew in the ranks of the German divisions."

Other correspondents described the terror of war, its filth, fear, and loneliness, its comradeship, heroism, and humor; the hours and hours of boredom, and the moments of indescribably exhilaration. There was John Hersey on Guadalcanal, Joe Liebling in North Africa; there were John Dos Passos, Ernest Hemingway, John Steinbeck, Ed Murrow, and others less famous. Some were killed. Of these, perhaps the best, and certainly the GI's own personal favorite, was a middle-aged newspaperman named Ernie Pyle, who wrote with compassion and distinction and who followed the "mud-rain-frost-and-wind-boys," as he called them, right up until the day that he was shot and killed by a sniper's bullet on the Pacific Island of Ie Shima.

Pyle wrote: "I believe that I have a new patience with humanity that I've never had before. . . . I don't see how any survivor of war can ever be cruel to anything, ever again." When he was buried, the following inscription was put on his grave marker: "At This Spot the 77th Infantry Division Lost a Buddy, Ernie Pyle. 18 April 1945."

Among the hardiest of those who sought to describe the war were the photographers, many of whom were in the heart of the action, and who, often as not, remained anonymous. Perhaps the best of them was Hungarian born Robert Capa—who survived the war, despite, the risks he took, only to be killed in Indochina in 1954. Capa was determined to immortalize "the little man whose future was at stake in a world he could not change."

Sergeant George Baker was another who set out to accomplish the same thing, but in quite a different fashion. He created the indestructible "Sad Sack," whose comic-strip adventures appeared in the Army magazine *Yank*. But the man who did more than anyone to immortalize the American infantryman was Bill Mauldin, a boyish looking GI who drew cartoons for the Army newspaper, *Stars and Stripes*. Mauldin was only twenty when he went overseas and rapidly became the best-known American war cartoonist, a kind of reincarnated Bruce Bairnsfather, the British cartoonist of the First World War. He captured the grim wit of the foxhole in a way loved by the enlisted men themselves, detested by some of their officers. The secret of his humor and of its impact among the men was that it was caste-conscious; it said to the enlisted man, "I'm with you, and only we together know what it's all about." His two cartoon characters, Willie and Joe, became the heartbreaking and hilariously funny heroes of an army that was fighting hard as it could, with little fanfare and a lot of griping, to get the job over with and get home, *alive*.

After the war Mauldin wrote a book, *Up Front*, which included the pick of his cartoons and his own comments on the war. What he had to say, like his drawing, put the "glories" of life at the front on their proper level. For example: "It's a little better when you can lie down, even in the mud. Rocks are better than mud because you can curl yourself around the big rocks, even if you wake up with sore bruises where the little rocks dug into you. When you wake up in the mud your cigarettes are all wet and you have an ache in your joints and a rattle in your chest."

There were only three punctuations to the dreary life of a front-line infantryman: relief, wounds, or death. A Marine's grave marker on Guadalcanal summarized the period in between:

And when he gets to Heaven,
To Saint Peter he will tell:
One more marine reporting, sir—
I've served my time in Hell.

As the first shiploads of coffins began coming back to the United States, they brought home to Americans the hard truth of war as nothing else could—not even those letters and telegrams being delivered to so many front doors: "We regret to inform you . . . ." As the death toll steadily mounted, little-known villages that were tucked away in obscure corners of the country suddenly felt as if they had suffered some biblical plague. Salinas, California, with a population of 11,586 and Harrodsburg, Kentucky, with 4,673, respectively contributed 150 and 76 men to the tragedy of Bataan.

There was a determined effort by the American command and its Graves Registration Service to keep track of all those who died, even when their remains were unidentifiable. Nevertheless, there were places in Europe and on islands in the Pacific where trenches were dug, the bodies dumped in after identification had been removed, a row of crosses put up, and a dog tag hung on each cross. And the sailor's grave, as always in war, was the sea. Before it was all over, 201,367 Americans were killed, more than the battle dead of the Union and Confederate armies in the Civil War.

Those who lived simply stumbled back from the edge of the

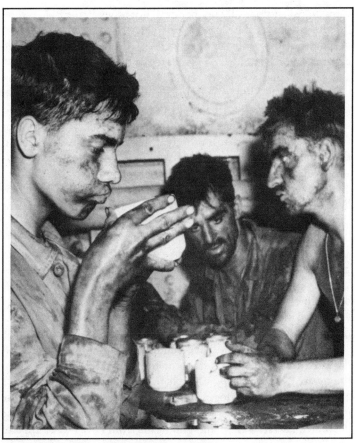

The men in this photograph have just
been through two days and two nights
of fighting on Eniwetok Island in the
Marshalls, in February, 1944. They are
members of the 22nd Marine Regiment, and
the battle was their first combat. There
was generally plenty of talk about combat,
but nearly always by men who had not as
yet experienced it. After they had, they
preferred to talk about other things.

canyon, psychologically neither dead nor alive. Ernie Pyle wrote: "In their eyes as they pass is not hatred, not excitement, not despair, not the tonic of their victory. There is just the simple expression of being there as if they had been doing that forever, and nothing else." Pyle also said: "A soldier who has been a long time in the line does have a 'look' in his eyes that anyone who knows about it can discern . . . it is a look that is a display room for what lies behind it—exhaustion, lack of sleep, tension for too long, weariness that is too great, fear beyond fear, misery to the point of numbness, a look of surpassing indifference to anything anybody can do." (It was a "look" that the GIs called "combat fatigue" or "nervous in the service" and that, by 1945, had translated itself into mental collapse for some five hundred thousand men.)

The incredible psychological pressures of war produced a strange form of spiritual bends in a good many men, who, when granted a momentary release from duty, sought to express their very joy in survival, sometimes in the age-old ways of the soldier, other times in fashions that seemed almost inexplicable. The GIs celebrated their triumph over death or masked their fears or fought their boredom in wild ecstasies of gambling, often playing for stakes they never would have believed possible in their civilian days. After all, what was three or four thousand dollars, when they were used to putting up their lives? And along with the dice and poker went the glossy photographs of American glamour girls—the "pin-up"—or the snapshots of sweetheart or wife that decorated barracks walls and bulkheads from Fort Dix to Bizerte to Ulithi. As a sentimental reminder, if all this was not enough, the names of girl friends, dogs, home towns, and cartoon characters and a lively variety of pet slogans were inscribed on the sides of tanks and airplanes.

Wherever they went in a bewildering and foreign world, the Americans often befriended ragged, big-eyed children, giving them candy bars and chewing gum. Also, wherever they went, they sought strong drink and feminine companionship. In North Africa they bought huge quantities of terrible home brew from Arab traders. In Italy they purchased all the grappa in sight, naming it Kickapoo Joy Juice after a concoction served in a well-known comic strip. The Canadians, for their part, distilled a wicked drink called "Steam," and an Iroquois sergeant among them was widely known as "C.P.R." (Canadian Pacific Railway) because he always "had steam up." Out in the Pacific, Marines and sailors improvised every imaginable means of producing a potion with a kick in it. One technique was to filter hair tonic through bread and then mix it with grape juice. Like virtually every other drink devised in the Pacific, it was known as "Jungle Juice."

In England and, after their liberation started, in Italy and France, the juxtaposition of GIs and old, hitherto stable societies produced jealousies and conflict, heightened by emotional strains and contrasting economic levels. Quarrels over women erupted as normal peacetime sexual morality lapsed into confusion, and as different army pay scales gave the Americans an advantage in entertaining that they were quick to use. One sour complaint among Britons was: "The trouble with you Yanks is that you're over-paid, over-sexed and over here." The GIs quipped back: "You're sore because you're under-paid, under-sexed and under Eisenhower."

Still, it is doubtful whether any army of such numbers or such power ever behaved better or, for that matter, was so well received, even among conquered enemies. The GI came and went, in Europe and the Pacific. He took home new notions about the earth, about people who were not American, not rich, not powerful, who represented a different race or faith. He left behind some of his own ideas and a great many dead comrades. He also left behind a curious marking that was chalked on rocks, on city walls, on lavatories: "Kilroy was here." No one ever found out for sure who Kilroy was, where he came from, or why anyone would care enough about him to scrawl his name across half the globe. But that Kilroy was there was absolutely certain; and if he had not made the world safe for democracy, he had at least helped to rid it of inhuman despotism.

XIII
The Air War

The waiting hours: The American crew
assigned to the 96th Bomb Group watch for
the return of bombers. Their crash truck is
loaded with fire-extinguishing foam.

L ike nearly every part of the Nazi war machine, Adolf Hitler's much publicized *Luftwaffe* was built for a short conflict, a blitzkrieg. The *Führer* was confident of quick triumph. Not until 1942 did he make any plans to modernize his aircraft; and by then it was too late. In 1940, an official directive of the Berlin Air Ministry ordered the postponement of work on all planes that would not be operational within two years. The directive explained: "Such types will not be wanted after the war."

From 1939 to 1941, the *Luftwaffe* controlled the skies on each front. But in 1942 things began to change. Germany found itself engaged in a four-front aerial war: over England, over North Africa, over the Soviet Union, and over the Reich itself. In 1939, Göring had pompously boasted: "If bombs drop on Germany, my name is Meyer." By 1942, sardonic Germans were calling him "Herr Meyer" night after night.

As the British and, later, the Americans intruded ever more deeply and persistently—even to Berlin—Göring moved his fighter squadrons into occupied nations facing Britain and established a primitive early warning system. When the Allied bombers headed east for German targets, they were hit first by these "outer" squadrons and then met by successive fighter wings.

But the *Luftwaffe* was extensively overcommitted by 1942, and the size and scope of Allied raids, smashing railway yards, factories, and cities from Cologne to Berlin, brought the war bitterly home to the German nation, making a mockery of all the Nazi regime's grandiose promises of security. There were public calls for retaliatory strikes on Britain, just as the British had demanded similar strikes on Germany during their arduous year 1940–41, but the *Luftwaffe* no longer had enough planes and pilots to satisfy any such craving for revenge. In October, 1942, Göring was forced to confess in a speech broadcast from Munich: "There are those who ask why we do not go in for reprisals. The answer is simple: it is because most of our bombers are needed more urgently in Stalingrad and in the Caucasus. . . . The winner in this war will be the side which knows how to concentrate its strength at the critical point in the battle. Our cities in the West and the Northwest have to stand up to hard blows, but I have come away from my many visits to them with the firm conviction that their morale is equal to the trial."

An initial hint of what lay in store for Germany occurred on the night of August 24, 1940, when a small number of R.A.F. planes for the first time fought their way to Berlin. The damage caused was negligible; but the wail of sirens, the groping fingers of searchlights, and the grunt of antiaircraft guns made the heady Germans think. By November 13, 1940, the British had mastered the art of piercing the distant German capital's defenses. On that night, Molotov had been bargaining with Ribbentrop for spheres of influence in a conquered world. The two ministers and their staffs were forced to take shelter, but Ribbentrop assured his guest that Britain was finished. Molotov shrewdly inquired: "If that is so, why are we in this shelter, and whose are these bombs which fall?" Those were the last significant Nazi-Soviet talks. They failed, and the world, as it turned out, was not to be conquered. Churchill remarked with relish: "We had heard about the conference beforehand and, though not invited to join in the discussion, did not wish to be entirely left out of the proceedings."

The R.A.F.'s harassing raids increased in 1941 as the *Luftwaffe* was drawn into Russia, and by 1942, enough British planes and pilots had been prepared for broad-scale strategic bombing. On May 30, 1942, came the first of the war's vast saturation raids: a thousand English planes attacked Cologne and left the Rhineland city blazing.

Soon afterward came a succession of hammer blows that devastated Berlin, Hamburg, Dortmund, Leipzig, Essen. The R.A.F.'s Sir Arthur Harris reported that his planes were destroying two and a half German cities a month and warned the Germans that they had but two alternatives, annihilation or surrender. The nation suffered thousands upon thousands of killed and wounded, but German morale and Nazi discipline held firm.

But the British did not limit themselves to city-smashing. They struck power plants, radar stations, railroads. In one sensational raid, carefully prepared and using specially tested projectiles, the R.A.F., on May 16, 1943, blew up the Möhne dam, on which four million Germans and the Ruhr industrial complex depended for water and energy. This daring operation was led by Wing Commander Guy Penrose Gibson, who received the Victoria Cross, and who was shot down and killed in a later action. As

Gibson flew his Lancaster up and down the dam, he saw the water of the dammed lake rising "like stirred porridge in the moonlight, rushing through a great breach." A few minutes later, he reported: "The valley was beginning to be filled with fog and . . . we saw cars speeding along the roads in front of this great wave of water chasing them. . . . I saw their headlights burning and I saw water overtake them, wave by wave, and then the color of headlights underneath the water changing from light blue to green, from green to dark purple until there was no longer anything except the water bouncing down."

The Germans had to stand up to an Allied strategy in which the British bombed by night and the Americans by day. This pattern was the result of a compromise to an argument between the Royal Air Force and the U.S. Army Air Forces.

The original argument was propounded by two resolute advocates of air power, the R.A.F.'s Sir Arthur ("Bomber") Harris, and Carl ("Tooey") Spaatz, who led the American bomber force based in Britain. Harris believed that if German cities were pulverized, German morale would crack. Furthermore, he argued, it would be foolish to accomplish the job by day bombing, which cost too heavily in planes and trained crews. Spaatz, on the other hand, refused to limit himself to the night-bombing methods of Harris or to broad metropolitan targets. He claimed it was unrealistic to assume that the Germans would knuckle under once their cities were smashed, just as it had been unrealistic for the Germans to assume that Britain would quit when it was being hammered by the *Luftwaffe*. He insisted on pinpoint bombing in long-ranging day raids that would knock out vital industrial and transportation centers.

When the United States entered World War II, determined to concentrate on destroying Germany before Japan, the initial burden fell upon the U.S. Army Air Corps. Its first effective unit in Europe was the Eighth Air Force, organized on January 28, 1942, and in May placed under the command of Spaatz, who established a series of bases in Britain with headquarters at Bushy Park, near London.

From the start, the Americans were given wholehearted cooperation by the battle-tested R.A.F., but there was no letup to the British argument against daytime raids on Germany. But Spaatz

The ground crew of the B-24 Liberator
Shoot Luke carefully check over their
plane following its safe return from
its twenty-seventh mission. The U.S. Army
Air Corps entered the war committed
to a strategy of high-altitude daylight
precision bombing. In contrast, Britain's
nighttime saturation bombing proved to be
indiscriminate; the darkness that provided
precious cover also obscured the target.

was eager to use his planes, particularly the B-17, for the pin-point work they had been built for.

Nowadays the B-17 "Flying Fortress" seems almost as diminutive and archaic—in comparison with the swept-wing, swing-wing, and delta-wing bombers that have survived into the missile age—as the strut-and-piano-wire biplanes of World War I. Yet it was a remarkable weapon for its time, built to fly high and fast, its hydraulic turrets fitted with pairs of .50-caliber Browning machine guns that swung simultaneously against attacking planes, permitting the tight echelons of bombers to spit out a storm of concentrated fire. Furthermore, the B-17 was equipped with the precise Norden bombsight, which, its admirers claimed, could "drop a bomb in a pickle barrel." Spaatz proved that, by formation flying and with added protection from long-range fighters, his planes could force their way through to chosen targets. On September 8, 1942, the Washington and London high commands agreed to go ahead with American day bombing, coordinated with Britain's night raids. Still, as late as the Casablanca conference in early 1943, Churchill expressed his conviction that the results of day assaults were too meager to justify their cost.

But Churchill finally agreed to try United States strategy. As a consequence, the Allies worked out a program of "around the clock bombing." Germany was pounded night and day. When the sun went down over Hitler's *Festung Europa*, Royal Air Force Stirlings and Lancasters rumbled through the Rhineland mists and on to Saxony and Brandenburg. And when, through the swirling smoke, the sun arose in the east again, American Liberators and Flying Fortresses came roaring down the aerial avenues. A complicated timetable was devised to avoid congestion of the narrow air space above the British Isles. But despite the tremendous accomplishments of strategic bombing, its effectiveness versus the cost has continued to be a matter of debate among military experts.

By 1943, the Eighth Air Force could concentrate on weakening the *Luftwaffe* and gradually softening up German defenses for the ultimate land invasion. That August 17 —one year after twelve United States planes first struck Germany—three hundred and seventy-six Eighth Air Force bombers hammered Regensburg and Schweinfurt, where Nazi fighters and the ball bearings for their engines were manufactured. Casualties were very heavy, and sixty of the planes on the missions did not come back. After the war Adolf Galland, the famous *Luftwaffe* flying ace, wrote that the first raid on Schweinfurt came as a real shock to the German high command. "If the German ball-bearing industry, their Achilles' heel, were to be destroyed or paralyzed, then the armament production of the whole Reich would suffer heavily. Speer [Albert Speer, who ran Hitler's armament program], in a postwar report, pointed out that with a continuation of the raids the German armament industry would have been essentially weakened within two months, and in four months would have come to a complete standstill. But luckily the first raid on Schweinfurt and Messerschmitt-Regensburg proved a disaster for the enemy. . . ."

Initially it seemed that the offensive could not be maintained. As it turned out, within four months, a fuel container known as the drop-tank became available to extend the range of American fighters. Thereafter, U.S. Thunderbolts and Mustangs could travel half again as far beside the lumbering B-17's and B-24's. The speedy Mustang, World War II's longest-range fighter, became known to bomber crews as "little friend."

The British likewise improved the deadliness of their nocturnal armadas. They developed the Beaufighter, which could accompany night bombers for six hours without refueling, and whose sophisticated radar equipment spotted Nazi planes in the foggy dark. Thereafter, without cease, the two air forces roared over Germany. During the "Big Week," February 19–25, 1944, the R.A.F. put twenty-three hundred bombers over Germany at night, and the American Air Force, thirty-eight hundred during daytime. Desperately seeking to fend off this particular series of assaults, the *Luftwaffe* lost four hundred and fifty planes—a rate it could not long sustain. By that same summer, Göring's air fleet had been crippled. Eisenhower was able to reassure his D-Day troops in early June, "If you see fighting aircraft over you, they will be ours."

Typical of the combined Anglo-American air strategies were the attacks on Hamburg, Germany's principal seaport, which housed some the the Reich's biggest oil refineries, and on Ploesti, the Rumanian oil-producing center on which Hitler drew heavily for fuel. Hamburg was easily identifiable to bombers coming in across the North Sea's open water or groping up the Elbe.

During daylight hours, American bombers battered its refineries and U-boat pens; at night its docks, refineries, and dwellings were savagely hammered by British heavy bombers flying in close formation and employing for the first time a very simple but highly effective method of fouling the enemy's radar. The planes dumped huge batches of tinfoil of the right length and width to float slowly down over the target as a shield against radar waves. German fighter defenses and flak directed by radar were thus knocked totally out of whack. The R.A.F. alone, in four raids between July 24 and August 3, 1943, killed an estimated forty-three thousand people in the grand old Hanseatic city. This terrible event became known to Germans as *"Die Katastrophe."* Countless lives were snuffed out by lack of oxygen in the fire storm produced in Hamburg. After *Die Katastrophe*, one Hamburg woman watched rescue workers stack corpses in trucks, then shivered and said: "If there were a God He would have shown some mercy to them." An elderly man replied: "Leave God out of this. Men make war, not God."

The decision to risk heavy losses by bombing Ploesti was made at the Trident Conference in Washington, May, 1943, and the attack was launched that August 1 by a force of one hundred and seventy-eight American B-24 bombers taking off from Libya. A small raid had already been staged by thirteen Liberators (B-24's) on June 11, 1942, but it did little damage. Indeed, it had the adverse effect of encouraging the Nazis to strengthen Rumania's antiaircraft defenses.

The 1943 raiders took off from Benghazi for a fifteen-hundred-mile flight across the Mediterranean and the German-occupied Balkans and met successive fighter attacks long before they approached their target. Nevertheless, they fought their way through, and soon the refineries and oil tanks were covered with brilliant orange flame and billowing black smoke. The damaged wreaked was substantial, but losses were severe. Four hundred and forty-six of the 1,733 men on the mission were killed, and only 33 of the original 178 planes came through it to fly again. Many planes were shot down over Rumania (where 108 men were imprisoned) and Bulgaria, while others gradually collapsed into the Aegean as they struggled to make their way back toward Africa. Still others found haven in neutral Turkey, where the crews were well received and interned in comfort.

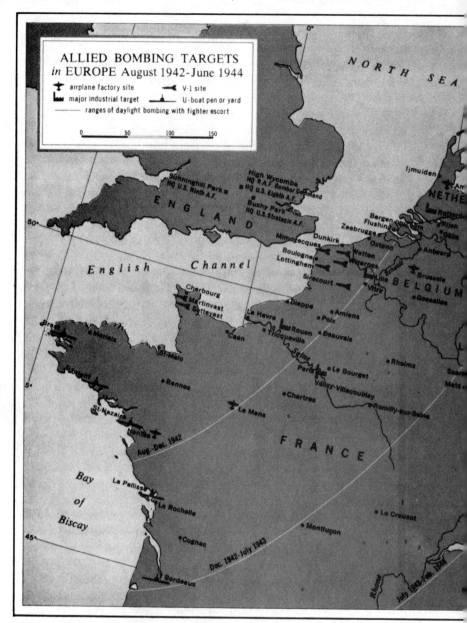

ALLIED BOMBING TARGETS
in EUROPE August 1942-June 1944

airplane factory site · V-1 site
major industrial target · U-boat pen or yard
ranges of daylight bombing with fighter escort

0   50   100   150

NORTH SEA

Ijmuiden

NETHE

ENGLAND

Sunninghill Park
HQ U.S. Ninth A.F.

High Wycombe
HQ R.A.F. Bomber Command
HQ U.S. Eighth A.F.

Bushy Park
HQ U.S. Strategic A.F.

50°

English   Channel

Mimoyecques
Dunkirk

Bergen
Flushing
Zeebrugge
Oostend

Boulogne
Lottingham

Watten
Wizernes

Antwerp

Lille

BELGIUM

Brussels

Siracourt

Gosselies

Cherbourg
Martinvast
Sotteyast

Dieppe

Vitry

Le Havre
Caen

Amiens

Poix

Brest

Morlaix

Ticqueville

Rouen

Beauvais

Rheims

St-Malo

Lorient

Perros

Le Bourget

5°

Rennes

Velizy-Villacoublay

Romilly-sur-Seine

Metz

Chartres

St-Nazaire

Le Mans

FRANCE

Nantes

Aug.-Dec. 1942

Bay

of

Biscay

La Pallisse

Le Rochelle

Le Creusot

Montluçon

45°

Cognac

Dec. 1942-July 1943

Bordeaux

The Allied strategists stressed the need
for a massive, sustained air offensive
to cripple the German war machine.

Although Hitler's defeats in Russia and the Mediterranean meant that the perimeter of air space that he had to defend was contracted, he was able to muster fewer and fewer fighters. And although the largely obsolescent Soviet Air Force of some twelve thousand combat planes had been eviscerated by the Nazis in 1941, new designs were created. Modern types began to emerge from Siberian factories: the highly maneuverable MIG and all-weather YAK fighters; the clumsy but invincible Stormovik. Little by little, a resurgent Soviet Air Force took its toll of the *Luftwaffe*, and "General Winter," Russia's oldest and most vicious ally, froze it into immobility. During the cold months of 1942–43, *Luftwaffe* operations on the Soviet front were cut to 25 per cent. By 1943, furthermore, the Russians began to receive substantial reinforcements of American P-39's, P-40's, A-20's, and B-25's, and British Hurricanes.

After V-E Day, *Luftwaffe* officers agreed with one of their number: "There is no doubt that the Americans harmed us most. The Russians were negligible as far as the home front was concerned, and we could have stood the British attacks on our cities. But the American devastation of our airfields, factories and oil depots made it impossible for us to keep going."

What really brought the *Luftwaffe* down was the application of a successful Allied strategy. Like determined dogs hounding a dying stag, American, British, and Russian fighters slashed away at their victim while American and British bombers prevented him from regaining sustenance. Had the Germans been able to shake free and concentrate on one single front for sufficient time, they might have achieved a major aerial victory. But the combination of losses to the west, south, and east and the destruction of replacement centers gradually whittled the mighty *Luftwaffe*. By the war's last year, it was almost helpless to defend Germany. In one American and two British raids on Dresden, February 13–14, 1945, one hundred and thirty-five thousand people lost their lives.

German scientists sought to recapture the upper hand by ingenuity. They developed and actually produced impressive numbers of the Messerschmitt 262 jet, which could easily kill normal propeller-driven fighters, thanks to its astounding speed—540 miles per hour. But production was hampered by Hitler's insistence on giving priority to the manufacture of bombers and the *Vergeltungswaffen*, or revenge weapons—the V-1 and V-2, with which he wanted above all to punish Britain's civilian population.

The *Führer* became obsessed with this idea. When *Luftwaffe* generals and Göring explained the immense value of the ME-262 in staving off Allied attacks, Hitler became furious. "I want bombers, bombers, bombers," he shouted. "Your fighters are no damned good!" He refused for almost half a year even to look at a test flight; then he promptly commanded that the new jet be converted into a bomber, for which it had neither the range nor the load capacity.

His view of the V-1 and V-2 was equally illogical. At first he remained convinced that the war could be won without bothering to give priority to experimental weapons. When the first doubts of victory finally began to bother him, he ordered sudden mass production of the V-2. Walter Dornberger, a scientist involved in the project, complained that he himself had not envisioned the rocket as an annihilation weapon. Hitler replied: "No, I realize that *you* didn't think of it! But I did."

Both V-1 and V-2 originated at the experimental center of Peenemünde, on the Baltic. The V-1, dubbed "Buzz Bomb" by the British, was a pilotless plane loaded with explosives, of which more than eight thousand were aimed at London in Hitler's frenzy for vengeance. However, many went astray (one even hit Hitler's bunker) or were shot down, and only 2,420 reached their target. These did extensive but far from crippling damage.

The V-2 was more frightening, a rocket forerunner of the long-range ballistic missile. It carried a tank of liquid oxygen that allowed it to fly above the earth's atmosphere, and it was aimed from fixed positions, like long-range artillery. Fortunately, Hitler, by according priority of materials and labor to conventional arms, deferred assembly-line production of this terrible instrument until it was too late for it to have a material effect on the war's outcome. By then, Allied reconnaissance and espionage had learned of the Peenemünde experiments and located many rocket sites under construction. As a result, bomber raids concentrated on these targets in 1943 and 1944, killing many leading scientists and reducing the power of the V-weapons counteroffensive. Only about eleven hundred V-2's were successfully exploded in England. They destroyed hundreds of buildings, caused thousands of casualties, but did not materially alter the war's course.

Preparations for American involvement in the Asian air war

were going on before the United States actually became a belligerent. A retired Air Corps officer named Claire L. Chennault had formed a flying Foreign Legion for Chiang Kai-shek in his struggle against Japan. This formation was soon destroyed, but with Washington's permission, Chennault recruited new American volunteers from an organization with the cover name of Central Aircraft Manufacturing Company (CAMCO). Washington loaned Chiang the money to buy one hundred Curtiss P-40 Tomahawks and to hire pilots.

This force, called the American Volunteer Group (AVG), was shipped in small batches to Burma, under assumed identities, and began training in September, 1941. The pilots had scarcely completed their course when Pearl Harbor came, and they went into action as the Flying Tigers, so called for their winged tiger insignia devised by the Walt Disney Studios. These Flying Tigers became romantic heroes, and they were an important morale factor back home. It was somehow comforting to know in December, 1941, that a group of American fliers were shooting down Zeros. The AVG subsequently became the Fourteenth U.S. Air Force. It was the the first Pacific air formation to employ rockets, and it also introduced an internationally integrated unit, the Chinese-American Combat Wing.

The air war in Asia was from the start a paramount factor both over sea and over land. Its importance can be summed up simply by two terminal events—Pearl Harbor and Hiroshima-Nagasaki. They signify the enormous change that occurred so rapidly in control of the skies.

When the Pacific conflict started in 1941, Japan held a perceptible lead in numbers of planes and crews who were veterans of the China campaign. The Japanese Army and Navy together had some three thousand operational aircraft and twice that number of pilots with at least five hundred hours flying experience. (These original pilots were far more skilled than the Americans had imagined; but the quality of their replacements declined.) Japan was already producing four hundred and twenty-five planes and two hundred and twenty-five pilots each month. The United States possessed fewer than nine hundred planes in the Pacific area. A heavy proportion of these were destroyed in Honolulu and the Philippines during Japan's initial surprise attacks. Furthermore, although the early American fighters were sturdier

A B-24 above Italy, wing torn by flak and
on fire, begins its plunge to the earth.
Flying a B-24 or B-17 was hard work for all
aboard, and there was always the dread
certainty that many would not be coming back.
Fliers died in many ways, sometimes in
an instant as bomb loads were hit, sometimes
with their planes in flames or spiraling down
with a wing or tail blown off.

and more heavily armored, none of them could rival the maneuverability of the famous Japanese Zero.

Nevertheless, as the immense United States production facilities began turning out vaster numbers and ever better plane types, the balance began immutably to shift. Japanese aircraft strength attained an approximate top level of four thousand, but by the end of 1944, the United States had about ten thousand war planes plus eight thousand transports at its disposal in the Pacific. These included the fastest propeller fighter ever built, the Mustang, and, in the end, the B-29 Superfortress, which carried out the A-bomb raids. From a steadily constricting circle of land bases on the Pacific Islands, from China, from India, and eventually from Burma, the U.S. Army Air Corps moved in ever more menacingly, while Admiral Nimitz's immense carrier task forces sailed closer and closer to Tokyo itself.

The B-29 was the ultimate air weapon of World War II, even more important than Germany's V-2 because the latter, although it served as forerunner for ballistic missiles, came too late and did too little damage. The B-29 developed from General "Hap" Arnold's insistence on a superbomber that could fly farther and with a bigger load than any other aircraft. It was blueprinted in 1940, before the United States was in the war. By the time it was in production, it had become a sixty-ton machine, capable when loaded of flying sixteen hours without stop. The first of these monsters was sent to India in April, 1944, and enormous airfields were built for them both in eastern India and western China. The first actual Superfortress raid was on June 5, 1944, from India to the railroad marshaling yards of Bangkok. Ten days later, another raid took off from the Chinese base network against Yawata, the Japanese steel center on Kyushu Island. But it was only after Major General Curtis E. LeMay, only thirty-eight years old, took over the XX Bomber Command and began to use it for close-formation daylight raids, a tactic he had mastered while serving with the Eighth Air Force in England, that the B-29's began to do their most terrible and insistent damage.

The monster planes were shifted from the China-Burma-India theater to the XXI Bomber Command in Saipan, Tinian, and Guam as soon as aviation engineers, hard on the heels of the conquering Marines, had managed to carve sufficiently large air dromes out of the jungles and atolls of the Marianas. At last, by November 24, they began their final campaign in earnest with a raid on the aircraft plants outside Tokyo. From then on, relentlessly, they were employed with increasing force against plane factories and harbors of Japan's home islands, hammering the main cities one by one.

In 1945, tons of explosives made of jellied gasoline and magnesium began to whistle down on Tokyo, Kobe, Nagoya. Indeed, on August 2, just four days before Hiroshima disappeared beneath the first insidious mushroom cloud, eight hundred and fifty-five Superfortresses wiped out six Japanese cities in one single massive operation. It was thus entirely plain before the first nuclear bomb was dropped that the so-called conventional plane using the so-called conventional explosive was, all by itself, a weapon of staggering destructive capacity. The bomber, so long considered the ultimate in strategic might, had reached its moment of total and awful triumph.

XIV
The Home Fronts

A Norman Rockwell poster shows the end
toward which all of America was striving.

Adolf Hitler's early successes on the battlefields of Europe and Russia brought with them a wave of support in Germany, even from those who hitherto had been reluctant to accept his brutal Nazi system. And as Hitler set about remaking Europe for Germany's benefit, life on the German home front seemed to be picking up, to the benefit of all. In fact, at first, with the help of loot from conquered areas, redirected Continental factory and farm output, the planning of an efficient and highly centralized Berlin Government, and the use of enslaved laborers from subject territories, the *Führer's* Third Reich flourished, and no one seemed displeased about that. Moreover, inherent German patriotism, martial spirit, and a habit of obedience were gradually shaped by *Gestapo* rigor and diabolically effective propaganda into a national instrument that brooked no opposition to the regime or whatever it was up to, including its most heinous offenses of human decency: extirpation of Jews, enserfment of foreign civilians, mockery of a free press, and a growing intolerance of religion. Although a very small German underground existed inside the Reich and was in touch with such distinguished *émigrés* as Ernst Reuter, future mayor of West Berlin, and although this underground included certain brave and renowned individuals, such as Carl Goerdeler, ex-mayor of Leipzig, and Pastor Dietrich Bonhoeffer, it was ineffectual. The terror mounted. Indeed, in 1944, one out of every twelve hundred German adults was arrested for political "offenses"—the latter being equivalent to the former.

D'Olier's *U.S. Strategic Bombing Survey* carefully analyzed this dictatorial system. It pointed out: "This elaborate machinery of control and compulsion was surrounded by a fringe of terror, symbolized by Gestapo, Elite Guards and the concentration camp. Although only very few actually knew much about the conditions in concentration camps, rumors and half-knowledge provided a powerful deterrent. . . . A stark fear of the unknown or partly known, increased by the observable severity of official punishment meted out to political offenders, enhanced and perhaps even exaggerated the demonstrable power of the control groups, and tended to cover up real gaps in their control. . . . The propaganda machine managed to persuade the man in the street for a long time that, for better of for worse, he was 'in for it,' because the world was bent on destroying Germany and the Germans. . . . Once the war was well under way, the Germans who enjoyed any advantage of position or economic status had a vested interest in German victory."

The German people accustomed themselves, without seeming aware of the fact, to living in a spiritual hell long before Allied power turned it into a physical hell. The appalling deeds of their masters at home and their soldiers abroad escaped the majority or were viewed with a deliberately blind eye. If the Germans ate less well, if they dressed in ersatz materials, if they relinquished the last vestiges of freedom, they were fed, clothed, and excited by dreams of triumph and a thousand-year Reich.

As a consequence of both their courage and their ignorance, the morale of the Germans withstood the ardors of Allied air raids, even though, as these increased, disillusion and doubt were privately nourished. Slowly a condiment of bitter humor was added to the diet of destruction. By the time Berlin was becoming a shambles, its citizens were caustically reminding each other of the *Führer*'s architectural forecast: "Give me four years and I promise you you won't recognize your towns." Outside one leveled warehouse, a sign was prominently posted: "Open day and night now."

In his desperate effort to regain the initiative after the tide began to turn, Hitler filled Germany with forced labor to replace drafted workers. By early autumn, 1944, some seven and a half million foreigners had been rounded up in occupied Europe and shipped to the Reich in boxcars, to a brutal half-life of endless toil, semistarvation, illness, and in the end, often death. To these were added about two million prisoners of war, many of whom, in violation of the Hague and Geneva conventions, were made to work in ordnance plants.

One military memorandum, dated June 12, 1944, brusquely ordered: "Army Group Center intends to apprehend forty to fifty thousand youths from the age of ten to fourteen . . . and transport them to the Reich. . . . It is intended to allot these juveniles primarily to the German trades as apprentices. . . . This action is not only aimed at preventing a direct reinforcement of the enemy's strength but also as a reduction of his biological potentialities."

It was not until after the war, during the war criminal trials, that the full horror was exposed. A doctor assigned to inspect foreign laborers in a Krupp factory reported at Nuremberg: "Upon my first visit I found these females suffering from open festering wounds and other diseases. . . . They had no shoes and went about in bare feet. . . . Their hair was shorn. The camp was surrounded by barbed wire and closely guarded by S.S. guards."

There was deliberate official encouragement to maltreat war prisoners—above all the unfortunate Russians, of whom more than two million died after capture. But Nazi bosses did not want the German people to become too exercised by public brutality. Heinrich Mueller, then *Gestapo* chief, warned his subordinates: "It was particularly noted that when marching, for example, from the railroad station to the camp, a rather large number of prisoners collapsed on the way from exhaustion, either dead or half dead, and had to be picked up by a truck that followed the convoy. It cannot be prevented that the German people take notice of these occurrences."

The captive hordes, both military and civilian, sought desperately and frequently to escape. But this was especially difficult because of close police supervision, added to constant exhaustion from sickness and hunger. Western prisoners were far better treated than those from Slavic nations. Through the Red Cross they had more care and closer contact with home. Not only did they organize effective means of spreading true war news, but there were many famous escapes. The Germans took ruthlessly repressive measures. Fifty British fliers caught in 1944 after fleeing their camp at Sagan were murdered at Hitler's personal order. The *Führer* commanded: "All enemies on so-called commando missions in Europe or Africa challenged by German troops, even if they are in uniform, whether armed or unarmed, in battle or in flight, are to be slaughtered to the last man." General Jodl prudently added these underlined words: *"This order is intended for commanders only and must not under any circumstances fall into enemy hands."*

Despite this horror, the moral rot, the suffering and the constant bombing, the Reich's formidable war machine rolled on. During the first four years of war, ammunition production multiplied 2.6 times, artillery 4.8 times, armor 8.7 times and aircraft 2.7 times. Albert Speer, youthful Nazi Minister of Arms and Munitions, saw to it that whatever happened in the totalitarian state, ordnance production increased. D'Olier's *Survey* found that despite intensification of Allied bombing and huge *Wehrmacht* losses, "the German army [as distinct from the *Luftwaffe*] was better equipped with weapons at the beginning of 1944 than at the start of the Russian War." The only serious shortage was in steel, although the *Luftwaffe* also was hampered by inadequate aircraft types, a result of Hitler's original conviction that the conflict would not be a long one.

The Germans were politically and intellectually benumbed by the time the war ended. Interrogated prisoners later conceded their folly. Elite Guard General Petrie said: "Propaganda was everything. We had to depend on it, and we took it as fact when we saw it printed." Franz Hofer, regional Nazi leader in Austria's Tyrol, acknowledged: "We believed in what the propaganda told us. It worked on us rather than on you." And Lieutenant General Huebner admitted: "We believed they [the Propaganda Ministry] must have known something, else they wouldn't have made such statements."

When Japan entered the war, its masses, also reared in a heritage that emphasized their superior qualities, were likewise easily subject to propaganda. After their first startling successes, there seemed to be little anxiety about the nation's future. The first shocking awareness of potential trouble came on April 18, 1942, when Doolittle's bombers suddenly pecked at Tokyo. One capital resident later said: "We finally began to realize that all we were told was not true—that the Government had lied when it said we were invulnerable. We then started to doubt that we were also invincible."

After Midway, after Guadalcanal, after successive German setbacks in the West, these doubts grew, but it was only on June 15, 1944, when sixty-eight Superfortresses struck Kyushu, that the Japanese people saw what lay in store. Tokyo was forced to tell them that "since the outbreak of the East Asian War everyone has recognized the difficulty of avoiding air attacks." The press began to talk of "a front behind the lines" and to exhort each civilian to remember he was "a warrior defending his country." Tokyo radio often broadcast an inane chant:

Why should we be afraid of air raids?
The big sky is protected with iron defenses.
For young and old it is time to stand up;
We are loaded with the honor of defending the homeland.
Come on, enemy planes! Come on many times!

Forced by Nazi soldiers to leave their
homes, this terrified little boy and some
of the families of this Polish town obey
with their hands raised over their heads.
Sometimes whole neighborhoods were lined up
against a wall and shot. More often, Jews
were rounded up and shipped in boxcars to
a death by disease, starvation, torture,
machine gun, or gas chamber.

And the planes came, more of them and more often. Air raid drills were frequent, even at night. Women were made to practice running uphill, bearing buckets of water; sandbags and pails were placed outside homes; enormous instruments resembling fly swatters were distributed to beat out flames.

By 1943 life was distinctly more austere. The rice reserve disappeared. Food became perilously scarce; the hungry were everywhere. Rations of electricity and gas became more strict. Women were asked to do without their colorful kimonos, and civilian consumption of cloth fell 95 per cent. Black market profiteering spread. Foreign Minister Shigemitsu wrote in his memoirs "To live at all, the people reverted to a primitive existence. . . . They had never quite understood what the war was all about. To them the war was not theirs but a military war. . . . discipline suffered, while public resentment against the Army and Navy grew apace. As these social disturbances grew, the gendarmerie and police went ruthlessly about their task of enforcing the powers of the Army in order to whip the people on to further exertions."

Until 1944, Tojo's officer-dominated dictatorship remained politically secure. Backed by the powerful Imperial Rule Assistance Association, it had gained 80 per cent of the seats in the Diet early in the war and later had persuaded Japan's skeptical industrial barons, the *zaibatsu*, that the glorious economic program for subduing East Asia was bound to succeed. The Japanese stock market continued to boom. But Tojo made the same mistake as Hitler, failing to expand war production at a time when he had opportunity to do so. By 1944, when Japanese industry had achieved maximum efficiency, Allied successes were amputating Japan's access to raw materials. The air offensive against the home islands had cut output by 60 per cent before the war ended.

In its initially successful attempt to achieve economic self-sufficiency, Japan had sought to stress its "liberating" role and to loosen East Asia from the grip of the colonial Westerner, who was depicted as a racial enemy in much the same sense as the Nazis depicted the Slavs. Tokyo's propaganda stressed American immigration restrictions and anti-Negro prejudice, British arrogance in India and Malaya, Dutch brutality in Indonesia. One result of this was to encourage cruelty to white war prisoners.

The Japanese military code disapproved of the practice of surrender, and Tokyo had never signed the Geneva convention. Thus it did not feel bound to Western conventions of humane warfare. Massacre, hunger, torture, and sheer callousness often marked treatment of Allied captives.

Japan's racist tenets at first succeeded in attracting the support of anti-imperialist Asians. They gained initial lip service from nationalist leaders such as Indonesia's Sukarno and Hatta, India's Subhas Chandra Bose, the Burmese revolutionists, and the bewildered followers of Premier Chang Ching-hui in Manchukuo (Chinese Manchuria) and Wang Ching-wei, puppet prime minister of occupied China. But this racist appeal dwindled together with the legend of Tokyo's invincibility. Japanese brutality, tactlessness, and indifference and a determination to "Nipponize" conquered areas soon antagonized the new revolutionary movements. They began to react against Tokyo's secret police, the *Kempeitai,* quite as strongly they had opposed their previous white masters; only now, thanks to war, they had arms with which to express political opinions. When Japan, isolated and smashed, went down amid a sea of enemies, included among them were millions of Asian peoples who, for a short period of time, had been subjects of the Greater East Asia Co-Prosperity Sphere.

On the Allied side, morale in Russia was at first severely shaken during the war's early months, although it remained constantly high in Britain and never faltered in the United States. The war in the Soviet Union came after Stalin had spent seven years repressing his subjects, murdering thousands, sending millions to prison camps, and spreading fear through a muted nation.

However, any initial hopes there may have been for a better life under the Nazis were short-lived, and Stalin focused his propaganda on national rather than ideological themes. The monolithic Soviet state harnessed everyone to the war effort. Women were mobilized to run tractors on collective farms. Those not fit for military service, the wounded, and the very old were conscripted into the labor force and were called upon to fight in emergencies like the battles for Leningrad and Moscow.

Most Soviet citizens, even those who bitterly resented Stalin, dug in with grim determination, living on the edge of starvation, often cut off from news of soldier relatives. In blacked-out Moscow during December, 1941, I was once arrested for "smoking ostentatiously" in the darkened, snow-filled streets. When a woman approached me, begging for food, I gave her the ruble equivalent of two dollars. She spat and said: "What can I do with that? Give me bread." During the 1941–42 winter, the foreign press was billeted in Moscow's Metropole Hotel and given privileged meals. Among items regularly served was a fruit dish so filled with worms that we dubbed it "motorized compote." At official Government banquets for visiting statesmen, the sallow waiters customarily stole scraps. We used to save bread and sugar for our secretaries; nevertheless, mine, originally a hefty woman, lost forty pounds during the war's first two years.

The Soviet home front was resolute, bitter, and marked by a wild hatred of the Germans that exceeded anything in Britain or America. I visited a hospital most of whose patients were members of tank crews who had suffered terrible face wounds and were being restored by plastic surgery. Except for those completely blinded, all of these men, some without jaws, some without noses, some without ears, expressed but one aspiration: to get back to the front and kill more Nazis. And as the Red Army regathered and surged forward on the attack, a new aura of confidence started to spread through the ravaged, suffering nation. At night, batteries around the Kremlin began to boom salutes to victories, and the country's war songs assumed a note of savage joy.

The British, an inherently less emotional people than the Russians, showed a comparably less frantic reaction both in adversity and success. Under Churchill's incandescent leadership, they managed to meet the challenge of 1940 alone and virtually unarmed, yet with a striking national calm. They simply refused, for the most part, even to contemplate the thought that they might lose the Battle of Britain, even though, for quite some time, logic argued against victory.

Britain adopted a system of tightly rationing food, shoes, and household goods. Gasoline and textiles were rigidly restricted, newspapers and magazines thin. The B.B.C. assumed an immense new importance as the essential organ for both informing and entertaining the English people and their restless allies in occupied Europe.

The British survived two aerial ordeals—the Blitz and the V-1, V-2 terror—with courage and endurance. Good naturedly they went into shelters or helped local police forces as air raid wardens and fire-fighting patrols. Somehow they managed to get to work despite scrambled transportation systems. Beside the ruins of their dwellings, they cheered Churchill as he visited his home front, cigar between clenched teeth, giving his victory signal.

As early as 1940, life had become appallingly thin and threadbare, and it was to remain so until long after the war ended. Shipping on which the island lived was almost wholly devoted to essential cargoes, and the treasury was bare. Housing was strained as buildings in cities were destroyed by bombing, families were evacuated to the country to be billeted with others, and the United Kingdom filled with troops mustered by the Americans, Canadians, Poles, and Free French for the final invasion.

Women played a far greater role than ever before, taking jobs as chauffeurs, laborers, ferry pilots, wardens, and farmers, and asserting a new and energetic independence of their own. Most important, the old social structures and traditions of personal diffidence were broken down as rich and poor rubbed shoulders in air raid shelters. The atmosphere of the English pub, with all its cozy intimacy, managed somehow to grip the nation in its time of most arduous difficulty. "Roll Out the Barrel" and "Kiss Me Goodnight Sergeant Major" were sung in dire moments with as much fervor as "God Save the King" when theater curtains rolled down early to allow the audience time to get home before the *Luftwaffe* arrived.

Unlike its Allies and its enemies, the United States lived a comparatively paradisiacal existence during World War II, the sole important island of unabated security in a total conflict. As such, its function was not only to furnish vigorous new manpower but to serve as an unassailable arsenal. President Roosevelt made this clear in his famous January, 1942, address to Congress, in which he promised that the United States would produce, by 1943, an annual one hundred and twenty-five thousand airplanes, seventy-five thousand tanks and eight million deadweight tons of shipping. He called in a Sears Roebuck executive, the shrewd, flat-voiced Midwesterner Donald Nelson, asked him how he liked the title "War Production Board," and, when Nelson approved it, said: "*You* are the chairman."

Soon the clatter of hammers, the clash of gears, and the sputtering of foundries encompassed the country. Locomotives, planes, trucks, steel landing mats, telephones, aluminum sheets, radar,

The ration stamp became a necessity, for among items on the rationed list were meats, butter, sugar, coffee, almost all canned and frozen foods, gasoline, and shoes. Still, the United States home front suffered little. Food was rationed, but no one went hungry. The United States, unlike her allies Britain and Russia, never had her continental territory violated, cities bombed, or civilians slain.

and above all guns and ammunition poured out in measureless quantities. On October 27, 1944, Roosevelt proudly told his fellow citizens: "The production which has flowed from this country to all the battlefronts of the world has been due to the efforts of American business, American labor and American farmers, working together as a patriotic team." It was a fine statement, even if not entirely accurate as, inevitably, there had been friction along the way between labor and management and government. (At the start of the war, the AFL and the CIO had agreed to a no-strike pledge, and union officials, if not all unions, lived up to it. The one major exception was John L. Lewis, who took his coal miners out on strike four times during the course of the war.) And if the size of the output was staggering, so also was its cost: between 1941 and 1945, the national debt rose from forty-eight billion to two hundred and forty-seven billion dollars.

To help foot the bill, Americans at home paid higher taxes and bought some six billion dollars worth of war bonds. They also put up with the few deprivations the war put upon them: ration stamps and shortages of butter, gasoline, textiles, meat, cigarettes, automobiles and automobile tires, apartments, refrigerators—the list went on and on. The Government's Office of Price Administration fixed the cost of certain consumer goods, and all too often shoppers were wearily reminded: "Don't ya know there's a war on!"

Newspapers, magazines, radio, and cinema joined to remind the nation of bleaker realities beyond our fortunate continent. Documentary films like *The Fighting Lady* and *The Battle of the Beaches* and Hollywood films like *Hitler's Children* and *Mrs. Miniver* recalled the ruthlessness of battlefronts and the suffering of foreign friends. There were even appallingly crude propaganda movies designed to stir up sympathy for the unhappy Russians. One of these, *Mission to Moscow*, was taken to the Soviet capital by its "hero," former ambassador Joseph Davies, an innocent admirer of Stalin, and shown in the Kremlin, to the Politburo's amusement.

Once it really got into the fight, the United States went at it with a violent, aggressive, uninhibited vigor that astonished both friends and enemies. It was not only the extent of this effort that was impressive, but also its ingenuity. One observer remarked: "The Seabees could probably have erected the pyramids on any of our beachheads had such construction been adjudged militarily desirable." The whole nation pitched in. The undrafted population floated from city to city and factory to factory as new enterprises sucked up energy. Washington's broad avenues, which had not yet managed to dispose of World War I's temporary buildings, were packed with mushrooming clusters of new offices. Almost overnight, the inrush of a new bureaucracy swelled the capital from an overgrown village to an underdeveloped metropolis.

Servants, nursemaids, clerks, cooks, doormen, messengers abandoned nonessential jobs and flocked off to war plants, where girls and old men hammered, riveted, and operated cranes. The impact on American habits was profound and permanent. Women who had known little except how to run a home became familiar with the time clock and fat pay checks. (Though fifteen million men were in uniform, the total labor force was greatly expanded, thanks in good part to the addition of some six million women.) When the war ended, families who had been accustomed to servants often found that they no longer had them, and that they could do without them.

There was also a minor revival of the speakeasy philosophy of prohibition days as some citizens preferred not to honor certain laws or adhere to certain patterns of patriotic behavior urged by the Government. Hoarding went on in a good many communities; ration stamps and tokens were bargained off. Novel black markets sprang up in everything from beef to tires. The same taxi driver who had once guided fares to illicit booze joints now took them to illicit gas stations. Bellboys managed to produce cigarettes, and butchers found fat steaks—for a price. And with the nation busily at work and wages higher than ever before, there was plenty of money around.

A tremendous exuberance gripped the population, which showed its pride over the achievements of its soldiery, confidence in its ability to surmount unexpected problems, eagerness to tackle unfamiliar enterprises, and an absolute lack of inhibition. It was also true that the thirties had been lean years indeed; it was wonderful to be back at work again in full force. In his last Navy Day speech before his death, Roosevelt mirrored some of this spirit. He proudly pointed out that, apart from its battlefield successes and its large industrial production, the country's achievement "has meant establishing for our Army and Navy supply lines extending over fifty-six thousand miles—more that twice the circumference of the earth. It has meant establishing the lines of the Air Transport Command—one hundred and fifty thousand miles of air supply system running regularly."

In distributing favors among World War II belligerents, fortune was generous to the United States. The American Dream of isolation was to a large measure preserved throughout much of the conflict, in the sense that we were never occupied like so much of Europe and Asia and never pounded by aerial attacks. We experienced victory without having pondered defeat. And we emerged ebullient, confident in our global position and in the belief that at last this earth had become politically habitable. For a few brief years, we felt assured that if again a malefactor disturbed this pleasant horizon, we alone possessed in our atomic treasury the power that could squash him.

XV

Assault on Fortress Europe

The devastation in this London street
attests to the omnipotence of the German
V-2, a forty-six-foot, fourteen-ton rocket
packing a high-explosive warhead.

By the spring of 1944, Hitler's chain of fortifications around Europe, from the Channel on the west to the Apennines and Aegean Islands on the south and the Vistula on the east, was formidable but uneven. Behind these strategic positions, the firmness of Nazi control was corrupted as internal forces of liberation organized with ever-mounting effect. All through France, the Maquis and saboteurs and spies of the resistance prepared for the final struggle. Similar if smaller undergrounds seethed inside Holland and Norway. Armed units, largely Communist-led, sprang up in Nazi-controlled northern Italy. In the Balkans, despite quarrels between Communists and anti-Communists, vigorous bands were active in Greece, Albania, and Yugoslavia, where Tito's partisans had created history's most effective guerrilla army. Even Poland, barely accessible to Western help, had a notable military underground. Finally, added to occupied Europe's fevered restlessness, Hitler's satellites, Hungary and Rumania, had already begun secret negotiations with Allied agents in the hope of buying back respectability.

These widely scattered freedom forces had developed apace since 1942, when Stalin first began to clamor for a second front. He suspected that the West was secretly delaying a cross-Channel invasion in the hope that Germany and Russia would batter each other to death—the reverse of what he himself had once hoped to promote between Germany and France. In the spring of 1942, Britain and the United States, in fact, were wholly in favor of such a second front and had been working on various plans for many months. But it became increasingly evident that neither the troops nor the technical equipment yet existed for any operation sufficiently large to stand a chance of success. Churchill had no intention of sacrificing another generation of young Englishmen on any enterprise as barren as those of World War I, and Roosevelt soon discovered that America, heavily engaged in the Pacific, was short on warships and landing craft.

Therefore, although Allied planners continued to contemplate a future landing in France, in the end they settled on a large commando sortie against Dieppe, on the coast of France, in August, 1942. A raiding force of five thousand men, primarily Canadian, attacked Dieppe, and more than half of these were killed, wounded, or captured.

That France should be the target of a later and larger assault was agreed on by both Washington and London. Planning was started on what would be known as Operation Overlord. In late 1943, at Cairo, Roosevelt and Churchill agreed that Eisenhower should command the operation. A few days earlier, at Teheran, they had informed Stalin that the cross-Channel invasion would take place in the spring of 1944.

Fresh from victories in Africa and Italy, Eisenhower set up headquarters in England in March. On February 12, 1944, he was ordered: "You will enter the continent of Europe and, in conjunction with the other United Nations, undertake operations aimed at the heart of Germany and the destruction of her armed forces."

On January 17, 1944, he took command of Supreme Headquarters, Allied Expeditionary Force—henceforth known as SHAEF—which replaced a planning group under Britain's Lieutenant General Sir Frederick Morgan that had been working on invasion blueprints for a year. Eisenhower expanded the scope of their provisional plan and, after long consultation with logistical and meteorological experts, decided to invade in June. Some sixty miles of beaches along Normandy's Cotentin Peninsula were chosen as the assault area, even though they were relatively distant, subject to heavy surf, and short on port facilities. The latter problem, it was hoped, could be solved by towing two prefabricated, concrete harbors, known as "Mulberries," to the scene.

The Dieppe raid had incited the Germans to expand their Atlantic Wall, but it also gave the Allies a more accurate idea of the kind of tactics needed to break through the Nazi defense shell. As a consequence, not only was the unprecedented idea of an invading force bringing along its own seaports adopted, but new kinds of landing craft to disembark heavy vehicles as well as troops close to the shore, amphibious vehicles, including the awkward DUKW, and flail tanks to beat out mines with whirling chains were developed by inventive technicians, as well as a trans-Channel fuel pipeline called PLUTO (Pipe-Line Under the Ocean). Allied ingenuity seemed limitless. For a time the British even considered constructing enormous aircraft landing platforms of frozen sea water and sawdust.

The invasion buildup was enormous, and all southern England gradually became one huge military encampment. Ports filled up with transport ships; airfields became packed with fighters and bombers; the pleasant English countryside was cluttered with parked tanks, trucks, jeeps; and urban areas were jammed with billeted troops. By early June, nearly 3,000,000 Allied soldiers, sailors, and airmen were ready for the assault. The actual attack was to be accomplished by 176,475 men, 20,111 vehicles, 1,500 tanks and 12,000 planes. Eisenhower subsequently recalled: "The mighty host was tense as a coiled spring, and indeed that is exactly what it was—a great human spring coiled for the moment when its energy should be released and it would vault the English Channel in the greatest amphibious assault ever attempted." It was Eisenhower's plan to drop three airborne divisions in Normandy to cut up German communications and block reinforcement, then to land his first five divisions on the Normandy shore between Caen and Cherbourg Peninsula.

Such monumental preparations could not, of course, be kept from German intelligence. Everyone knew the invasion was coming. But the vital factors of exactly when and where were unknown to the enemy, and these secrets remained essential to success. The Allies worked out several careful deception plans. An actor who resembled Montgomery was sent to North Africa to attract Nazi attention to the Mediterranean. A skeleton American First Army Group was set up along England's southeastern coast, dummy tanks were deployed to fool *Luftwaffe* reconnaissance, and fake messages were radioed for the benefit of German interceptors. Rumors and Allied bombing raids strongly hinted at attacks against the Pas de Calais, Holland, and even Norway. The Germans were confused enough to withhold vital reserves until certain that the Normandy landings indeed represented the main Allied offensive.

Field Marshal Gerd von Rundstedt, who had been called out of retirement to command the German forces in the West, had no use for Hitler's Atlantic Wall of concrete fortifications as an effective way to stop the Allies. His idea was to hold his strength well back from the beaches and to fight decisive battles at places of his own choosing. Hitler, however, in the fall of 1943 had put the daring Rommel under Rundstedt to act as the principal chief of operations. Rommel inspected the Atlantic defenses, found them sadly lacking, and went to work. For six months, half a

This photograph captures a seemingly
uneventful D-Day landing of U.S. troops
on the Normandy Coast. Men died uselessly
when they left their landing craft too
soon and stepped into water over their
heads; others fell into underwater shell
craters and drowned. Deadly storms of
enemy fire swept the beaches with little
letup as the assault waves moved inland.

million men labored constructing giant pillboxes and murderous hazards of every variety. Rommel placed little reliance on static defense alone. The only way to defeat an Allied landing, he argued, was to meet it head on and destroy it. "The war will be won or lost on the beaches," he told his aide. "The first twenty-four hours of the invasion will be decisive." He erected advance barriers at beaches where he though a debarkation likely. He booby-trapped and flooded rear areas where airborne landings might come. He gathered available armor, guns, rockets, and mortars, then positioned reserves to strike either at the mouth of the Somme, where he expected the principal landing, or at Normandy, where he looked for a subsidiary thrust.

Hitler guessed more shrewdly. Over a month before D-Day, he reckoned that Eisenhower would seek his main lodgment in the Cotentin Peninsula. His intelligence service even gained advance knowledge of the two lines from Paul Verlaine's poem, "Chanson d'Automne," that would alert the French underground to imminent assault. But Allied deception measures and the weakness of *Luftwaffe* reconnaissance (there were only one hundred and nineteen German fighters along the Channel, against about five thousand for the Allies) left the *Wehrmacht* command bewildered when the signal came.

The weather had turned unfavorable. Rommel decided that the invasion could not come immediately and drove back to Germany on June 4 to join his wife on her birthday on June 6, and to see Hitler. As a result, he would be twenty-four hours late in getting back to the front. His strategy of immediate riposte was thus to begin a day late. As for Hitler, on the morning of D-Day he was fast asleep at his headquarters, doped with barbiturates; no one thought it was wise to awaken him.

Eisenhower had decided, after intensive consultation, that because of the tide schedule, the most feasible days for landing were June 5, 6, or 7. Sunday, June 4, a gale blew up, but forecasters predicted clear weather Tuesday morning, to be followed by more bad weather. Faced with the choice between a possible critical delay or a gamble with the elements, he decided to go. Early June 6, the largest amphibious force ever seen, including four thousand ships and covered by eleven thousand planes, hurled itself against the Atlantic Wall of which Hitler had boasted: "No power on earth can drive us out of this region against our will."

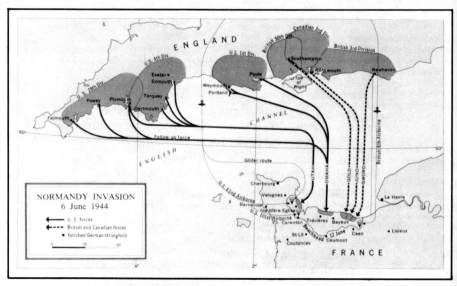

NORMANDY INVASION
6 June 1944

← U.S. forces
←--- British and Canadian forces
■ fortified German stronghold

0   25   50

The breakout of the Allied assault on
Fortress Europe did not come until late
July, from St. Lô, when American armor
and infantry swept southward, isolating
the ports of Brittany as they had already
sealed off Cherbourg on the Cotentin
Peninsula. Then they swung to the east,
pivoting on the British forces under
Montgomery, who shoved steadily against
the Germans in the area northwest of
Paris. In mid-August the *Führer*'s enraged
refusal to authorize retreats resulted in the
capture of one hundred thousand surrounded
German soldiers near Falaise. Meanwhile,
on August 15, a combined French and American
army commanded by General Alexander Patch
landed on the Mediterranean coast of France
and, bolstered by some fifty thousand troops
of the French Maquis, pushed rapidly
northward. Ten days later, Paris was
liberated, and the Allies pushed on with
hardly a break in stride. By mid-September
Hitler had withdrawn to the West Wall,
along the German border. There was talk
among the Allies of the war ending before
Christmas, but the *Führer* already had plans
under way for a massive counterattack
in the Ardennes to begin a few days
before the holidays.

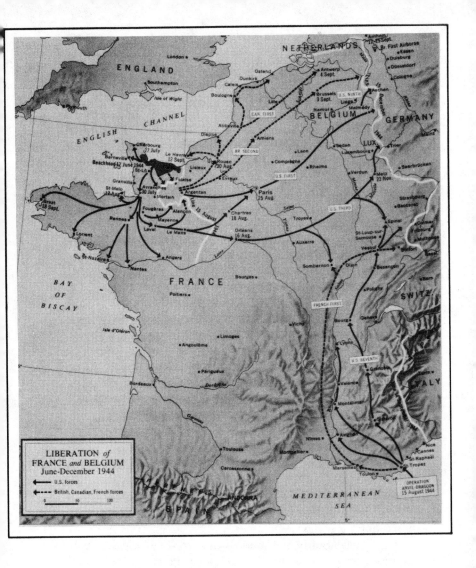

LIBERATION of
FRANCE and BELGIUM
June-December 1944

→ U.S. forces
--→ British, Canadian, French forces

0   50   100

It was 3:32 A.M. New York time when a radio flash announced the invasion and Eisenhower's Order of the Day: "The tide has turned. The free men of the world are marching together to victory." A few hours later, President Roosevelt led the American people in prayer: "Almighty God: Our sons, pride of our Nation, this day have set out upon a mighty endeavor, a struggle to preserve our Republic, our religion, and our civilization and to set free a suffering humanity. . . ."

As the invasion armada headed toward France on the evening of June 5, American and British paratroopers and glider units landed in pell-mell confusion behind the German lines and scattered through the darkness. When Major General Maxwell Taylor dropped with his staff and found only a handful of enlisted men, he commented wryly: "Never have so few been commanded by so many."

Before daylight on the sixth, despite the tangle, an initial lodgement had been successfully achieved. Then, as they peered from their pillboxes, the Germans suddenly saw a galaxy of ships of different sizes and shapes sliding out of the early morning mist. By 5:30 A.M., the assault units were headed for shore. They pushed across the beaches and fought inland to the isolated paratroopers.

Gradually, swarming with men, tanks, and amphibious supply carriers, the beachheads expanded: the Americans at Utah and Omaha beaches, the British at Gold, Juno, and Sword. Tanks flailed through mine fields, and infantry scrambled over underwater and shore obstacles to burst through to the *bocage*, Normandy's stiff hedgerows. Unbelieving peasants greeted their liberators: "*Ah, mon Dieu, ne nous quittez pas maintenant*" ("My God, don't leave us now").

By nightfall nearly one hundred and fifty-five thousand Allied troops were ashore and had taken some eighty square miles of France. The invasion had achieved complete surprise, and within a few days, it was evident that the Allies were in France to stay. Lieutenant General Hans Speidel, Rommel's chief of staff, subsequently acknowledged: "The first phase of the invasion ended with an obvious military, political and psychological success for the Allies. . . . From June 9 on, the initiative lay with the Allies." When Rommel and Rundstedt warned Hitler that the position was critical, the *Führer* shut them up. He repeated his familiar instruction: hold at all costs.

A week after D-Day, the Nazis produced their last trump, something new in warfare, the V-weapons. London was once again battered from the air, but this time by little jet-engined V-1 "buzz bombs" that by the end of the summer had killed more than six thousand people and destroyed some seventy-five thousand buildings. But Hitler's passion for revenge obscured his military logic. While London lived through the V-1 terror, the great embarkation ports of Southampton and Portsmouth were spared. By September, when the *Führer* unleashed the big, long-range V-2 rocket bombs, it was too late to alter the war's outcome.

A few days after the first V-1 hit England, an event took place inside Germany that, had it succeeded, might have ended the war in Europe that year. The rather disorganized anti-Nazi conspirators who had been intermittently plotting against Hitler recruited a resolute professional Army officer, Lieutenant Colonel Count Klaus von Stauffenberg, a brave soldier who had lost an eye, a hand, and two additional fingers fighting for his fatherland, and who loathed the *Führer*. Together with General Friedrich Olbricht, Deputy Commander of the German Home Army, Stauffenberg planned a coup d'état. He personally would undertake to murder Hitler, and once word of his deed had been flashed by the code word "Walkyrie," Olbricht and other commanders in the conspiracy would quickly seize control of the Reich.

The landings in France and the rapid Soviet advance prompted Stauffenberg to move swiftly, before the Allied position became so powerful that a post-Hitler government could not hope for compromise. Therefore, when summoned to a meeting at Hitler's East Prussian headquarters, he took a briefcase containing a time bomb. He intended to leave this inside the concrete bunker where such conferences were normally held, and then to leave. Although the place of the meeting was changed to a wooden guesthouse, Stauffenberg followed his plan, placed his briefcase underneath the oaken conference table, just six feet from Hitler's legs, then left the room.

At 12:37 P.M., July 20, there was a tremendous explosion. Four men were killed, twenty wounded. That there were no more casualties was due to someone's accidentally having shifted the briefcase. Hitler, although partly protected by the table, was temporarily paralyzed in one arm, and also burned and deafened.

Heusinger, not a member of the conspiracy, told me years afterward: "When I came to I did not immediately known what had happened. I was lying on my back with a weight on my chest. I pushed myself upward and realized I was using someone's head as a support. My hand was full of hair. When I looked down I saw it was Hitler's."

Stauffenberg had confidently flown back to Berlin, but Olbricht received a telephone message telling him the *Führer* was alive. As the conspirators issued and countermanded confused orders, loyal Nazi units moved to round them up. Some, including Olbricht and Stauffenberg, were immediately shot. Others committed suicide. Rommel, who was suspected of being directly involved in the plot (which he was not), was offered the chance to take poison and thus save his family from retribution. It was announced that he had died of wounds suffered in an automobile accident, and he was given a hero's funeral. A huge *Gestapo* roundup took place; almost fifteen thousand suspects were arrested, and perhaps as many as five thousand were put to death. Some of the more distinquished plotters were tried in a specially constituted "People's Court," humiliated, and then slowly strangled on meathooks. Their agony was filmed on Hitler's order, and the film was then show to selected military audiences as a warning.

While the Nazis crushed their opponents at home, Eisenhower moved as rapidly as his logistical difficulties permitted into the second phase of his plan. This phase had two objectives: the capture of Cherbourg, and the buildup of sufficient forces and matériel to break out toward Germany. By June 27, when General "Lightning Joe" Collins's U.S. VII Corps took Cherbourg, there were a million Allied troops in Normandy. Ordering Montgomery's British and Canadian forces to hold a "hinge" at Caen, in the first week of August Eisenhower sent his blitzkrieg expert, Patton, swinging southward, eastward, and around to envelop the main German army. As his command car moved through fields of burning rubble and blackened German corpses, Patton shouted above the roar of his artillery: "Compared to war, all other forms of human endeavor shrink to insignificance. God, how I love it." He wrote to his wife: "Peace is going to be hell on me."

Then, before dawn on August 7, the enemy counterattacked from the town of Mortain, striking toward Avranches on the

Outside Carentan, France, ten miles inland
from the invasion beaches, a French peasant
prays over the body of a young American
soldier killed in front of the man's home.
Allied casualties continued to mount as
armies pressed into the Norman countryside.
But by June 17, the day this picture was
taken, Rommel and Rundstedt recognized the
futility of trying to contain the Allies
and urged a withdrawal. Hitler refused.

sea. With Patton completing his end run and Montgomery ready to push in from Caen, it seemed that the Germans were about to be caught in a mammoth envelopment. But Montgomery was slow to close the German escape corridor in the Falaise gap. He was sharply criticized for this caution. Eisenhower and Omar Bradley both felt that he had let far too many enemy troops break out of the trap. Bradley wrote in his memoirs: "If Monty's tactics mystified me, they dismayed Eisenhower even more." The arrogant Patton proposed to Bradley: "Let me go on to Falaise and we'll drive the British back into the sea for another Dunkirk." Even so, eight infantry and two panzer divisions were obliterated. The liberation was off and rolling well.

On August 15, the Nazis were struck another blow, a landing in southern France known as Dragoon. Churchill, who had argued against this invasion, considered it at least well named, "because I was dragooned into it." A fleet of over fifteen hundred ships, including nine aircraft carriers, arrived off the Riviera between Toulon and Cannes. The landing took place with minimal resistance. Helped by French Maquis and resistance agents, the American Seventh Army, under Lieutenant General Alexander Patch, and General Jean de Lattre de Tasigny's French First Army rolled up the Rhone Valley and, within a month, joined Patton's forces north of Switzerland at Épinal, giving the Allies a continuous line from Switzerland to the Atlantic.

As the Germans retreated toward the Rhine, the fate of Paris became a matter of acute military concern. Eisenhower, who was primarily interested in destroying the German armies, had no desire to become involved in any subsidiary operation, no matter how important sentimentally or politically, or to assume the logistical burden of feeding four million Parisians. He sent precise orders to General Pierre Koenig, commander of the French Forces of the Interior (F.F.I.), that "no armed movements were to go off in Paris or anywhere else" until he had given a specific command. However, without Eisenhower's knowledge, de Gaulle secretly instructed Koenig to seize the capital as soon as he could and told General Jacques Leclerc, whose armored division was under Eisenhower, to ignore SHAEF discipline if necessary and march on the capital.

The combination of French chauvinism outside and inside Paris precipitated an attack. The Paris police went on strike, and three thousand armed gendarmes seized the prefecture on August 19.

The following day, although ordered by Hitler to devastate the city, its commander, General Dietrich von Choltitz, negotiated a surrender that permitted him to withdraw the occupying garrison while leaving Paris undestroyed. Eisenhower was forced to accept human and political reality. On August 25, Leclerc, followed by the U.S. 4th Infantry Division, entered the City of Light and formally accepted Choltitz's surrender. The next day Patton sent a message to Eisenhower: "Dear Ike: Today I spat in the Seine." And de Gaulle, amid loud acclaim, marched down the Champs-Élysées and established his hold on France.

Liberation of Paris involved many troops and much fuel, and it undoubtedly delayed the rush toward Hitler's Rhine defenses. Bradley later wrote: "We needed just two more weeks of gasoline [to reach the Rhine]. . . . Those were my thoughts about Paris. I didn't want to lose those two weeks there, and perhaps we did."

As summer ended, German territory was being terribly constricted. The Russians drove in hard from the east, and Tito's Yugoslav partisans were carving up *Wehrmacht* units in the Balkans. The Fifth and Eighth armies in Italy, although weakened by Dragoon, nibbled through Tuscany toward the Po. And Eisenhower's steadily growing forces pushed into Belgium and, from Switzerland northwestward, established themselves near the Rhine.

Eisenhower's plan to approach Germany along an extensive front was hotly disputed by Montgomery, who wanted a narrow, concentrated thrust at Berlin. Montgomery recounts: "I was unable to persuade the Americans to take the risk—which, in any case, was practically nil. So it was *not* done, and the war went on into 1945—thus increasing our post-war political problems, and tragically wasting a great many valuable young lives." In any event, his idea was dismissed by SHAEF, primarily for reasons of logistics. The Allied armies were outrunning their supply system. Eisenhower preferred prudence, and to shore up his line for the final penetration of the Reich, he decided to consolidate his position along the Rhine. By September he resolved on the capture of that great river's Dutch debouchment by an extensive airborne operation aimed at the Dutch towns of Eindhoven, Nijmegen, and Arnhem, while obliterating Walcheren Island, where a tough German force was preventing the use of Antwerp, Belgium's main port.

A German V-2 has just exploded at a major
intersection in Antwerp, situated on a
main supply line to Holland. To impede the
British route through the city, the Germans
launched increasing numbers of flying
bombs. Most of Holland's towns had been
spared the war's devastations, but Allied
efforts in the fall of 1944, and the German
resistance that they engendered, erupted
in many places into chaos and calamity.

The air drop on the Low Countries was only a partial success and ended inconclusively. Although some twenty thousand men took part, Arnhem, the British objective, was fiercely defended by the Germans, and Britain's First Airborne Division lost three fourths of its roster.

By October the Americans had captured their first German city, Aachen, ancient citadel of Charlemagne. They moved on into the Hürtgen Forest, where they battled through snow-covered mine fields, taking heavy losses. It was at this stage that Hitler decided on a bold counterthrust, which he called "Watch on the Rhine," to pierce the Allied lines where they joined in the Ardennes Forest. His objective was to break through to Antwerp, severing Eisenhower's supply lines and perhaps sufficiently demoralizing the West to prepare the way for a negotiated peace. In mid-September a group of high-ranking commanders, including Field Marshal Model and General Jodl, began work on highly secret and comprehensive plans. Then, on December 11 and 12, at his Eagle's Nest headquarters near Frankfurt, the *Führer* received the division commanders who would be involved in the crucial operation.

An important aspect of the Ardennes campaign was called "Greif," which under the famous S.S. adventurer, Otto Skorzeny, would befuddle the Allies with specially trained, English-speaking troops wearing American uniforms. This scheme was largely frustrated, despite the fact that, when a Nazi officer was captured with operational orders for "Greif" in his possession, a wave of suspicion swept the American lines that anyone might be a German agent. Rundstedt scraped up twenty-four divisions, and masses of armor moved to the takeoff line under cover of heavy forest and a continuing fog. On the morning of December 16, eight panzer divisions broke through weak Allied defenses on a seventy-mile front.

The attack was a total surprise and at first achieved astonishing success. However, the Americans around the crossroads town of Bastogne created a bristling hedgehog position, and the offensive slowly began to lose steam. Eisenhower sent Patton to relieve Bastogne, whose commander, Brigadier General Anthony McAuliffe, had answered a German surrender demand with the now famous laconic reply: "Nuts." What became known as the Battle of the Bulge, because of its initial dent in the Allied line,

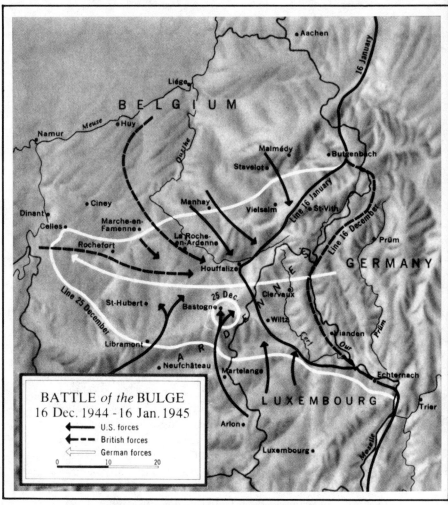

BATTLE *of the* **BULGE**
16 Dec. 1944 - 16 Jan. 1945

- ← U.S. forces
- ◀--- British forces
- ⇐ German forces

0   10   20

The Battle of the Bulge, Hitler's massive
counteroffensive, was to be a surprise
thrust of great power, sending panzer
divisions and infantry bursting through
Belgium's Ardennes Forest to cut the Allied
forces in two at the most weakly held
part of their front. The sudden onslaught
immediately shattered the front line.
However, after the Germans' initial,
shocking success between December 16
and 19, Montgomery's armies on the north
and Bradley's on the south squeezed hard,
forcing the Germans to withdraw.

petered out in a succession of sharp counterattacks. The Germans, faced with no alternative to disaster, drew back inside the Reich in January, 1945.

Through 1944, Hitler had fought back with increasing frenzy. In the spring he had occupied Hungary to curb Danubian collapse. When the Atlantic Wall fell, he had ordered the destruction of London by V-weapons, and of Paris by S.S. demolitions. He had sought to terrify internal opposition by appalling cruelty. He even had managed to launch one final military offensive. Yet when the year ended, it was clear that he was doomed. That last December, General Hasso von Manteuffel was impressed by the *Führer*'s "stooped figure with a pale and puffy face, hunched in his chair, his hands trembling, his left arm subject to a violent twitching which he did his best to conceal, a sick man apparently borne down by the burden of his responsibility."

XVI
Closing in on Japan

A fighter ace aboard the fleet aircraft carrier *Lexington* during the attack on Saipan proudly indicates his six "kills."

A t the start of 1944, the Western powers, having forged an iron ring around the Japanese Empire, were beginning to screw it tight like some immense garrote. All the outer island bastions had been reconquered, from the Solomons to the Aleutians. The Allies were pushing slowly forward in the Burmese jungles; Japan's huge land army was still bogged down in China, robbed of any clear victory; and Tokyo was forced to remain ever more on guard in the north, where the Soviet Union, having repulsed Germany in distant Europe, once again became a menace along the Manchurian frontier and opposite the northern Japanese islands.

Of all these widespread fronts, by far the most important was that on the ocean itself. In the two years since Pearl Harbor, much to Japan's astonishment, United States industrial energy had produced an incomparable new fleet and new air forces and the American high command had developed a technique of island-hopping amphibious advances, moving westward across the Pacific. The Third, Fifth, and Seventh fleets, reorganized in March, 1943, by Admiral Ernest J. King, Chief of Naval Operations, were assigned special carrier task forces bearing F6F Grumman Hellcat planes that were at last able to outfight the Japanese Zeros. There were also new torpedo planes and dive bombers. A generation of fairminded commanders had assumed direction of this new kind of naval war: Admirals Halsey and Spruance; Vice-Admirals Marc A. Mitscher and John H. Towers; Rear Admirals Arthur W. Radford, Frederick C. Sherman, Alfred Montgomery, and Charles Pownall. Together with the Marine Corps and MacArthur's army, they had devised the famous leap-frog method of circumventing enemy strongholds, harrying them with bombing attacks and landing far behind them on islands that could provide airfields and ports from which to stage further advances. By 1944, thousands of square miles of contested waters had been reconquered. American naval strength had become paramount on the world's seas: some forty-seven hundred vessels, including six hundred and thirteen warships, and more than eighteen thousand aircraft. By late summer of 1944, almost one hundred U.S. fleet and escort carriers were roaming the Pacific.

From the start, as they planned their offensive, the Joint Chiefs of Staff foresaw that Japan itself would have to be bombed mercilessly prior to any climactic invasion, in order to wear down the defending army and disrupt communications and the ability to move reserves against a landing. At first it was hoped that such an aerial assault could be mounted from eastern China, and blueprints were drawn up for the eventual capture of a South Chinese port to supply such an operation. In 1943, the high command had hoped to work toward this by occupying Luzon, in the Philippines, and Formosa. And though Admiral King originally had wished to save time by bypassing the Philippines, it was decided in March, 1944, to take those islands where we had suffered such a humiliating defeat. MacArthur was ordered to prepare a Luzon invasion for February, 1945, while Nimitz would simultaneously attack Formosa. In the end, the Formosan project was dropped and the date for the Philippine invasion advanced. But first it was necessary to secure more advanced bases in the western Pacific from which to counter Japanese air and naval attacks.

Therefore, on June 15, 1944, just as Eisenhower was consolidating his Normandy beachhead, Nimitz's forces hit Sapian in the Marianas, some thirteen hundred miles east of the Philippines and more than three thousand miles west of Hawaii. Saipan was defended by thirty-two thousand Japanese under the elderly Lieutenant General Yoshitsugu Saito. An armada of five hundred and thirty-five ships, commanded by Admiral Spruance, carried one hundred and twenty-seven thousand men, of whom two thirds were Marines. Four days after the landing, the Japanese fleet steamed into the area, and in a hot, cloudless sky with optimum visibility, the most intensive carrier battle of the war took place, an event the Americans promptly called the Great Marianas Turkey Shoot. During two days of fighting in the air above Saipan and at sea, the United States forces lost one hundred and thirty aircraft, against almost five hundred Japanese land- and ship-based planes. The Imperial Fleet limped back in the direction of the Philippines and, with scarcely any remaining fighter protection, lost three carriers on the way. The air was cleared, and the path to the Marianas at last lay unhindered.

The fighting on Saipan itself was ferocious. The Japanese staged successive banzai attacks, particularly against the U.S. 27th Division. But the defenders fought with more ardor than skill and in three weeks' time were overwhelmed. Saito himself had no wish to outlive his troops. On July 7, as the end neared, he

This Marine on Saipan is caught by the photographer in the moment he sags after being struck by a Japanese mortar-shell fragment. The picture is blurred because the concussion from the shell explosion jarred the camera. From June 15, 1944, the start of the Saipan landings, enemy fire was ferocious, but by July 9 the island fell under American control.

knelt on the floor of his cave command post and, shouting "Hurrah for the Emperor," stabbed himself with his ceremonial sword. His principal officers followed suit. Admiral Nagumo, who had commanded the carrier strikes at Pearl Harbor and at Midway and was at this time in command of a small-craft fleet at Saipan, shot himself.

The American forces started mopping up isolated pockets of resistance, and when they had finished, they counted 23,811 Japanese dead. Among the casualties were hundreds of Japanese civilians who had taken refuge along the pitted line of escarpments on Saipan's northern shore. When they saw that all was lost, they disregarded the surrender appeals of the Americans and set about the ghastly business of mass suicide. In one of the war's most dreadful episodes, they hurled babies down from cliffs and jumped after them, or blew themselves up with grenades. United States losses on Saipan were also heavy: more than 16,000 casualties, including 3,426 deaths.

On July 23, Marine Lieutenant General Holland M. ("Howling Mad") Smith continued the Marianas offensive by seizing Tinian. He lost only one hundred and ninety-five dead against almost thirty times that number of Japanese. On August 10, Rear Admiral W. L. Ainsworth reoccupied Guam, the last of the Marianas, after almost three weeks of combat.

Here again there was a tough, swirling struggle. Even cooks and clerks were at times thrown into action when Japanese counterattacks pierced the American lines. Bulldozers sealed hundreds of snipers in caves, while ferocious night banzai charges were cut down by Marine riflemen and machine-gunners. When the Marines finally entered Agana, the island capital, a combat correspondent reported that they "found nothing there." But there was more than a little joy among the victors when they discovered that Guam had been Japan's main liquor dump for the central Pacific and was rich in Scotch, rye, bourbon, beer, and sake.

Thus by August the Marianas as well as the Gilberts and strategic airfields along the northern coast of New Guinea were in American possession. The British general Orde Wingate's famous raiding forces had chopped deep into northern Burma. Merrill's Marauders, the comparable U.S. force, were working with Chinese troops to safeguard the new Ledo Road, designed to connect South China and Allied bases in India.

But although the Japanese were being slowly driven westward

and northward in the waters of the Pacific, on the Asian mainland their strength was largely intact. These mainland forces blocked further advances in Burma. And, fearing the long-range B-29's that the Air Corps was just bringing into action from India and China, the Japanese overran seven Chinese airfields where Chennault's Fourteenth Air Force had been established to support Chiang Kai-shek. This China offensive was, in fact, the most serious Tokyo managed to launch during the final two years of the war. Driving southward from Hunan Province and westward from Canton, battle-hardened divisions expelled Chiang from much strategically valuable territory and delayed the opening of overland communications between China and Calcutta, India.

One result of Japan's 1944 land campaign in Burma and China was a change in the Allied command structure for Southeast Asia. When it was agreed that an American would command the invasion of Europe, the British, who had hoped for Sir Alan Brooke, were somewhat disappointed. As a result, they were given the consolation prize of Southeast Asia, and Lord Louis (later Earl) Mountbatten was placed in charge of that difficult theater. He established headquarters first at Delhi and subsequently at Kandy in Ceylon and resolved to be as diplomatic as possible with his independent-minded American subordinates, above all the headstrong "Vinegar Joe" Stilwell.

This was no easy undertaking. Stilwell's own posthumous diaries confirm that he felt scant loyalty either to the dashing royal admiral, whom he somewhat scornfully called "Looie," or to his plans. Nor, for that matter, did Stilwell's successor, Major General Albert C. Wedemeyer, improve relations much, despite his more agreeable manners. Stilwell was recalled in late 1944, and to improve operational control after the Japanese drive, his former command was divided between Wedemeyer, in charge of the China theater under Chiang, and Lieutenant General Daniel I. Sultan, another American, in charge of the Burma-India theater.

Despite their resurgence in China and their relative success in holding the Burma front, the Japanese saw quite plainly that their fate hung upon the outcome of the Pacific Ocean campaign. Following the loss of Saipan and the obvious harbinger of disaster in the first B-29 raids on Japan, the Tojo Government fell. It was replaced by a cabinet, under the venerable General Kuniaki Koiso, that was clearly lacking in confidence of final victory, if not yet ready to seek peace. The new Navy minister, Admiral Mitsumasa Yonai, asked his fleet commander, Admiral Soemu Toyoda: "Can we hold out till the end of the year?" Toyoda replied: "It will probably be extremely difficult to do so."

At this juncture the United States amphibious giant leapt forward once again in a huge stride, ignoring the isolated Japanese strongholds of Truk and Rabaul far to the east and striking the Palau Islands in the direction of the Philippines. This offensive opened at Peleliu in mid-September, 1944. Some forty-five thousand Marines and soldiers hit the tiny island and were immediately faced with stiff resistance. The brutal, difficult battle lasted a month. A particularly tough defense was put up by the island garrison along a cave-pocked massif dubbed Bloody Nose Ridge by the Americans, who lost almost eighteen hundred dead and another eight thousand wounded. More than eleven thousand Japanese were killed.

Slowly the gateway to the Philippines was opening. That sprawling cluster of islands, once Spanish and later under American suzerainty, held the strategic key to Southeast Asia, the South China coast, and Japanese Formosa. In an effort to gain Filipino cooperation, Tokyo had established a puppet government in October, 1943, under José Laurel, a rich nationalistic and anti-American politician. However, his regime failed to gain any substantial popularity. With the assistance of American agents, armed resistance movements sprang up in the mountains, in hinterland villages, and, underground, in some cities. As early as March, 1944, Imperial General Headquarters acknowledged that "even after their independence, there remains among all classes in the Philippines a strong undercurrent of pro-American sentiment. . . . something steadfast, which cannot be destroyed. . . . Guerrilla activities are gradually increasing."

Defense of the archipelago was in the hands of Field Marshal Hisaichi Terauchi, whose main combat strength was the Fourteenth Army under General Tomoyuki Yamashita, Japan's most celebrated general. Yamashita, who had conquered Singapore, bragged that he would issue to MacArthur the same ultimatum he had presented to the British General Percival: "All I want to know from you is yes or no." The Japanese had established numerous strongpoints, airfields, and naval bases throughout the islands, but their primary concern was to hold Luzon at all costs.

Tokyo very properly assumed that MacArthur had meant what he said in 1942 when he had promised to return. Imperial Headquarters had drawn up the plan—called *Sho-Go* ("Victory Operation")—for a "general decisive battle" that was to smash any American assault along the vast island chain starting at the Philippines in the south and ending at the Kuriles in the north. The operation was to start just as soon as the intentions of the Allies became clear.

On October 6, 1944, the Japanese ambassador in Moscow learned from the Soviet Foreign Office that the U.S. Fourteenth and Twentieth air forces were about to start heavy bombing offensives designed to cut off the Philippines. After studying American fleet movements and spotting a large assemblage of transports near Hollandia and Wakde, off the north coast of New Guinea, Imperial Headquarters calculated that the invasion would aim at Leyte and begin during the final ten days of October.

Tokyo was right. However, for fear of committing his main fleet too soon, before being certain of MacArthur's precise target, Admiral Toyoda, the cautious Japanese naval commander, did not begin to move his forces until American warships were discerned approaching Leyte Gulf, north of Mindanao. It took four days before the Imperial Fleet was in position to make its final challenge against the U.S. Third and Seventh fleets.

American preparation for the landing had been careful and extensive. All through mid-October, air strikes hammered up and down the Philippines, more or less as had been predicted by the astonishingly indiscreet Soviets. Admiral Mitscher's Task Force 38 attacked Japanese airfields as far north as Formosa, destroying or crippling an estimated three thousand Japanese aircraft.

But only after the first large elements of MacArthur's liberating army had landed on Leyte did the Imperial Navy begin its desperate riposte. In the last days of October, some 70 Japanese warships and 716 planes, split into three separate commands, opposed 166 American warships and 1,280 planes in the greatest naval battle of all time, the Battle for Leyte Gulf.

Toyoda, following the Japanese *Sho-Go* plan, split his fleet into three separate forces. A small Northern Force under Vice-Admiral Jisaburo Ozawa, made up mostly of carriers without planes, was used as a decoy to lure Halsey's Third Fleet northward and away from the Leyte Gulf beachhead and its supporting Seventh Fleet under Vice-Admiral Thomas C. Kinkaid. Meanwhile, Vice-Admiral Takeo Kurita, whose Singapore fleet then constituted

Fleet carriers, led by the *Essex*, steam
somewhere in the Pacific in November, 1944.
Each fleet aircraft carrier was a huge and
complex creation, an intricately organized
floating community of almost three thousand
men who were needed to keep it functioning.
These ships existed for a single purpose: to
get planes into the air and down again.

60 per cent of Tokyo's major naval units, was to take his Central Force through San Bernardino Strait between Luzon and Samar and come down into Leyte Gulf from the north. At the same time, a smaller Southern Force under Vice-Admiral Shoji Nishimura was to come through Surigao Strait and enter Leyte Gulf from the south. The beachhead with its unloading ships, caught between the two of them, would be wiped out, and so would Kinkaid's Seventh Fleet. Then when Halsey returned, they would fall on him and destroy him.

So went the plan. Under some circumstances it might have succeeded. Without Japanese air power, it was doomed. The Americans struck first. Kurita, steaming in from the west, was detected by two U.S. submarines, which sank two of his cruisers and disabled a third. The next day, in the Battle of the Sibuyan Sea, one of the Japanese Navy's greatest battleships, *Musashi*, was sunk by American carrier planes.

But now Halsey fell for Ozawa's decoy trick and ran off north in pursuit, leaving San Bernardino Strait unguarded. And Kinkaid steamed south, rightly guessing that another Japanese force might try to come through Surigao Strait. There, on the night of October 24–25, his Seventh Fleet destroyed Admiral Nishimura's Southern Force. Nishimura had come under attack by American destroyers and PT boats as he steamed through the straits and had already lost three destroyers before he came up to the Seventh Fleet. As he approached, Rear Admiral Jesse Oldendorf, who was in tactical command, performed the classical maneuver of capping the T: as each Japanese vessel came up, the guns of the entire Seventh Fleet concentrated on it. The entire Japanese force, except for one destroyer, was wiped out.

The next day, Admiral Kurita brought his Central Force, still powerful and consisting of four battleships, six cruisers, and numerous destroyers, through San Bernardino Strait and found himself near a force of sixteen escort carriers with their destroyer escorts. The carriers were divided into three tactical units; one, called Taffy 3 and commanded by Rear Admiral Clifton Sprague, almost immediately came under fire from the guns of the Japanese force. After a heroic battle, in which the planes of all sixteen carriers as well as the destroyers of Taffy 3 took part, Kurita finally broke off the action. One American carrier and three destroyers had been sunk and other ships badly hurt, but three enemy cruisers had also gone down. Kurita could have gone in and shelled the defenseless beaches, but instead he turned and retired west.

Later he explained that intercepted messages had led him to believe a large American force was on its way to cut him off.

The Battle for Leyte Gulf marked the first appearance of kamikaze, or suicide, planes. On October 19, Vice-Admiral Takijiro Ohnishi had met with senior commanders at Mabalacat fighter base in the Philippines and announced: "With so few planes we can assure success only through suicide attack. Each fighter must be armed with a 550-pound bomb and crash land on a carrier deck." This was the origin of the technique of kamikaze, which means "divine wind." The word refers to a typhoon that blew away a Mongol fleet which had sailed to invade Japan in the Middle Ages.

Even while Admiral Clifton Sprague's carriers of Taffy 3 were fighting with Kurita's force, the escort carrier *Santee* of Rear Admiral Thomas Sprague's Taffy 1, a few miles away, was hit by a suicide plane. It thus became the first ship to be crashed by a kamikaze. The time was 7:40 A.M. Soon afterward, another kamikaze hit the *Suwannee* in the same force. Then, just before 11:00, when Kurita had turned away and Taffy 3 was counting her wounds, she came under attack. Five kamikazes either did minor damage to carriers or were shot down, but a sixth crashed through the flight deck of the *St. Lo*, set off bomb and torpedo explosions, and sent her to the bottom. Thus Japan first tested what was to become one of her most terrible weapons.

The kamikaze pilots pressed home their attack with great persistence and resolve. From that moment until the war was actually ending, it was considered a great privilege among young Japanese airmen to volunteer for these one-way missions. Farewell letters written by these pilots to their families have since been collected. One said: "Think kindly of me and consider it my good fortune to have done something praiseworthy." Another sadly reflected: "Every man is doomed to go his own way in time." Still another pilot concluded the last page of his diary: "Like cherry blossoms/In the spring/Let us fall/Clean and radiant." All were in their early twenties.

Although they could not turn the tide of war and although they were shot down in droves by the concerted antiaircraft fire of the vessels that they attacked, the kamikazes did great damage, above all later on at Iwo Jima and Okinawa. Before the conflict ended the following August, the kamikaze special attack corps had sunk or damaged more than three hundred U.S. ships and had exacted some fifteen thousand casualties. On the eve of the

No rows of white crosses mark the graves
of men who pay the price of victory at
sea. Those who die on the deep lie in the
deep. Wrapped and weighted in their canvas
shrouds, the bodies of Coastguardsmen from
the crew of the transport USS *Callaway*
await commitment to the ocean. They were
some of the hundreds of U.S. sailors killed
by kamikaze attacks during the invasion
at Luzon's Lingayen Gulf in the Philippines.

final surrender, when he committed hara-kiri, Ohnishi, who had first conceived of the idea of a flying suicide corps, wrote: "They fought well and died valiantly with faith in our ultimate victory. In death I wish to atone for my part in the failure to achieve that victory. I apologize to the souls of those dead fliers and to their bereaved families."

Halsey to the north meanwhile had discovered Ozawa's decoy force and exacted swift revenge. He sank four carriers, a cruiser, and two destroyers. Thus, in the entire series of battles off Leyte, Japan suffered immense naval losses which it could ill afford. Unfortunately, despite the magnitude of the great victory, it soon became a matter of acid argument among the admirals. Just the way Bradley and Patton blamed Montgomery for allowing the encircled Germans in Normandy to flee through the Falaise gap, Kinkaid blamed Halsey for falling for the Japanese trick and not blocking the San Bernardino Strait. Through that strait, the badly mauled Kurita was able to escape with four capital ships, about all Tokyo had left. Halsey in turn resented that he could not finish off Ozawa's force but had to return urgently southward to help out Kinkaid. In any case, the strategic results of the combined victory were enormous. The naval power that Japan had first established in 1905 by sinking a mighty Russian fleet was finally and irreparably crushed.

Even more immediately important, however, was the fact that the Imperial Navy had wholly failed to interrupt the American landings on Leyte by sinking the assembled transports and supply ships. The liberation of the Philippines was now well begun. Carrying out the pledge he had made at Corregidor, MacArthur had returned and planted the Stars and Stripes on Filipino soil, nine hundred and forty-eight days after he had been ordered to leave by President Roosevelt.

On October 20, the charismatic old general waded ashore on the Leyte beach of Palo, and shortly afterward, in a sudden monsoon rain, he stood by a truck-mounted microphone and broadcast: "This is the Voice of Freedom, General MacArthur speaking. People of the Philippines: I have returned! . . . At my side is your President, Sergio Osmeña, worthy successor of that great patriot Manuel Quezon, with members of his Cabinet. The seat of your Government is now, therefore, firmly reestabished on Philippine soil." Yamashita managed to reinforce his garrison, and the last grim phase of the Asian campaign started.

On October 21, MacArthur occupied Tacloban airport. By early November, he had expelled his enemies from the island's southern and northeastern sectors. By now the guerrilla movement was producing aid on Leyte and becoming increasingly active on the other islands. The Japanese sought desperately to contain and reverse MacArthur's surge and, despite their loss of control over the sea passages, attempted to bring up reinforcements. However, on the night of December 6–7, almost exactly three years after their first raids on the Philippines, they lost six warships crammed with soldiers and supplies. The following week, an additional three transports were sunk, and Yamashita's position became hopeless. By December 16, the Americans had taken Ormoc, and by the end of the month, organized resistance had ceased on Leyte. MacArthur had already moved on to Mindoro and was starting his preparations for the final assault on Luzon and the capital, Manila.

By the time the Leyte struggle ended, the Japanese had lost 56,263 dead against only 2,888 Americans, an impressively disproportionate victory. Only 389 Japanese had, however, surrendered. Marshal Terauchi, lacking the necessary naval support to move his troops from one island pocket to another and hammered by constant aerial attacks, withdrew to the Asian mainland and established headquarters in Saigon.

In his report on the war, General Marshall recalled that at the end of the Leyte battle, men of the U.S. 32nd Division found a letter written by an unknown Japanese soldier. It read: "I am exhausted. We have no food. The enemy are now within 500 meters of us. Mother, my dear wife and son, I am writing this letter to you by dim candlelight. Our end is near. What will be the future of Japan if this island should fall into enemy hands? Our air force has not arrived. . . . Hundreds of pale soldiers of Japan are awaiting our glorious end and nothing else. This is a repetition of what occurred in the Solomons, New Georgia and other islands. How well are the people of Japan prepared to fight the decisive battle with the will to win . . . ?"

By the time the fighting in Leyte Gulf and on Leyte Island was over, not only did the Philippines lie open; Japan itself was naked, unprotected by its customary shield of naval power, exposed to assault from almost anywhere. The answer to the Japanese soldier's question would come soon—and terribly.

XVII
Smashing the Third Reich

Churchill, Roosevelt, and Stalin pose at
Yalta, in February, 1945, where they held
the most fateful meeting of the war.

By early 1945, the military situation required the principal Allied leaders to meet and settle three terminal problems. They had to arrange how to wind up the war in Europe without any ugly incidents when their armies came together in the Continent's heart. They had to decide on the division of the spoils of victory. And they had to coordinate a final offensive against Japan.

The site chosen for this biggest and most fateful meeting of World War II was Yalta, on the Black Sea shore, in Russia's recently liberated Crimea. On February 4, Roosevelt, Churchill, and Stalin gathered with their staffs in palaces that once were tenanted by vacationing czars, but which by then were in a sorry state, thanks to the Nazi occupation. The palaces themselves were still standing, but the rest of Yalta was destroyed. (Roosevelt was outraged by this "reckless, senseless fury" of the Nazis, as he was later to report to Congress.) Indeed, the Soviet Government had to requisition furniture, chambermaids, and waiters from Moscow's principal hotels and hastily dispatch them to the Crimea in order to make its guests comfortable.

Much has been written about what was decided at Yalta, and earnest men still argue whether its decisions were wise or necessary. Above all, it is contended that Yalta gave Moscow too much and thus helped to produce the Cold War.

At the time, a foolproof understanding was not all that neat and easy to arrange. Germany was still very much alive and fighting desperately with its V-weapons. The advancing Western armies were hampered by supply problems; they had been hit hard at the Battle of the Bulge and had still to cross the Rhine. The Red Army, which had borne the brunt of Hitler's fury, was now in control of Bulgaria, Rumania, Poland, and East Prussia. Perhaps most important of all, Roosevelt did not yet know whether secret nuclear experiments going on at home would produce a workable atomic warhead in time to guarantee Japan's collapse without direct invasion and enormous American casualties. Nonetheless, certain facts now can be seen with clarity.

Churchill's last efforts to induce Roosevelt to push eastward and save much of the Balkans and Germany from Soviet occupation had failed for reasons previously described. Roosevelt himself was a tired, frail man. When he later addressed Congress, this proud, brave cripple for the first time publicly referred to "the ten pounds of steel on the bottom of my legs."

Stalin, on the other hand, was calm, confident, and wholly assured that his unilateral aims were at last on the verge of success. He felt that he could insist on Anglo-American acceptance of these aims. That spring, before the conflict ended, he was to tell Marshal Tito: "This war is unlike all past wars. Whoever occupies a territory imposes his own social system. Everyone imposes his system as far as his army can advance."

Churchill could do little in the contest between Roosevelt and the laconic, resolute Stalin. Anthony Eden, who had his own prejudices, subsequently complained that Roosevelt displayed a certain frivolity when dealing with the fate of nations.

A redoubtable effort has been made by Roosevelt's admirers to demonstrate that Stalin made more concessions at Yalta than did the West. Among the concessions they enumerated are final arrangements for the United Nations, closer military coordination, and French participation in the occupation of Germany. Edward Stettinius, the Secretary of State, claimed that the Yalta agreements "were, on the whole, a diplomatic triumph for the United States and Great Britain. . . . The real difficulties with the Soviet Union came after Yalta when the agreements were not respected."

The Americans sought at Yalta to insure Russia's promised aid against Japan, after a German surrender, while keeping Moscow's voice muted on the fundamental problems of China's political future and the division of the Japanese Empire.

The Big Three exchanged briefings on their offensives against Germany and agreed to synchronize them. They decided that the defeated Reich would be divided into four occupation zones (France's to come from Anglo-American territory), and that reparations should include "the use of German labor." They endorsed a new Provisional Government for Poland that would include both Soviet-sponsored Communists and émigré representatives from London. They accepted an eastern Polish border along the Curzon Line, with unspecified accessions in the west at Germany's expense. Free elections were pledged for eastern Europe. And in Asia, Russia was promised the return of all lands and concessions lost in the disastrous 1904–5 Japanese war.

Appended to these accords were three secret understandings. The Anglo-Americans and the Russians agreed to exchange each other's civilians as they were rounded up in Germany. This, of course, meant a Western obligation to send back to the U.S.S.R. many thousands of deserters and political refugees, who were to suffer on their return. The second secret understanding—secret until France could be informed—arranged a voting formula with a veto for permanent members in the Security Council of the proposed United Nations. In the third secret understanding, Russia formally promised to enter the war with Japan "in two or three months after Germany has surrendered."

Even before Yalta, the grand coalition had begun to coordinate its final military assault on Germany, closing the vise from west and east. On January 6, 1945, Churchill had asked Stalin in a special message to renew the Red Army offensive and thus relieve pressure on the Western Front. When Stalin promised a new thrust along the Vistula, Churchill wired: "May all good fortune rest upon your noble venture." As for the poor Poles, over two hundred thousand of them had been allowed to die futilely in Warsaw in the fall of 1944, when an uprising of their underground Home Army, first encouraged by Moscow, was then denied desperately needed Soviet aid. The Home Army leadership would undoubtedly prove troublesome when it came to establishing a Communist-controlled government in Poland; so Stalin dismissed their brave efforts as an "adventuristic affair" and did little to help. The Red Army stalled on the Vistula and did not enter the capital until the Nazis had crushed the rebellion early in October. One desperate Polish patriot wrote:

We are waiting for thee, red pest,
To deliver us from black death.

On January 12, the Russian drive began on a huge front between the Danube and the Baltic. The most famous Russian commanders were engaged: Zhukov, Rokossovski, Vassilevski, Konev. The target was Berlin.

According to the official Soviet history, the Russians had now mustered an overwhelming superiority over the Germans: "5.5 times more men . . . 7.8 times more guns, 5.7 times more tanks, and 17.6 times more planes." They ground on across Poland and into the Prussian province of Brandenburg.

Hungary, which since 1943 had sought intermittently to sign an armistice with the West in secret negotiations at Istanbul, surrendered to Moscow January 20, 1945. Nazi units, however, held

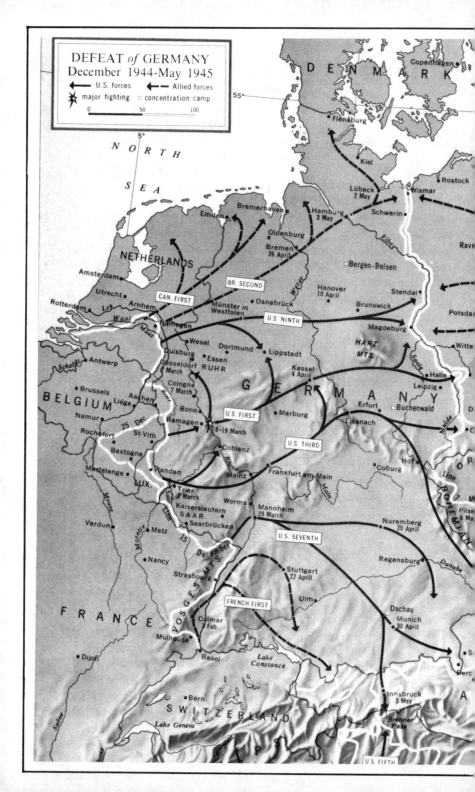

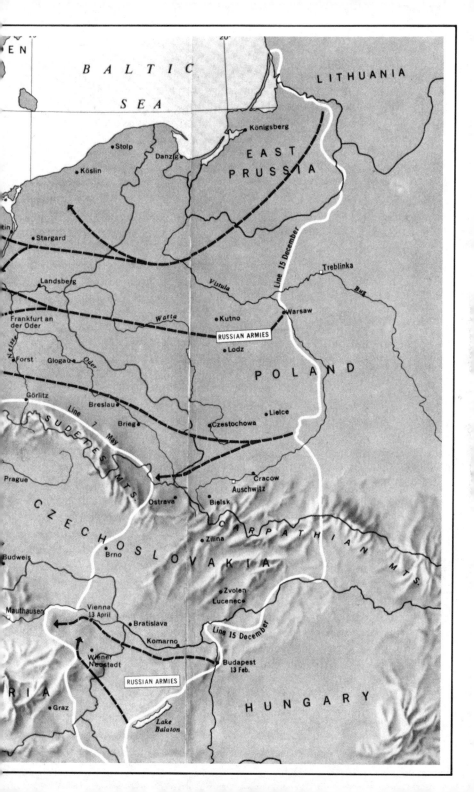

on in Budapest until February 13, ruining that splendid city in the process. The Yugoslav partisans and a few regiments of Bulgarians, who had now turned against Hitler, joined the Red Army as it smashed up into Austria. Subservient governments were established by Russian henchmen in Sofia, Bucharest, Budapest. Coalitions clearly dominated by Communists took over in Poland, Yugoslavia, and the Slovakian portion of Czechoslovakia.

Although Patton's American tanks had reached western Chechoslovakia, they were halted by a decision from Washington, which wished at all costs to avoid any accidental collision between the U.S. and Soviet forces as they advanced toward each other.

By April 13, the Soviet juggernaut had taken Vienna. Three days later, far to the north it began to storm in force across the Oder River. By April 21, Zhukov reached the outskirts of Berlin, and the European war's last great battle started. Marshal Ivan Konev in his memoirs recalls that he and Zhukov had been summoned to the Kremlin on April 1 and told that "the Anglo-American command was preparing an operation aimed at capturing Berlin and with the object of capturing it before the Soviet Army." (Possibly this referred to the Montgomery plan already long since rejected by Eisenhower.) Stalin then turned to his two greatest marshals and asked: "So who's going to take Berlin then, we or the Allies?"

Stalin suspected the German generals of preferring to surrender to the West, in search of a deal to contain the Soviet advance. Furthermore, the Allies, after destroying the Ardennes counteroffensive, had started smashing forward again at a fast clip, driving down the Moselle and Roer rivers into the Rhine Valley. In February, Montgomery's tanks had managed to squash through the flooded delta country around Nijmegen as the U.S. First Army pushed steadily toward Cologne. The Germans retreated to the eastern bank of their most famous river, the Rhine, and waited for the first attempts to cross.

On March 7, 1945, Eisenhower benefited from a remarkable bit of luck. While the U.S. 9th Armored Division was rumbling toward the town of Remagen, a German prisoner warned his captors that in forty-five minutes, at precisely 4:00 P.M., the great bridge spanning the swollen Rhine there would be blown up. The Americans raced to seize it. Although two demolitions charges exploded with minor damage, they captured the span intact,

In stacks, the dead at Gusen concentration
camp in Austria await burial. As the Allied
forces drove deep into Germany, they came
across these camps and, aghast, revealed
the full depravity of Hitler's Third Reich.
The horrors are well known now, but not
less shocking: the bodies piled in heaps,
the living who were little more than skin
drawn over skeletons, the gas chambers, the
crematories that burned day and night.

crossed it, and established a stronghold on the other side of Hitler's last natural defense in the west. Hitler was furious. He set up a special court-martial to try the officers in charge of the bridge, and four of them were executed. He then fired Rundstedt and replaced him with Kesselring, who later said: "Never was there more concentrated bad luck at one place than at Remagen."

From then on, the German collapse accelerated on all fronts. In northern Italy, the U.S. Fifth and British Eighth armies launched a new spring offensive against the twenty-six Nazi divisions that were holding a line along the Po and the passes leading north-ward into German Austria. One by one, the famous cities that still were being held by the Nazis in the name of Mussolini's rump Fascist Republic fell: Bologna, Ferrara, Modena, Mantua, Verona, and finally, Genoa and Milan.

Collapse of the Italian front had been hastened by a fascinating secret negotiation. Since late summer, 1944, the Nazis had made various efforts to sound out their different enemies on a possible separate peace. Ribbentrop, apparently with Hitler's blessing, had explored the chance of compromise with Moscow. Himmler, perhaps hoping to save his own skin, sent the S.S. General Karl Wolff to northern Italy to try to make an arrangement with the Italian partisans. When this failed, Himmler's principal Italian representative, Colonel Friedrich Dollmann, together with Wolff's adjutant, contacted an American O.S.S. agent in the Swiss bor-der city of Lugano. Wolff himself was smuggled to Switzerland, where, on March 8, he was received in Zurich by Allen Dulles, head of O.S.S. operations for Europe. On March 19, still in Switzerland, Wolff met two Allied generals wearing mufti, one of whom, Lyman Lemnitzer, was to become chairman of the U.S. Joint Chiefs of Staff and after that NATO commander. By the end of April, terms of capitulation had been substantially agreed upon. They were finally implemented May 2.

Meanwhile, from their Rhineland bridgehead, the Allies swept northward to encircle and reduce the Ruhr, where so much of Hitler's arsenal had been made. Eisenhower methodically envel-oped one German army after another, thus preventing any final Nazi withdrawal to a northern or southern redoubt. Just as he would earlier have preferred to bypass Paris, he now preferred to avoid a race for Berlin, despite all its political and symbolic importance. His aide, Captain Harry C. Butcher, wrote that for Eisenhower, "the taking of Berlin would be a mere show; what he wanted to do was to end the war as quickly and economically in lives as possible."

Concentrating on this desire for speed and low casualties, the Supreme Allied Commander set and sprang a series of swift traps. His Ninth and First armies joined east of the Ruhr and captured that sprawling complex of factories and four hundred thousand German troops. His Sixth Army Group swung southward toward Switzerland and on to the Austrian border. The Twelfth Army Group ground eastward to the Elbe, the final juncture for a meeting with the Russians.

As the Americans, British, and Free French broke through the walls of Hitler's Third Reich, they discovered to their horror that even the most ghastly tales about Nazi atrocities were understatements. One after another they penetrated the unbelievable hells of Buchenwald, Dachau, and Bergen-Belsen, while the Russians, approaching from the east, entered the death mills of Lublin-Maidanek and Auschwitz.

In these and numerous other concentration camps, the Nazis incarcerated, starved, and murdered more than ten million human beings, including six million of Europe's Jews, for the crime of being what Hitler considered "inferior" by blood or for having opposed his rule. All of Germany's renowned efficiency was employed to perfect the operation of these abattoirs. Men, women, and children were forced against their will to work for the slave empire, were tortured in its name, and were finally killed by it. Often, most appalling of all, their corpses were boiled for soap, their hair was used for mattresses and the fillings in their teeth for the system's gold hoard. Sometimes, their tattooed skins were used to decorate lampshades. Never had there been so immense a crime.

After he had seen his first concentration camp near the aristocratic town of Gotha, Eisenhower cabled Washington and London to send journalists and members of Congress and Parliament to Germany. "I felt," he later wrote, "that the evidence should be immediately placed before the American and British publics in a fashion that would leave no room for cynical doubt."

As these diabolisms were uncovered, an event occurred that tended to enhance bitter emotions among the conquering armies. On April 12, 1945, a tired and prematurely old Franklin Roosevelt was resting at Warm Springs, Georgia, when suddenly he complained: "I have a terrific headache." Two hours later, he was dead of a cerebral hemorrhage. His death was succinctly announced in the regular Army-Navy casualty lists: "Roosevelt, Franklin D., Commander in Chief, wife, Mrs. Anna Eleanor Roosevelt, the White House."

Churchill called this "a loss of the British nation and of the cause of freedom in every land." Chiang Kai-shek began a fast and meditation. The streets of Moscow were filled with weeping men and women. Goebbels telephoned Hitler with delight: "My *Führer*, I congratulate you! Roosevelt is dead! It is written in the stars that the second half of April will be a turning point for us." Hitler himself issued an Order of the Day describing Roosevelt as "the greatest war criminal of all times." And Harry Truman, a modest but decisive man, moved into the American seat of power to usher the world into the atomic age.

Roosevelt died at Warm Springs in what for him was a tranquil haven and knowing that his cause had won. Such was not to be the fate of the Axis dictators.

Mussolini was the first to go. By the end of April, as the allies were approaching Milan, last big city of his puppet Republic, and as partisans were swarming up to the Swiss border, the *Duce* sought the mediation of the archbishop of Milan, Ildefonso Cardinal Schuster. At the archbishop's palace he discovered that the Germans were already in the process of surrendering. He then telephoned his wife to say farewell, gathered money and some of his secret files, and took off northward with a few followers and his young mistress, Clara Petacci. On April 27, his little caravan joined a German antiaircraft battery retiring toward the Tyrol. They were soon stopped by a partisan roadblock. Mussolini disguised himself in a German helmet and military overcoat, but at the village of Dongo he was recognized and seized. On April 28, near lovely Lake Como, the *Duce* and his mistress were stood against a wall, read the death sentence by Colonel Valerio (Walter Audisio), the partisan commander, and shot. The bodies were trucked to Milan, kicked, beaten, and strung up by the feet in front of a gasoline station.

When Hitler received the news, he knew that his turn had come. The Battle of Berlin was raging all around him, though his Chancellery still defended against the Russians. On April 29, he dictated his personal will and his political testament. He named

At 7:09 A.M. by the mantel clock, Harry
Truman is sworn in as the thirty-third
President during a brief ceremony attended
by a score of officials and members of
Congress. This man, who shortly would have
to decide whether to use the atomic bomb,
did not even know on April 12 that such a
device existed. "Last night the whole
weight of the moon and stars fell on me,"
he told the press. "Please pray for me."

Martin Bormann, the number two Nazi, as his executor and expelled Göring and Himmler from the party because of their disloyalty to his frenzied last-minute commands. He appointed Grand Admiral Karl Doenitz President of the Reich and Supreme Commander of the Armed Forces. He made a last appeal against "international Jewry" and then concluded: "I myself and my wife—in order to escape the shame of overthrow or capitulation—choose death." His wife was plump Eva Braun, whom he married the day before his suicide.

Hitler ordered that his favorite Alsatian dog be poisoned, and poison was distributed to his secretaries. Then, early in the morning of April 30, he shook hands with remaining members of his entourage and retired with Eva Braun. Goebbels, Bormann, and a few other Nazi bosses were left behind to send the final telegrams. About 3:15 that afternoon, Eva Braun, sprawled on a sofa, took poison. At 3:30, Hitler, seated at a table near her, shot himself in the mouth with a pistol. The corpses were taken into the Chancellery garden by Bormann, Hitler's valet, and a surgeon, placed in a Russian shell-hole, doused in gasoline, and burned. Goebbels had an S.S. orderly shoot him and his wife after she had poisoned their six children. Bormann disappeared without a trace.

By the time of Hitler's death, thousands of Berliners were scurrying from their besieged capital in a hysterical effort to avoid Soviet retribution, as, block by block, floor by floor, the troops of Zhukov and Konev bored through the burning city.

An officer with a German tank unit at Tempelhof airfield kept a diary which gives some faint idea of that last terrible fight: "We retreat again, under heavy Russian air attacks. Inscriptions on the house walls: 'The hour before sunrise is the darkest,' and 'We retreat, but we are winning.' . . . The night is fiery red. Heavy shelling. Otherwise a terrible silence. . . . Women and children huddling in niches and corners and listening for the sounds of battle. . . . Nervous breakdowns. The wounded that are not simply torn apart are hardly taken in anywhere. The civilians in their cellars are afraid of them. Too many of them have been hanged as deserters."

On May 2, Berlin at last fell.

For a few days disconnected fragments of the *Wehrmacht* thrashed about in isolated sectors between the Austrian Tyrol and Scandinavia. Bormann had sent Doenitz Hitler's last message saying: "Grand Admiral Doenitz: In place of the former Reich Marshal

Göring the *Führer* appoints you as his successor. Written authority is on its way. You will immediately take all such measures as the situation requires." Doenitz, whom nobody bothered to tell that Hitler was dead, wired back: "My *Führer!* My loyalty to you will be unconditional."

Hitler's Thousand-Year Reich lasted a bit more than twelve years. The Doenitz Reich survived Hitler by a week. The German radio announced that the *Führer* had died "fighting to his last breath against bolshevism." It said nothing of suicide. Doenitz went on the air to regret the "hero's death" of Hitler. He publicly hinted at the desire to arrange accommodation with the Western Allies against "the advancing Bolshevik enemy." On May 5, Admiral Hans von Friedeburg even sought an eleventh-hour deal at Eisenhower's headquarters in Rheims while all German forces in northwest Germany, Holland, and Denmark were already capitulating.

Friedeburg hoped to stall negotiations long enough to bring the maximum number of troops and refugees westward, eluding Russia's grasp before the fighting ceased. Eisenhower, however, threatened to close the entire Allied front against such refugees unless there was an immediate, total cease-fire. On May 5, Army Group G, comprising all German forces in Austria, yielded to the Sixth Army Group. The actual surrender came at 2:41 A.M., May 7, 1945, in a modest schoolhouse at Rheims.

Friedeburg, Field Marshal Alfred Gustav Jodl, and his aide, Major General Wilhelm Oxenius, signed the terms. Eisenhower refused to attend in person. Instead he sent British, French, Soviet, and American emissaries to accept unconditional surrender of all German forces to both the Western Allies and the Soviet Union, together and simultaneously. When the brief ceremony ended, Jodl said with much difficulty: "With this signature, the German people and armed forces are, for better or worse, delivered into the victor's hands." The Allied representatives made no comment. The Germans were then conducted to Eisenhower's office and asked if they understood what they had signed. "Ja," said Jodl. Next day, to symbolize unity among the victors, the ceremony was repeated in Berlin, where Zhukov signed for the Soviet Union. May 8 thus became the historical V-E Day.

London, Paris, New York, Moscow, the entire world, save for Japan, rejoiced in the news. Eisenhower told his troops in a Vic-

Celebrators on New York's Wall Street on
V-E Day cheer the victory in Europe. On
May 7, 1945, the remnants of Hitler's
Third Reich surrendered unconditionally.
The reaction to the news was much the same
in all the Allied countries: an outpouring
of unrestrained happiness.

tory Order of the Day: "Let us have no part in the profitless quarrels in which other men will inevitably engage as to what country, what service, won the European war. Every man, every woman, of every nation here represented has served according to his or her ability, and the efforts of each have contributed to the outcome." President Truman said to the American people in a radio address: "We must work to bind up the wounds of a suffering world—to build an abiding peace, a peace rooted in justice and law. We can build such a peace only by hard, toilsome, painstaking work—by understanding and working with our Allies in peace as we have in war."

In Moscow, crowds, which had been expecting the great news almost hourly since Berlin's fall, swarmed into Red Square, brushing aside enormous police reinforcements. A thousand guns fired thirty rounds each to signalize "complete and total victory."

The announcement came long before dawn, and thousands of people poured into the streets wearing everything from pajamas to fur coats. The crowd stayed on and on and grew ever larger. There had been no such demonstration in Moscow since the Revolution's earliest wild days. Hordes gathered in front of the British and American embassies, and whenever a foreigner was spotted, he was gently plucked up by a hundred hands and passed along with cheers. George Kennan, U.S. chargé d'affaires, made a speech from the embassy balcony, where the Red banner hung beside the Stars and Stripes. Roars went up: "Long live Truman!" "Long live Roosevelt's memory!" "Long live the great Americans!"

Far away, on America's Pacific Coast, a conference was meeting at San Franscisco to create the United Nations. From April 25, not long after Roosevelt's death, until June 26, shortly before the first nuclear device was exploded in secret, the world's new leaders argued about the structure of the organization they were building. The debated the "fundamental human rights" to which they would henceforth dedicate themselves, rights including "social progress and better standards of life" and "the equal rights of men and women." At the insistence of a Republican member of the United States delegation, Senator Arthur H. Vandenberg of Michigan, one word was added to the list—"justice."

XVIII
The End of the Rising Sun

On August 9, 1945, Nagasaki became the victim of the second atomic bomb. Five days later came the surrender of the Japanese and the end of World War II.

Even before the mopping-up had ended on Leyte in the Philippines, MacArthur sent Lieutenant General Walter Krueger's Sixth Army on a long, hooking loop through Surigao Strait, the Mindanao Sea, and on to Lingayen Gulf and Luzon, key to the whole Philippines archipelago. On January 9, 1945, some sixty-eight thousand Americans began clambering ashore on the vulnerable Lingayen beaches in what became the largest United States land campaign of the Pacific War. (More American forces were engaged in Luzon than in either Africa or Italy.)

Krueger's objective was Manila, the national capital and a magnificent port. But Krueger was opposed by an impressive army under General Yamashita, comprising two hundred and fifty thousand men divided into three groups: Shobu Group of one hundred and forty thousand men in the North Central sector, defending Lingayen Gulf; Kembu Group of thirty thousand men, defending the network of airbases around Clark Field; and Shimbu Group of eighty thousand men in southern Luzon.

Despite their size and dispositions, Yamashita's troops had already been weakened by harassing guerrilla attacks and steady United States air bombardment, and they were unable to stop Krueger. By January 31, the Americans had moved deep into the Central Plain and had expelled the Japanese to the mountainous north and east. They prepared for the final drive on Manila, timed to coincide with an Eighth Army drive across the base of the famous Bataan Peninsula, which had begun with landings at San Antonio Bay on the twenty-ninth.

On February 3, the U.S. 1st Cavalry Division reached the outskirts of the capital, but it took twenty-nine days to complete the occupation against desperate house-to-house resistance. When the rubble of Manila finally was freed on March 4, several Japanese units on Luzon remained in effective condition, and Yamashita continued fighting from stronghold pockets until the very end of the war. But MacArthur had achieved his principal goal, and he set about establishing on Luzon a great base from which to invade Japan itself.

Two weeks after returning to the capital where he had spent so many years, MacArthur was back on Corregidor. He issued an order: "Hoist the colors and let no enemy ever haul them down."

At last, on July 5, he was able to announce that the campaign was over. In the Philippines the Americans had annihilated four hundred and fifty thousand of the Emperor's best remaining troops.

It was Admiral Spruance, a quiet, philosophical, but resolute sailor, later a highly successful diplomat, who had helped dissuade Nimitz and Washington from the original plan of moving directly to Formosa instead of to the Philippines. So when Iwo Jima and Okinawa were chosen for invasion right after Luzon, it was fitting that Spruance's Fifth Fleet should land the V Marine Corps, which was under Major General Harry Schmidt, on Iwo. D-day was February 19.

Only seven hundred and seventy-five miles from Honshu, a main island of Japan, the barren, volcanic island of Iwo Jima was of particular importance to the B-29 offensive. It was being used by the Japanese as a radar warning station and as a base for fighter interceptors. But even more important, once captured, its three airfields could be employed by P-51 Mustangs to provide fighter escort for the huge B-29's as they flew the thousand-mile return trip to their bases in the Marianas to the south. The eight square miles of Iwo were defended by more than twenty thousand valiant Japanese under Lieutenant General Tadamichi Kuribayashi. The island had been well prepared with extensive mine fields, lengthy underground tunnels, and communications systems protected by artillery fortified with concrete made from the island's black volcanic ash.

Initially, there was virtually no Allied cover on the exposed beaches, and the conquest of the ugly little island presented the Marine Corps with the largest bill of its brave and bloody history. The Marines took Iwo inch by inch, crawling forward on their stomachs or behind tanks that bogged down in the volcanic ash. Men with rifles and flame throwers fought their way from pill-box to foxhole, climbing the dominant defensive feature, rocky Mount Suribachi, where on February 23, after three days of furious combat, the Marines hoisted the Stars and Stripes and photographer Joe Rosenthal of the Associated Press took one of the war's most famous pictures. To secure the island took a total of 26 days and 20,965 American casualties, including 6,821 dead. Lieutenant General Holland M. "Howling Mad" Smith commented succinctly: "The fighting was the toughest the Marines ran across in 168 years." The price of Iwo came high, but by the war's end,

24,761 B-29 crewmen had used its airfields for emergency landings.

By now, the Pacific offensive was working like a one-two punch. On March 26, 1945, Lieutenant General Simon Bolivar Buckner's Tenth Army landed its 77th Division in the Kerama Islands, west of Okinawa, principal center of the Ryukyu chain. The small islands were quickly subdued and became a seaplane base and anchorage for supply ships during the operation. At the same time, Marines took the nearby Keise Islands, artillery was emplaced, and Okinawa, just eight miles away, came under direct attack.

Okinawa was a rather poor chunk of land comprising some seven hundred square miles, but its strategic value was immense. It was only three hundred and fifty miles from Japan proper, and it had good harbor facilities and plenty of room to stage troops. It would provide an ideal jumping-off place for any invasion of Japan. This island was the stake of the war's last and biggest amphibious assault. Vice-Admiral Richmond Turner had elaborated the actual operations plan for its capture on February 9, ten days before the Iwo Jima landing. He arranged concentric invasions by forces under himself, Spruance, Mitscher, and Buckner (who commanded seven Marine and Army divisions).

The mere fact that Japan's defenses had been constricted by a tightening ring and that the Japanese therefore could no longer pretend feints and diversions worried the invaders. They were aware that Lieutenant General Mitsuru Ushijima, Okinawa's commander, had more than one hundred thousand men and three thousand aircraft at his disposal, and that the kamikaze menace, originated at Leyte and embellished at Iwo Jima, would now, surely, reach a ferocious peak.

The Okinawa landing began at 8:30 A.M., April 1, Easter Sunday. By the time the battle ended, eighty-two days later, over three hundred thousand troops were on the island. During the first hours of the invasion, the American commanders, who were expecting immediate resistance as at Iwo Jima, were surprised to find almost no opposition on the beaches. In fact, there seemed to be little opposition anywhere. Five hours after the Marines were ashore, they had captured one vital air strip and not a shot had been fired.

If everything seemed to be going much too easily, it was because Ushijima had pulled back to the southern part of the island.

The first assault wave heads ashore at
Iwo Jima on D-Day, February 19, 1945.
The Marines moving inland were pinned
down by an enemy they could not see; low
hummocks of sand were the tops of pillboxes,
with their gun slits only a few inches
above ground. Japanese artillery on Mount
Suribachi, the island's one peak (shown
here), rained shells onto the congested
landing beach with devastating effect.

He had decided on a defense in depth designed to attract the main assault forces and then cut them off, instead of risking piecemeal losses to heavier American naval artillery and air power. Five days elapsed while the Marines muttered that Okinawa was "the screwiest damned place in the Pacific." Then the Japanese struck. On April 6 and 7, nearly seven hundred enemy aircraft, including some three hundred and fifty kamikazes, pounded the American beachheads and the task forces assembled offshore.

The first five hours of the battle that was designed to smash the American invaders of Okinawa took a toll of six American ships and 135 kamikaze pilots. The Japanese committed their largest battleship, the 72,908-ton *Yamato*, without air cover and with fuel enough only for a one-way trip. On April 7, despite its screen of eight destroyers and the light cruiser *Yahagi*, it was sunk in less than two hours—along with four destroyers and the *Yahagi*. The Imperial Fleet was gone.

From then on, the land conquest of Okinawa proceeded in a bloody series of pushes. The Americans first reduced the northern defenses and then turned southward. The ultimate and most fiercely defended position was in the ancient city of Shuri, a center of pre-Chinese, pre-Japanese culture. There Marine flamethrowers burned their way through dugouts in immemorial cemeteries. When the last strongpoint on Kiiyama Peninsula fell, 110,071 Japanese were dead, nine for every American. Buckner was among the Americans killed. Before dawn on June 22, Ushijima and his principal subordinate, Lieutenant General Cho, knelt in full dress uniform before their headquarters cave and cut out their entrails.

The persistent thrust of American sea power, whose destruction had been calculated at Pearl Harbor, closed in upon Japan's Pacific fringes, backed up by an ever-encroaching land power and formidable air power. What was left of an Asian front simply fell apart. While B-29 bombers continued their pulverizing operations from the Marianas, the stalemate in Burma and, ultimately, China, had turned into a Japanese retreat.

Along the Manchurian-Soviet border, where a truce of mutual convenience had been arranged between Moscow and Tokyo, a day of reckoning was due. As disaster loomed over Germany, it became increasingly necessary for Japan to keep ground forces opposite the border. As early as the spring of 1944, the Japanese

General Staff had begun plans for defense against a Russian attack. At Yalta Stalin had promised—as booty for joining the Pacific war—the Kurile Islands and southern Sakhalin (which had been lost to Japan in 1905), as well as Russian privileges in Chinese ports and railways. On April 5, 1945, Molotov informed the Japanese embassy in Moscow that the U.S.S.R. was denouncing its Neutrality Pact because the situation had "radically changed." On May 15, Tokyo annulled its alliance with a German state that had ceased to exist. But the gesture was meaningless; it was quite apparent that a new front soon would open, at a most disastrous moment for the Emperor. The Japanese sought to stave off the reckoning by sending out peace feelers, but to no avail. When the Big Three victors met at Potsdam in July, Stalin told the British and Americans of these overtures. Truman then confided to Stalin the secret that the United States possessed a "new" bomb that could have a decisive effect on the war. But he avoided disclosing the weapon's full import.

While Tokyo alerted its Manchurian army, it was facing accumulating difficulty in China itself. A 1944 offensive there had not succeeded in altering the strategic balance. Despite mutual recriminations, both Mao's Communists and Chiang's Kuomintang armies continued to nibble at areas occupied by a Japan that no longer had troops to spare. By early 1945, Mountbatten's forces had managed to open land communications between Burma and China. Mountbatten flew to Manila, where MacArthur promised to help prevent the Japanese from reinforcing their Singapore and Malayan garrisons. At Potsdam, Marshall authorized Mountbatten to assume over neutral Siam (Thailand) whatever control he required and to plan for eventual operations in formerly Dutch Sumatra and in French Indochina, whose territory was thereby withdrawn from MacArthur's supervision.

By this time, Japan's most dreadful tribulations had begun. General Curtis LeMay had made of the Marianas a massive Superfortress base. Once he had assembled there three wings of long-range B-29's, he began a devastating series of raids against Japan's helpless main island cities. Starting in February, 1945, employing a new bomb containing magnesium and jellied gasoline, bombers burned out factories, docks, urban areas, and Tokyo itself. Japan, with jerry-built houses and overconcentrated industrial centers, was peculiarly vulnerable to incendiary attack. LeMay

The crew of the USS *Bunker Hill* fights a
flight-deck fire after a Japanese suicide
plane dove into the ship on May 11, 1945,
off Okinawa. Almost four hundred officers
and men died, and with the carrier out
of action, Admiral Marc Mitscher, aboard,
transferred his flag to the *Enterprise*.

made the most of the situation, reducing the armament and crews of his planes so that they could carry a maximum weight of fire bombs.

In mid-March, he dispatched 334 B-29's from Guam, Saipan, and Tinian on the most destructive single bombing mission ever recorded. It did more damage than even the dreadful atomic explosions that were to wipe out Hiroshima and Nagasaki.

On the night of March 9–10, just after midnight, the pounding of Tokyo started amid a high wind. Within half an hour, the resulting fires had flamed wholly out of control. A factory worker who took refuge in a school compound later described his experience: "The fires were incredible by now, with flames leaping hundreds of feet into the air. There seemed to be a solid wall of fire rolling toward the building. All the windows were closed to prevent sparks from pouring into the rooms and setting the school ablaze. . . . Many people were already gasping for breath. With every passing minute the air became more foul. . . . the noise was a continuing, crashing roar. The great bombers were still coming over Tokyo in an endless stream. . . . Fire-winds filled with burning particles rushing up and down the streets. I watched people—adults and children—running for their lives, dashing madly about like rats. The flames raced after them like living things, striking them down. They died by the hundreds right in front of me. Wherever I turned my eyes, I saw people running away from the school grounds seeking air to breathe. They raced away from the school in a devil's cauldron of twisting, seething fire. The whole spectacle with its blinding lights and thundering noise reminded me of the paintings of Purgatory." A Japanese newspaperman wrote: "The city was as bright as at sunrise; clouds of smoke, soot, even sparks driven by the storm, flew over it. That night we thought the whole of Tokyo was reduced to ashes." The fire department estimated that the raid killed 97,000 people, wounded 125,000, and left 1,200,000 homeless.

One by one Japan's cities were reduced: Tokyo, then Nagoya, Kobe, Osaka. Each devastation was so terrible that currents of heat were flung upward into the sky, tossing the vengeful airplanes and tearing helmets from the heads of their crews. In one ten-day blitz, the Superfortresses wholly flattened thirty-two square miles of Japan's most important centers.

By April 6, MacArthur was given command of all U.S. Army

forces in the Pacific and was directed, with Nimitz, the naval commander, to prepare for the war's final operations. This task was rendered far easier than the Joint Chiefs of Staff could foresee by the accomplishment of a scientific miracle.

At 5:30 A.M., July 16, in a remote New Mexican desert, the first atomic device was placed upon a steel tower near Alamogordo Air Base and detonated. Under the direction of Dr. J Robert Oppenheimer, a theoretical physicist from the University of California, the July 16 test was successfully staged, producing what an official War Department release later described as "a revolutionary weapon destined to change war as we know it, or which may even be the instrumentality to end all wars."

Tentative manufacture of the bomb had been begun by General Groves's Manhattan Engineer District in 1942. American, British, and French scientists had pooled their knowledge, and following Fermi's 1942 chain-reaction experiment, the United States had built two gigantic plants at Oak Ridge, Tennessee, and Hanford, Washington, to separate a uranium derivative known as U-235 and to make plutonium. At Los Alamos, New Mexico, Oppenheimer established a laboratory to work on producing a warhead. However, until its actual testing in July, no one, not even its sponsors, could be certain that it would work. So secret was the project that only a handful of persons were even aware of its existence, and they did not include Harry Truman, then Vice-President. The day after Roosevelt died, Secretary of State James F. Byrnes told Truman of the coming experiment, but his first thorough briefing did not come until twelve days later, from Secretary of War Henry L. Stimson.

Pandora's terrible box opened—never again to be slammed shut—just as dawn unfolded July 16. As the countdown ended, Oppenheimer, standing with Groves in a distant control station, shouted, "Now!" The assembled officers and scientists peered through their dark glasses at the auroral burst of flame, and Oppenheimer thought of two passages from the Hindu epic, Bhagavad-Gita. One went: "If the radiance of a thousand suns were to burst into the sky, that would be the splendor of the Mighty One." The other: "I am become Death, the shatterer of worlds." A tremendous blast rushed out across the desert, and above it rose the first of those awful mushroom-shaped clouds.

Nagasaki lies shattered and scorched after a nuclear attack. Because the city is on uneven ground, sections were shielded from the blast, and casualties and destruction, although terrible, were less severe than at Hiroshima. Damage to industry, however, was greater. The day after the bombing, Emperor Hirohito broadcast to his people—the first time he had ever talked to them—to say that the years of fighting were ended.

It remained for Truman to decide if, how, where, and when this fantastic weapon should be employed. Twelve days before the test, Churchill had given the President British consent in principle to drop the bomb on Japan. Truman himself was to write in his *Memoirs*: "Let there be no mistake about it, I regarded the bomb as a military weapon and never had any doubt that it should be used." When he told Stalin about the bomb at Potsdam, Stalin replied that he hoped the United States "would make good use" of it.

There was some discussion among American leaders on what preliminary warning should be addressed to Tokyo prior to employment of the two bombs already being assembled on Tinian. Undersecretary of State Joseph C. Grew urged that Japan be alerted to its danger with a message indicating no insistence on the Emperor's abdication. Stimson echoed this view, but Byrnes opposed it. On July 26, the Potsdam Declaration was issued, with an ultimatum demanding that Japan surrender unconditionally or face complete destruction. Two days later, Premier Suzuki announced that his Government would ignore it. Lieutenant General Spaatz, by now Commanding General of the U.S. Army Strategic Air Forces in the Pacific, had been instructed to prepare to utilize the first of the two fabricated bombs after August 3, weather permitting, against one of four cities: Hiroshima, Kokura, Niigata, or Nagasaki. Following Suzuki's action, this order was confirmed. A B-29 from the 509th Composite Group, with a specially trained crew commanded by Colonel Paul W. Tibbets, Jr., was chosen for the first mission.

At 8:15 A.M., August 6, Tibbets released over Hiroshima a uranium bomb of the type called "Little Boy." He reported later: "As far as I was concerned it was a perfect operation." On August 9, a plutonium bomb known as "Fat Boy" was dropped on Nagasaki. The destruction in each case exceeded the most careful extrapolations of scientists, and it was hours before the mushroom clouds, smoke, and flames had sufficiently blown away to permit adequate photo reconnaissance.

It is impossible to convey the full meaning of these twin events. The casualty toll was staggering and, of course, fails to suggest the indescribable suffering incurred, but estimates claim—no one knows for certain—that from seventy to eighty thousand people were killed at Hiroshima and an equal number were injured, and that some forty thousand died at Nagasaki and about sixty thousand were injured.

Militarily, the denouement was swift. Truman announced: "We are now prepared to obliterate rapidly and completely every productive enterprise the Japanese have above ground in any city." On August 8, Molotov summoned in Ambassador Sato and informed him that the Soviet Union was declaring war. The very next day, three Russian army groups rolled over Japan's Kwantung Army and within a few days had penetrated deep into Manchuria. On August 10, Tokyo sued for peace on the basis of the Allies' Potsdam Declaration, but requested that Hirohito be retained as Emperor. (Truman, acting on advice from Grew, Stimson, and Leahy, came to the decision that this stipulation was in the best interests of the United States.)

The actual surrender was decided at a final meeting of the Supreme War Council, in the presence of the Emperor. Hirohito said: "I cannot bear to see my innocent people suffer any longer." Following a lengthy discussion, Suzuki rose and quietly remarked: "Gentlemen, we have spent hours in deliberation without coming to a decision and yet agreement is not in sight. You are fully aware that we cannot afford to waste even a minute at this juncture. I propose, therefore, to seek the imperial guidance and substitute it for the decision of this conference." He then advanced sadly to the throne. The diminutive Hirohito, by avocation a marine biologist, who kept a portrait of Abraham Lincoln in his study, said he felt compelled to accept the Allies' terms.

These terms stipulated that "from the moment of surrender the authority of the Emperor and the Japanese Government to rule the state shall be subject to the Supreme Commander of the Allied Powers." On August 15, in a taped radio message, his first direct voice communication with his people, the Emperor informed them that the war was over and it was time to "pave the way for a grand peace for all generations to come."

The Russians spurned the announcement as "only a general statement on Japan's capitulation." They continued their brief but fierce offensive. The Kwantung Army surrendered August 22, but Soviet airborne troops and the Red Fleet moved on to Dairen and Port Arthur in Manchuria and seized southern Sakhalin and the Kuriles. The Japanese fought sporadically until September 12. The Russians captured five hundred and ninety-four thou-

Japan had surrendered on August 14, but obeisance to military etiquette and the gravity of the circumstances required a formal ceremony, which took some time to assemble. On September 2, on the deck of the battleship *Missouri*, at anchor in Tokyo Bay, the surrender document was signed. "It is my earnest hope," said MacArthur, who presided, "... that from this solemn occasion a better world shall emerge."

sand Japanese and killed some eighty thousand, against their own losses of eight thousand dead and twenty-two thousand wounded. On August 26, Sir Frederick Browning, on behalf of Mountbatten, accepted the Japanese surrender of Southeast Asia in Rangoon. And, starting August 28, American troops began a mass and unopposed landing on Japan's home islands, occupying all strategic centers.

Although there were several separate Japanese capitulations on widely separated fronts—with China regaining sovereignty over Inner Mongolia, Manchuria, Formosa, and Hainan, and with Britain reoccupying Hong Kong and accepting a formal Japanese surrender in Singapore on September 12—the crucial and historical act confirming Imperial Japan's defeat took place aboard the forty-five-thousand-ton battleship, U.S.S. *Missouri*, on September 2, 1945, in Tokyo Bay.

The event was staged with a high sense of drama. Suzuki had resigned August 15. The new Premier, Prince Higashikuni, was able to avoid the capitulation ceremony for protocol reasons—he was the Emperor's uncle. Instead, the one-legged Foreign Minister, Mamoru Shigemitsu, wearing striped pants and top hat, limped aboard the *Missouri* from a gig that flew the Stars and Stripes, accompanied by General Yoshijiro Umezu, representative of the General Staff.

The *Missouri*, flagship of the U.S. Pacific Fleet, was flying the same flag that had waved over the Capitol in Washington the day Pearl Harbor was attacked. Jammed together on the deck was a mass of correspondents and Allied officers: British and Australians with scarlet band on their caps and collars; Gaullist French with vivid decorations; Dutch with gold-looped emblems; Chinese in olive drab; Russians in stiff shoulder-boards, headed by the obscure Lieutenant General Derevyanko; and the Americans, simply garbed in plain suntans.

After MacArthur had opened the ceremony with a brief and generous address, Shigemitsu, with great dignity, signed two copies of the surrender document in Japanese and English. Umezu followed. Then MacArthur strode forward, bringing with him two high officers who had been rescued from Japanese prisoner-of-war camps: Lieutenant General Jonathan M. Wainwright, whom he had been forced to leave behind at Corregidor, and Lieutenant General Sir Arthur Percival, the loser of Singapore.

MacArthur then signed, followed by Nimitz and the Allied delegates.

The handsome general, looking a generation younger than his years, said: "We are gathered here, representatives of the major warring powers, to conclude a solemn agreement whereby peace may be restored. The issues, involving divergent ideals and ideologies, have been determined on the battlefields of the world and hence are not for our discussion or debate. Nor is it for us here to meet, representing as we do a majority of the people on earth, in a spirit of distrust, malice, or hatred. But rather it is for us, both victors and vanquished, to serve, committing all our peoples unreservedly to faithful compliance with the understandings they are here formally to assume. It is my earnest hope . . . that from this solemn occasion a better world shall emerge . . . a world dedicated to the dignity of man. . . . Let us pray that peace be now restored to the world, and that God will preserve it always. These proceedings are closed."

XIX
The Legacy

Still reinforced and repaired, the Berlin
Wall, which was erected to prevent East
Germans from escaping to the western zone,
is a symbol of today's divided world.

On August 7, 1945, the day after Hiroshima, Stalin convened five leading Soviet physicists and, putting them under the charge of his secret police boss, Lavrenti Beria, ordered them to catch up with American atomic achievements. On July 10, 1949—from three to six years before Washington believed it possible—Russia exploded its first A-bomb. The United States reacted by testing an infinitely deadlier hydrogen bomb on November 1, 1952. Then, on August 20, 1953, Georgi Malenkov, the first post-Stalin premier, announced a similar Soviet test. The nuclear race was on and has yet to be halted.

Like its predecessor, World War II bequeathed to its survivors more problems than it settled—except this time there was a quantum jump. Even before the hot war ended, a cold war had started among the victors, and against this background loomed the stark fact that man had at last invented weapons able to destroy mankind. This had an immediate impact upon the power relationships of a perplexed and deeply wounded earth.

As early as the spring of 1945, President Truman, coached by Byrnes and Stimson on the diplomatic import of the nuclear secret, had decided that we were "in a position to dictate our own terms at the end of the war." On April 23, the new President received Molotov and addressed him sharply on the rapid and grave deterioration in eastern Europe. The Soviet foreign minister complained: "I have never been talked to like that in my life." Truman answered: "Carry out your agreements and you won't get talked to like that."

So, in an uneasy atmosphere of mutual mistrust, and with Yalta pledges violated by one side and atomic strength possessed by the other, the victorious armies started their military occupation of Germany. This moment had originally been foreseen with savage relish. The British harbored few generous thoughts toward any Germans; hatred burned in Russia; and in America, there was a bitterness unusual in our national character. Henry Morgenthau, Jr., Roosevelt's Secretary of the Treasury, wanted to turn Germany into a pasture. Roosevelt told his Cabinet that as far as he was concerned, the Germans "could live happily . . . on soup from soup kitchens."

Truman, however, discharged Morgenthau and, relying increasingly on the advice of Byrnes and Stimson, began at least a logical policy toward the Germans. The Russians, meanwhile, allowed their troops to take vengeance in rape and pillage before they settled down to looting everything that could be moved. There was a race by both victors, eastern and western, to capture equipment. In the Harz Mountains, the Americans located a cache of V-2 documents and also rounded up dozens of intact rockets. These, with the aid of some of Hitler's principal experts, eventually were developed into a United States missile system.

After much diplomatic bargaining, the American and British armies withdrew from advanced positions to their prearranged occupation lines. The zones both of Berlin and of Germany itself were taken over by the victors along frontiers that still exist today. But the wreckage of the Third Reich—what was left after Russia took East Prussia, and Poland moved to the Oder-Neisse border —remained partitioned. No formal peace was made. Byrnes was later to write: "We should recognize that the Soviet Union, alone of all the major powers, was not eager to obtain an early peace settlement." Thus, although settlements were arranged with Italy and the Axis satellites, the greatest nation in Europe's heart remained split in two. And as time went on, both Germanies tended to forget Hitler with what the Swiss theologian, Karl Barth, had called "the remarkable German quality of living down in the grand manner all unpleasant memories."

Those Nazi chiefs who had not already, like Hitler, Goebbels, and Himmler, committed suicide, were tried in a four-power court at Nuremberg under a new and ex post facto body of law dealing with aggressive warfare and "crimes against humanity."

On October 18, 1945, the prosecutors issued indictments against twenty-one Nazis, who were given thirty days to prepare their defense. On November 20, the accused were assembled in a mud-colored building—one of the few Nuremberg structures to survive the bombs—and the trial got under way. It lasted ten months. The details of what the Nazis had accomplished in their death camps, the so-called medical experiments they had conducted, their slave labor program, the horrors they had inflicted wherever they went, were, day by day, exposed in thousands upon thousands of words of testimony, motion pictures, and grisly exhibits. A war-weary world soon became all too familiar with the overwhelming and, alas, virtually incomprehensible statistics of the Nazi nightmare, and with the expressionless faces of the inconsequential-looking men in the prisoners' dock.

That vindictiveness was not the purpose of the trial was shown by the differences in sentences handed down. Some, like Hans Fritsche, an editor and propagandist, Franz von Papen, former chancellor and diplomat, and the financial genius Hjalmar Horace Greeley Schacht, were acquitted. The most odious were sentenced to death, including the S.S. boss, Martin Bormann, *in absentia*, and Göring, who managed to poison himself an hour before he was to have been executed. Ribbentrop, Kaltenbrunner, Rosenberg, Frank, Streicher, Frick, Sauckel, Seyss-Inquart, Keitel, and Jodl were hanged.

Prominent Japanese war leaders were similarly tried. Two committed suicide: General Shigeru Honjo and Prince Fumimaro Konoye, who had been premier three times. Seven were sentenced to hanging, including General Hideki Tojo. Tojo sought, unsuccessfully, to kill himself. Before he finally mounted the scaffold he wrote a farewell poem: "It is good-by./Over the mountains I go today/To the bosom of Buddha./So, happy am I." The Japanese said to each other: "Pity. Pity."

Both Germany and Japan were placed under military rule, although Truman's new tough policy kept Russian troops from participating in the Japanese occupation. Germany was truncated in the east and temporarily lost the Saar. Japan yielded all its mainland empire, the Kuriles, and southern Sakhalin Island, while Okinawa became to all intents an American strategic colony.

Immediately after the war ended, the Americans and British started a pell-mell demobilization. Despite the brief interlude in which Truman successfully reversed the policy of conciliating Stalin, the Yalta formula, as interpreted by Moscow and enforced by its military presence, became a pattern for the postwar map. Succeeding years demonstrated that there exists an inherent incompatibility between the Western demand at Yalta for "free and unfettered" elections in eastern Europe, and the concession that eastern European governments should be "friendly to the Soviet Union."

Fortunately, the United Nations, already born before the end of World War II, helped prevent the Cold War from turning into holocaust. Stimulated largely by the State Department under Secretary Hull, ardently embraced by Roosevelt, endorsed by Chur-

An undelivered speech by Franklin D.
Roosevelt, written shortly before his
death, reveals the original thought behind
the birth of the United Nations: "Today
we are faced with the pre-eminent fact
that, if civilization is to survive,
we must cultivate the science of human
relationships—the ability of all peoples,
of all kinds, to live together and work
together in the same world, at peace. . . ."

chill and accepted by Stalin, this organization grew out of a set of international conferences at a Washington, D.C., estate, Dumbarton Oaks, in 1944.

The United Nations was designed to include all peace-loving states but to leave with the great powers the authority to enforce peace. Although it failed to attain its dreams, it provided a valuable sounding board for world opinion and a center for secret crisis negotiations. And the mere existence of the U.N. in the stormy years since World War II has sometimes helped ease otherwise unendurable pressures.

These pressures have become increasingly complex. The strategic emphasis placed by the Allies on winning a hot-war victory in Europe before tackling Asia was continued into the cold war. Europe, with all its intellectual and industrial power, was from the start an area of primordial concern. Russia has always expanded more easily into Asia, where it could introduce a higher standard of living. But American policy forced it to concentrate on European problems, thus permitting in Asia the rise of Russia's most dangerous ultimate rival, China.

The United States wisely saw that it could not successfully survive the immediate postwar years as an isolated power, and that it required Europe's support. Therefore a series of diplomatically unprecedented commitments was made: the Truman Doctrine, to defend Greece and Turkey; the Marshall Plan, to reinvigorate Europe's latent strength; the North Atlantic Treaty Organization, to conserve that strength. Within a remarkably short time, Europe began again to speak with a proud and authoritative voice. Indeed, within another decade, the Continent was prepared to contemplate a different future, founded upon neither nationalistic rivalries, dissolved empires, nor American sustenance.

Meanwhile, Moscow pursued three fundamental policy tenets. The first was to regain all eastern European territory once held by the czars. Stalin took back Rumania's Bessarabian and north Bucovina provinces, eastern Poland, and the Baltic States. He also seized East Prussia, but left most of Finland intact, although it had been a Russian duchy. The second tenet was to insure friendship of eastern European lands by installing Communist regimes. The third tenet was to bind its ideological empire into an economic and military bloc.

Soviet attempts to expand were deliberately countered by an American doctrine of containment. Although within ten months of Germany's collapse the United States had reduced its forces in Europe from three and a half million to four hundred thousand men, a Communist guerrilla uprising in Greece was put down with American aid. Likewise, Soviet efforts to bully Iran and Turkey failed. Not until some years later—under Khrushchev, not Stalin—did Moscow discover how to gain a position in the Middle East by the simple device of exporting surplus arms.

It was in the East, not the West, that the major postwar problems ultimately assumed shape. Japan fell rapidly under American domination, which Russia was never able to challenge. General MacArthur, in charge of the Allied occupation, put through a remarkable democratization program, including a constitution insuring political freedom and outlawing war. The Emperor, probably to his intense delight, was stripped of all but symbolic status and allowed to go back to his passion of marine biology. Hirohito issued an Imperial Rescript saying that his ties with his subjects were "not predicated on the false conception that the Emperor is divine and that the Japanese people are superior to other races and fated to rule the world."

Although Russia could not meet the United States's Oriental challenge in Japan, it could in China. Stalin did not really formulate a consistent Chinese policy until after his troops had defeated the Japanese in Manchuria. Originally, indeed, he seemed to prefer Chiang Kai-shek to Mao Tse-tung, and the Chinese Communists complained about Moscow's "erroneous tendencies." But, from the moment that Mao's armies finally smashed the Kuomintang, the Russians sought to make China into communism's Asiatic counterpoise to United States island bastions from Japan to the Philippines.

Washington tried without success to frustrate the communization of China. A mission by General Patrick Hurley failed to resolve differences between Chiang and Mao. When General Marshall was dispatched on a similar enterprise, he announced a truce between the rival ideologists in early 1946; but this truce collapsed. By the end of 1949, the huge country was in Mao's hands.

Initially, Moscow seemed to be succeeding. But just at a time when Stalin's successors, aware of Russia's responsibilities as a nuclear power, were discarding both Stalinism and the belief in war's inevitability, China was accepting both theories. This contradiction produced an ideological schism more profound than any since Catholicism split between Rome and Constantinople.

What was originally, in the Cold War's first phase, a protracted conflict between the United States and the U.S.S.R. now seems, in retrospect, a relatively simple problem. Both sides recognized a balance of terror and managed to hold the essentials of what had become a postwar status quo. This was above all true for Europe, where armistice, if not peace, came before it came to Asia—in both the hot and cold wars.

Now there are other players in the game. The paramount pair of powers are paramount only in terms of ultimate implications, not in the application of their strength. Both America and Russia had, a decade ago, become accustomed to certain illusions. They each believed in their ability to shape the world. Both are coming to realize this is beyond their means. The quantum jump into perplexity achieved by World War II remains a blazing fact. All nations, giants and midgets, are caught up in destiny's whirlwind. New members knock at the door of the atomic club, and scientific genius races ahead far more rapidly than the political wisdom that must guide it.

CHRONOLOGY

1939

SEPTEMBER

1 Adolph Hitler starts World War II by attacking Poland at dawn. German forces, using planes and tanks in blitzkrieg tactics, cross the border and begin battles of annihilation with ill-prepared Polish troops.

3 Great Britain (11:15 A.M.) and France (5 P.M.) declare war on Germany. Australia and New Zealand join Allies. British ships at sea receive message, "Winnie is back" as Churchill becomes First Lord of the Admiralty. British blockade of German coast is proclaimed. German U-boat warfare begins with sinking of British liner *Athenia* off Ireland. Roosevelt says that U.S. will stay neutral, but that he "cannot ask that every American remain neutral in thought as well."

4 R.A.F. carries out first bombing raid of war, on ships in harbor at Wilhelmshaven.

5 Germans cut Polish Corridor, cross Vistula River, and bomb Warsaw. U.S. neutrality is proclaimed as official national policy.

6 Polish Government flees Warsaw.

7 British convoy system begins operation in North Atlantic.

8 Germans reach Warsaw. Roosevelt proclaims "limited" emergency.

10 British Expeditionary Force under the command of Lord Gort begins to land in France. Canada declares war against Germany.

13 Daladier forms War Cabinet in Paris and promises victory.

17 Soviet troops invade Poland from the east. U-boat torpedoes British carrier *Courageous* off Ireland.

18 German and Soviet troops meet at Brest-Litovsk in Poland.

28 Warsaw surrenders after being devastated by air attacks. In Moscow, Molotov and Ribbentrop sign treaty partitioning Poland. Blitzkreig has crushed Poland in less than a month of fighting. Nazi plans call for systematic annihilation of Poles, which will take 5,000,000 civilian lives.

OCTOBER

3 British units move into sector of Allied line on Belgian frontier. U.S. sets up Pan-American Security Zone to protect hemisphere.

6 Hitler, in Reichstag speech, makes "last peace offer" to Allies.

12 Chamberlain rejects Hitler's "last peace offer."

14 Lieutenant Günther Prien sneaks U-boat into supposedly impregnable British naval base at Scapa Flow and sinks battleship *Royal Oak.*

NOVEMBER

3 Stalin presents Finland with drastic territorial demands.

4 Roosevelt signs Neutrality Act, allowing belligerents to "cash and carry" American arms—which only the Allies are able to do.

8 Hitler escapes assassination in bombing of Nazis' Munich beer hall.

13 German planes raid Shetland Islands, the first time that bombs fall on British soil.

29 Stalin ends nonagression agreement with Finland.

30 Soviet troops invade Finland from Arctic Sea to Karelia.

DECEMBER

7 Russians reach Mannerheim Line on Karelian Isthmus, where the Finns are dug in for defense.

13 British warships drive German pocket battleship *Graf Spee* into Montevideo harbor after battering it in running battle in Atlantic.

14 Soviet Union is expelled from the League of Nations for acts of aggression against Finland.

17 German crew scuttles *Graf Spee* outside Montevideo harbor.

20 *Graf Spee* commander, Captain Hans Langsdorff, commits suicide.

22 Finns counterattack at Mannerheim Line; Russians pull back.

1940

JANUARY

2 Fighting rages in bitter cold along Mannerheim Line.

8 Food rationing begins in Britain.

11 Finns announce destruction of entire Soviet division.

20 Russians attack Finnish units in the region of Lake Ladoga.

26 U.S. commercial treaty with Japan expires, Hull notifies Tokyo that trade will continue on day-to-day basis. Russian drive near Lake Ladoga collapses.

FEBRUARY

9 Roosevelt announces that Sumner Welles will tour capitals at war in search of practical peace terms.

12 Expeditionary forces from Australia arrive at Suez.

17 British destroyer *Cossack* invades Norwegian waters to rescue 299 British POWs from German prison ship *Altmark.* Norwegian Government lodges formal protest.

25 Sumner Welles arrives in Rome.

26 Russians push Finns back in drive along Mannerheim Line.

MARCH

2 Sumner Welles arrives in Berlin to talk peace with Adolph Hitler.

11 Sumner Welles arrives in London.

12 Finns agree to Stalin's terms after Russians breach Mannerheim Line. Soviet Union takes 16,173 square miles, including Viipuri and the Karelian Isthmus. Finns living in ceded areas are advised that they will be allowed to resettle themselves in Finland.

18 Hitler and Mussolini hold much-publicized meeting at Brenner Pass.

20 Daladier falls, and Reynaud becomes Premier of France with flat commitment to win the war.

30 Japanese set up new puppet Chinese regime at Nanking.

APRIL

4 Chamberlain allots Churchill direction of British defense.

8 Allies announce that they have mined Norwegian coast to stop shipments of iron ore to Germany.

9 German forces invade Norway by sea and air at key points from Oslo to Narvik. Norwegians fight back, but Germans quickly take key airfields and harbors. Denmark, invaded at the same time, gives up without resistance.

10–19 British warships sink ten German destroyers in Battle of Narvik. British and French units land in Norway but are vastly outnumbered in almost every sector of the fighting.

17 U.S., concerned about Japanese movements in western Pacific, warns Tokyo not to use European war as a cover for aggression.

30 In Norway Allies pull back after decisive defeat near Trondheim.

MAY

1–3 Allies evacuate Namsos, and Norwegian army on Trondheim front gives up.

10 One of the most decisive days of the war. Hitler unleashes a shattering offensive in the west. Seventy-five divisions (ten armored and six motorized) and hundreds of planes support two major drives. While one force invades the Low Countries, the other strikes at France through the rugged hills of the Ardennes region, considered by the French high command to be impassable. German strategy is to flank the Maginot Line. Blitzkrieg moves so fast that the Germans break through Belgian fortifications along the Meuse River and the Albert Canal on this first day. In London, Chamberlain resigns, and Churchill becomes Prime Minister.

11 Allied troops move into Belgium. German commandos take Fort Eben Emael, key to Belgian defenses.

13 German panzers smash through thinly defended Ardennes. Churchill delivers his celebrated "blood, sweat and tears" speech.

14 Germans exploit their Ardennes break-through and cross the Meuse in force. Dutch surrender, and the *Luftwaffe* bombs Rotterdam, previously declared an open city. Between 30,000 and 40,000 people are killed during the attack. Queen Wilhelmina escapes to London. British Home Guard prepares for Nazi invasion.

17 Germans take Brussels and Antwerp. British begin to pull units back from their line in Belgium.

19 Germans drive deep into northern France. Weygand replaces Gamelin as supreme commander of Allied armies. Churchill tells Commons that French have pledged to "fight to the end."

20 Germans panzers reach Channel.

21 Germans take Abbeville and split the Allied forces.

23 Germans take Boulogne.

24 Germans take Calais.

26 British begin evacuation of trapped Allied soldiers from beach at French port of Dunkirk.

28 King Leopold of Belgium orders his army to surrender.

31 Allied troops are ordered to leave Narvik in Norway as the disaster in France grows by the hour.

JUNE

3 *Luftwaffe* bombs Paris.

4 Dunkirk evacuation ends as the last of the small boats from England leave the French coast under heavy fire. The operation has saved more than 300,000 British and French troops. Churchill tells the Commons and the world: "We shall never surrender."

5 Battle of France begins.

10 Germans break through the Weygand Line. Mass exodus from Paris jams the roads leading south. Among the refugees are members of the French Government, which transfers its headquarters to Orleans. Italy declares war on France and Britain. In an address delivered at the University of Virginia, Roosevelt declares: "The hand that held the dagger has struck it into the back of its neighbor."

11 Churchill confers with Reynaud at Briare and finds an atmosphere of defeatism. Weygand and Pétain are especially pessimistic.

12 Paris is declared an open city. Germans take Rouen and Rheims.

13 Germans cross Marne at Château-Thierry, famous American sector in World War I. Reynaud asks Roosevelt to send "clouds of planes," only to be told that the U.S. does not have them. At a meeting in Tours, the French Premier informs Churchill that France may be forced to conclude a separate peace with Germany.

14 German troops enter Paris and parade triumphantly down the Champs-Élysées.

15 Germans capture Verdun. F.D.R. sets up National Defense Research Committee and appoints Dr. Vannevar Bush as its chairman.

16 French resistance crumbles as Germans reach Loire. Reynaud rejects Churchill's offer of common Franco-British citizenship and resigns in favor of Marshal Pétain.

17 Pétain asks Hitler for an armistice and tells the French people, "We must stop the fight."

18 Churchill asks the British to rise to "their finest hour." De Gaulle uses the B.B.C. to appeal to the French to continue the fight. In Munich, Hitler and Mussolini confer on strategy. Molotov congratulates Hitler.

21 A triumphant Hitler presents surrender terms to French in historic railway carriage near Compiègne. France is to be divided into an occupied zone, including Paris and the Atlantic coastline, and an unoccupied zone over which Marshal Pétain will preside. French sign surrender the following day.

24 French sign armistice with Italy. Hitler declares that "the war in the West is won."

25 Japan, emboldened by French collapse, demands right to send troops into French Indochina.

28 British recognize de Gaulle as "leader of the Free French." Republican convention in Philadelphia nominates Wendell Willkie as 1940 candidate for President. Smith Act checks subversive activity in U.S.

30 Germans seize Channel Islands, the only British soil they will occupy in the course of the war.

JULY

2 Pétain sets up headquarters of his regime at Vichy, famous spa.

3 British warships sink or damage elements of French Navy at Oran, Algeria, to prevent them from falling into the hands of the Germans. Three battleships and one carrier are destroyed during the attack, which embitters future Anglo-French relations.

4 British seize all French ships in British ports to keep them from joining Vichy. Italians start drive against British in Sudan.

5 Vichy regime breaks off diplomatic relations with London.

10 Battle of Britain begins as *Luftwaffe* ranges over England's southern coast, hitting port facilities.

16 Hitler orders planning for Operations Sea Lion—invasion of Britain. Prince Fumimaro Konoye becomes Premier of Japan with a program of economy and peace.

18 Democratic convention in Chicago nominates F.D.R. as candidate for an unprecedented third term. British close Burma Road, main supply route to China, as peace gesture to Japan.

19 Hitler, in wildly applauded speech in Reichstag, appeals to the British to realize that they cannot win the war and predicts that Churchill will seek refuge in Canada.

20 Roosevelt signs bill calling for two-ocean navy. Four billion dollars are earmarked for two hundred vessels, including seven battleships.

21 Soviet Union absorbs Latvia, Lithuania, and Estonia.

30 Harry Hopkins, special assistant to the President, arrives in Moscow for talks with Stalin.

AUGUST

3 Italian forces invade British Somaliland from East Africa.

9 British garrison is withdrawn from Shanghai as Japanese moves in Far East become more menacing.

15 Two thousand German planes open Operation Eagle, to drive R.A.F. from the sky and prepare for invasion of Britain. Göring has some 2,500 planes for the battle, both bombers and fighters, while for defense the R.A.F. can muster only 700 to 800 fighters.

17 Hitler declares Britain subject to total blockade. Battle of the Atlantic grows increasingly intense as convoys duel with U-boats.

18 F.D.R. and Mackenzie King of Canada agree to set up a board for joint defense policy.

20 Battle of Britain rages on. Churchill salutes R.A.F. with the words: "Never in the field of human conflict was so much owed by so many to so few."

25 R.A.F. raids Berlin for the first time.

29 French Equatorial Africa declares allegiance to de Gaulle and his "Free French" movement.

30 Hitler forces Rumania to cede territory to Hungary and Bulgaria.

SEPTEMBER

3 Britain receives fifty overage destroyers from U.S. in return for bases in Newfoundland and the West Indies.

4 Hull warns Japanese against aggression in Indochina. General Antonescu becomes the head of the Rumanian Government.

6 Congress appropriates funds for two-ocean navy. King Carol of Rumania abdicates throne, under pressure, in favor of his son Michael.

7 *Luftwaffe* opens "London Blitz." Indiscriminate nighttime bombing kills over four hundred, injures over sixteen hundred.

12 Ambassador Grew warns Hull of possible Japanese retaliation in case of U.S. oil embargo.

13 Italian forces invade Egypt from Libya under orders from Mussolini to drive British out and secure Suez Canal.

15 R.A.F. attacks Continental ports and shipping from Boulogne to Antwerp, blasting "invasion coast" that Germans plan to use for Operation Sea Lion. *Luftwaffe* suffers prohibitive losses in the Battle of Britain. Churchill calls this "the culminating date" in the struggle for control of the air.

16 Selective Service is adopted in U.S. Men aged 21 to 26 are required to register for military training.

17 Hitler postpones Operation Sea Lion. R.A.F. victory over *Luftwaffe* has made impossible any cross-Channel invasion of Britain.

23 De Gaulle, supported by ships of the Royal Navy, tries to take

Dakar, French West Africa, but troops loyal to Vichy drive him off after brief fighting. British warships cripple the French battleship *Richelieu* at Dakar.

26 F.D.R. proclaims embargo on export of scrap iron and steel to all nations outside the Western Hemisphere except Britain. Japanese, after extorting agreement from Vichy, send their troops into Indochina.

27 Japan, Germany, and Italy sign Tripartite Pact pledging joint action if any member goes to war with U.S.

29 U.S. Marine detachment lands on Midway Island and begins erecting new defenses.

OCTOBER

4 Hitler and Mussolini meet at Brenner Pass amid talk of a fundamental change in Axis strategy. With Britain undefeated but on the defensive, Axis attention shifts to the Mediterranean and the Balkans.

7 Germans seize Rumanian oil fields to ensure enough fuel to keep their war machine going.

8 Japanese ambassador to U.S., Nomura, says embargo on iron and steel is an "unfriendly act."

10 *Luftwaffe* resumes heavy attacks on London but is hampered by fall weather.

15 U.S. embargo goes into effect.

16 Over sixteen million Americans register under Selective Service.

18 British reopen Burma Road as Japanese become more menacing.

21 Churchill addresses French people over B.B.C. and promises that they will be liberated one day.

24 Hitler confers with Pétain, who agrees to promote Nazi concept of New Order for Europe. Germany is to be dominant, France is to be a favored satellite of the Nazi state.

28 Hitler meets Mussolini in Florence. Italian troops in Albania cross the border into Greece.

29 First Selective Service numbers are drawn from goldfish bowl used for same purpose during World War I. British troops land in Greece.

31 R.A.F. bombs oil tanks in Naples.

NOVEMBER

1 Italian planes bomb Athens and Salonika and push their drive from Albania into Greece.

5 F.D.R. wins a third term in a landslide victory over Willkie, who carries only ten states.

8 R.A.F. bombs Munich beer hall, scene of Nazi celebrations.

10 Chamberlain dies at his home in Hampshire. He had been "deceived and cheated by a wicked man," Churchill says in reference to Chamberlain's diplomatic dealings with Hitler.

11 Latin Quarter students begin organizing first resistance cells in occupied Paris. British planes blast

Italian fleet anchored in Taranto harbor, and the Royal Navy gains almost complete domination of Mediterranean.

12 Molotov meets Hitler in Berlin. They fail to reach an agreement on stabilizing eastern Europe.

14 *Luftwaffe* hits Coventry with terror bombing that destroys most of city.

19 Greek counterattack routs Italian invaders and forces them into disorganized retreat.

20 Hungary joins Axis.

23 Rumania joins Axis.

DECEMBER

2 Greeks announce they have taken 5,000 prisoners on Albanian front.

3 Greeks capture Porto Edda in Albania and claim to have taken twenty-eight thousand prisoners.

6 Greek victories cause resignation of Marshal Badoglio as chief of staff of the Italian Army.

9 British Army of the Nile under Wavell counterattacks against Italian troops in North Africa.

11 Army of the Nile takes Sidi Barrani, capturing entire Italian garrison.

18 Hitler issues "Barbarossa" directive to his top military men. He says: "The German armed forces must be prepared to crush Soviet Russia in a quick campaign before the end of the war against England." He orders absolute secrecy in military preparations.

20 U.S. sets up Office of Production Management under William S. Knudsen to expedite shipments of material aid to Britain.

21 Hitler denounces U.S. policy and calls it "moral aggression."

23 Anthony Eden, who resigned from the Chamberlain Government because he could not accept appeasement, returns to Foreign Office under Churchill. Germans execute first Parisian for anti-German activity.

29 F.D.R. delivers a fireside chat in which he terms the Axis a real threat to America and calls upon Americans to turn their country into an "arsenal of democracy."

1941

JANUARY

5 British Army of the Nile captures Bardia and takes twenty-five thousand Italian prisoners.

6 In his annual message to Congress, F.D.R. mentions the Four Freedoms—of speech and worship, from want and fear—and calls them essential human rights. He asks Congress to pass legislation approving lend-lease aid to anti-Axis nations.

15 British forces based in Kenya and Sudan launch invasion of Italian East Africa and quickly penetrate into Ethiopia, the land of the deposed Emperor Haile Selassie.

19 Hitler decides to aid Mussolini in his Greek adventure. British troops invade Italian Eritrea.

22 British Army of the Nile captures Tobruk and many Italian prisoners.

24 Army of the Nile captures Derna.

29 Secret U.S.–British staff talks begin in Washington. There is much concern over "wolf pack" tactics of German U-boats in Atlantic, and over forays of battle cruisers *Scharnhorst* and *Gneisenau*. The talks produce the strategy of "Germany first" in case of U.S. involvement in the war.

FEBRUARY

7 Army of the Nile captures Benghazi.

9 Churchill tells Roosevelt: "Give us the tools, and we will finish the job."

12 General Erwin Rommel arrives in Tripoli to assume command of German-Italian forces.

26 British take Mogadishu, capital of Italian Somaliland.

MARCH

1 Bulgaria joins Axis.

5 British troops from North Africa land in Greece.

11 F.D.R. signs Lend-Lease Act, which gives him authority to sell, transfer, lend, or lease arms and supplies to nations whose defense is vital to U.S. Purpose: to help British when their credits lapse. Initial appropriation amounts to seven billion dollars.

24 Rommel and Afrika Korps open first offensive against British in Libya.

25 Yugoslav Government secretly joins Axis at Vienna conference with Hitler, who is confident that his Balkan flank is now secure.

27 Word of the agreement touches off a rebellion in Belgrade. The regent, Prince Paul, is forced out and Peter II declared king. General Simović and Cabinet proclaim Yugoslav neutrality.

28 British naval units shatter the remnants of the Italian Navy in Battle of Cape Matapan.

APRIL

3 Churchill sends Stalin warning of big German troop movements in eastern Europe. Stalin ignores warning. Army of the Nile, seriously weakened by detachment of units to Greece, retreats from Benghazi as Rommel continues to press on.

6 Incensed by the revolution in Belgrade and determined to help Mussolini, Hitler pours troops into Yugoslavia and Greece, thereby delaying Operation Barbarossa for several crucial weeks. Delay will make it impossible to complete Russian campaign before winter.

7 British forces enter Addis Ababa. They now have taken possession of all Italian East Africa.

9 U.S. undertakes defense of Greenland in return for the right to set up military bases there.

11 F.D.R. extends U.S. patrol zone in North Atlantic to longitude

26 degrees, nation's new "sea frontier."

13 Germans capture Belgrade. Russians sign treaty of friendship with Japanese Empire.

16 First lend-lease shipments of food arrive in Britain in time to prevent a critical shortage.

17 Yugoslav Government surrenders to Germans, but partisan guerrillas continue resistance in mountains.

18 British position at Mount Olympus becomes untenable, and a pullback to Thermopylae is ordered. Admiral Kimmel in Pearl Harbor proposes to Washington that a higher priority be given to Wake Island.

19 German flanking movement across Pindus Mountains compels British to retreat again. It is now obvious that Greece cannot be held.

20 Rommel's forces encircle Tobruk, which endures siege with support from Royal Navy.

23 Greeks surrender to Germans, and King George II flees to Crete. British problem now is to save as much of the expeditionary force as possible.

26–27 Main body of British force embarks from southern Greek ports in a "little Dunkirk." Some forty-three thousand get away; twelve thousand are killed or taken prisoner. German troops march into Athens.

29 Rommel's North African drive eastward grinds to a halt at the Egyptian border. He has outrun his

supplies in "a tactician's paradise and a quartermaster's hell."

MAY

2 British forces enter Iraq after Baghdad regime invites Hitler to send them military aid.

8 R.A.F. steps up assault on major German cities, hurls thirteen hundred planes against Hamburg and Bremen.

9 British advance through Iraq.

10 Rudolf Hess, Hitler's deputy, lands by parachute in Scotland after a solo flight from Germany. He brings a private peace plan to make Germany and Britain allies against Bolshevism. Churchill has him imprisoned; Hitler disowns him. *Luftwaffe* deluges London with incendiary bombs, starting thousands of fires and badly damaging, among hundreds of other buildings hit, the House of Commons. Londoners do not know it, but this is almost the last of the Blitz. Henceforth the *Luftwaffe* will be occupied in the east.

20 Germans invade Crete by means of gliders and parachutes —first major airborne invasion in history.

21 U-boat sinks American merchant ship *Robin Moor* off Brazil.

24 *Bismarck* sinks *Hood* after broadside gun duel between two of world's mightiest warships. British naval units converge on battle area off Greenland and begin chase of *Bismarck*.

25 *Bismarck* "disappears" in North

Atlantic after breaking through cordon of British vessels.

26 British plane spots *Bismarck* racing for French coast.

27 British air and sea forces sink *Bismarck* off Brest. F.D.R. declares Americans now face an "unlimited national emergency."

31 British forces in Iraq bomb airfields and enter Baghdad.

JUNE

1 British complete the evacuation of troops from Crete.

4 The "Woodchopper of Doorn" dies in Holland—former Kaiser Wilhelm II, who fled into exile on German defeat in World War I.

8 Free French, with British support, invade Syria in effort to break Vichy power in key region of Middle East.

16 U.S. closes German consular offices and orders Hitler's officials to leave the country.

17 Free French take Damascus. Auchinleck replaces Wavell in command of North Africa forces.

22 Hitler unleashes tremendous offensive against Soviet Union along two-thousand-mile front from Baltic Sea to Black Sea. In the north, Leeb commands twenty-nine divisions in drive from East Prussia toward Leningrad. In the center, Bock commands fifty divisions in drive from Poland toward Moscow. In the south, Rundstedt commands forty-one divisions in drive from Poland toward Ukraine. Nearly three thousand planes support invasion. Russians have about

the same number of troops and five thousand planes, but German blitzkrieg shatters defense in all three sectors of the battlefront.

24 Roosevelt promises American aid to Soviet Union.

JULY

1 Germans occupy Riga, capital of Latvia, and continue victorious advance along invasion front.

2 Japanese military forces take over French Indochina.

7 U.S. forces land in Iceland to relieve British troops there.

12 Vichy forces in Syria capitulate to de Gaulle's Free French troops. Russia and Britain agree on mutual aid pact against Germany.

16 Germans capture Smolensk on "Napoleonic road" to Moscow.

26 F.D.R. halts trade with Japan, freezes Japanese assets in U.S., nationalizes Filipino forces under MacArthur, commander in chief in Far East.

AUGUST

2 U.S. begins to ship supplies to Russia as impression grows that Stalin is facing disaster.

7 Stalin makes himself supreme commander of Soviet military.

9–12 F.D.R. and Churchill hold their first meeting aboard ship in Argentia Bay, Newfoundland.

14 Atlantic Charter, drawn up by F.D.R. and Churchill, is published. It calls for defeat of the Axis powers, and self-determination of nations as an international principle.

17 F.D.R. warns Japanese ambassador that U.S. will act if Japan attempts domination of Far East.

22 German Occupation authorities warn all Parisians to consider themselves hostages: multiple executions will follow every time a German soldier is killed by Resistance members.

25 British and Russian forces co-operate in invasion of Iran. Churchill and Stalin agree that the Nazi intrigues in Teheran must be stopped. Both want supply line through Iran to be kept open. Churchill wants to end the threat to India.

26 Russians, in full retreat before Rundstedt's advance, blow up great power dam on Dnieper River.

SEPTEMBER

1 Nazis intensify anti-Semitic campaign by forcing all Jews to wear yellow star on their clothing.

4 Germans throw siege lines around city of Leningrad.

11 F.D.R. announces "shoot on sight" order to U.S. naval forces finding Axis vessels in American waters.

16 Iranian Shah abdicates under British and Russian pressure. U.S. Navy aids Royal Navy by undertaking convoy duty in eastern Atlantic, assuming responsibility as far as Iceland.

19 Germans take Kiev, capital of the Ukraine, as Rundstedt advances across Dnieper River.

21 Germans isolate Crimea by breakthrough to Sea of Azov.

24 Stalin endorses Atlantic Charter, including provision about self-determination for all nations everywhere.

29 Harriman and Beaverbrook arrive in Moscow to find out from Stalin how Russians can be helped in the face of the German blitzkrieg.

OCTOBER

1 Moscow protocol provides for U.S.–British aid to Russia—war supplies for nine months.

2 Germans launch frontal drive on Moscow.

8 Germans capture Orel.

12 Germans capture Bryansk. Stalin issues order for the removal of most Government departments to Kuibyshev, on the Volga River.

13 Germans capture Vyazma.

14 German advance to within sixty miles of Moscow. Muscovites hasten defenses of their city.

16 Axis troops capture Odessa, seaport on the Black Sea.

17 U-boat damages U.S. destroyer *Kearny* off Iceland.

18 General Hideki Tojo becomes Premier of Japan, representing ambitions of the war party in the Japanese military establishment.

20 Stalin declares Moscow under a state of siege, but the German advance stalls against defense devised by General Zhukov.

25 Germans capture Kharkov, important Ukrainian industrial center.

31 U-562 torpedoes and sinks U.S. destroyer *Ruben James* off Iceland, with a loss of 115 Americans, more than two thirds of all aboard.

NOVEMBER

7 Stalin rouses the Russians with his "Holy Russia" speech. U.S. grants Soviet Union a billion dollars in lend-lease. Admiral Yamamoto sets date for Pearl Harbor attack—December 7.

9 Germans take Tikhvin, almost isolating Leningrad.

14 U-boat torpedoes British carrier *Ark Royal* off Gibraltar.

15 Germans begin siege of Sevastopol, Crimean bastion.

16 Germans capture Kerch on the Black Sea peninsula and resume their attempt to take Moscow.

17 Grew warns from Tokyo of possible Japanese sneak attack. U.S. repeals restrictive sections of Neutrality Act, allows American merchant ships to arm and carry cargoes to belligerent ports. Japanese Ambassador Nomura and special envoy Kurusu initiate talks with Secretary Hull in Washington. Demands of Premier Tojo include lifting U.S. embargo, stopping aid to China, and ending U.S. naval expansion in the western Pacific.

22 Germans capture Rostov on Don.

26 Hull offers Nomura and Kurusu renewed American trade in return for an end to Japanese aggression in Far East. None of them knows about Japanese task force

that set sail the day before from Kurile Islands. Admiral Nagumo has two battleships, six carriers, three cruisers, and nine destroyers. His military objective is the American base at Pearl Harbor.

27 Washington sends warning to U.S. Pacific commanders that war may be imminent.

DECEMBER

2 Tokyo rejects Hull's proposals and sends Nagumo radio message: "Climb Mount Niitaka." It means: "Attack Pearl Harbor."

3 Nagumo's task force crosses international date line, four days away from Pearl Harbor.

6 Roosevelt sends personal message to Emperor Hirohito, urging him to use his authority to keep the peace in the Pacific. At sea, Nagumo raises symbol of victory over his flagship—the banner of the Japanese Navy in 1905, when it had defeated the Russian Navy in the Battle of Tsushima, key victory in the rise of the Japanese Empire. Zhukov launches Russian counteroffensive after stopping the second German drive toward Moscow.

7 Japanese begin, at 7:55 A.M., sudden, devastating assault on Pearl Harbor. In less than two hours, planes and submarines from Nagumo's task force destroy or badly damage six American battleships, many smaller vessels, and over three hundred planes. Toll in American lives is about 2,400. Nagumo loses twenty-nine planes and four midget submarines. He leaves Pearl Harbor battered, U.S.

navy crippled, American people shaken by the catastrophe.

8 Roosevelt, in an address that terms December 7 "a date which will live in infamy," asks Congress to declare war on Japan. Congress does so with only one dissenting vote. Japanese planes bomb Guam and Wake Island installations. In Southeast Asia, Japanese forces invade Malaya and Thailand.

9 Japanese land on Gilbert Islands.

10 Philippine airfields are wrecked as Japanese forces land on Bataan Island off coast. Japanese storm ashore on Guam, force small American garrison to surrender. Makin Island in Gilberts is seized. Auchinleck's Eighth Army, counterattacking against Rommel's Afrika Korps, relieves besieged Tobruk.

10 British battle cruiser *Repulse* and battleship *Prince of Wales*, sailing without air cover, are sunk by Japanese planes off Malaya. Japanese attempt landing on Wake Island, are thrown back by Marine detachment. Destroyers lost in attack are first Japanese surface craft sunk by U.S. naval forces during the war. Hitler and Mussolini declare war on the U.S., keeping their promise to their Japanese ally.

12 In wide-ranging bombing attacks across Philippines, Japanese planes destroy American air power there. Japanese General Homma sends an assault wave ashore on Luzon, prelude to full-scale landings.

17 Admiral Chester Nimitz is named commander of U.S. Pacific Fleet, replacing Admiral Kimmel, who, along with General Walter Short, is relieved of his command and charged with "dereliction of duty."

19 Congress extends military draft to men aged 20 to 44. F.D.R. sets up Office of Censorship under Byron Price. Hitler, furious over Zhukov winter offensive, fires several generals and makes himself commander in chief of the German armed forces.

20 Admiral Ernest King becomes commander of U.S. Navy.

21 U.S. and British military men meet in Washington to plan common prosecution of the war. They set up Combined Chiefs of Staff, reaffirm "Germany first" policy, and earmark enough men and matériel to deal with Japanese in the Pacific.

22 Churchill arrives in Washington for talks with Roosevelt and other American leaders. Japanese land in force on Luzon and advance rapidly against MacArthur's outnumbered American and Filipino defenders.

23 MacArthur begins pulling his men back into Bataan. His strategy is to establish a short defense line across the peninsula. Wake Island falls to Japanese landing forces. Free French forces take over St. Pierre and Miquelon Islands.

24 British Eighth Army captures Benghazi in continuing offensive against Rommel's Afrika Korps.

25 British forces in Hong Kong surrender to Japanese. Russians establish bridgehead in Crimea.

26 Churchill addresses Congress, says war will be won in spite of almost daily defeats, expresses hope that Americans and British will "walk together side by side in majesty, in justice, and in peace."

27 Rationing begins in U.S. with automobile tires.

28 Manila, an open city, is savagely bombed by Japanese planes.

31 Nimitz assumes duties of his new naval command at Pearl Harbor.

1942

JANUARY

2 Japanese enter Manila. MacArthur now has his army entrenched on Bataan Peninsula.

11 Japanese take Kuala Lumpur and continue rapid advance down Malay Peninsula. British are in headlong retreat before an enemy they have completely underestimated. Japanese also begin penetration of Dutch East Indies with a landing on the island of Celebes near Borneo.

13 F.D.R. sets up War Production Board with Donald M. Nelson as chairman. His orders are to mobilize nation's resources for war.

20 Russians capture Mozhaisk in continuing winter offensive. In Berlin, Reinhard Heydrich tells secret conference of Nazi party leaders of Hitler's latest anti-Semitic decree—"Final Solution" through mass murder in concentration camps already established at places such as Auschwitz and Belsen.

21 Twenty-one American nations in Rio agree to break relations with Germany, Italy, and Japan. Rommel sends motorized reconnaissance in force through British lines near El Agheila. British advance units begin pell-mell retreat in fear of being cut off.

23 Japanese take Rabaul on New Britain in Bismarck Archipelago, and Kieta on Bougainville in Solomons.

24 Presidential commission headed by Supreme Court Justice Owen J. Roberts issues report after inquiry into circumstances surrounding Pearl Harbor disaster. Verdict: Kimmel and Short mainly responsible through failure to take adequate defense measures after warnings that Japanese might attack. Rommel makes strong armored thrust at Auchinleck's defensive line.

24–27 Battle of Macassar Strait is fought off Borneo. Allied sea and air forces hit enemy convoy in first sea battle in Pacific.

25 Japanese land on New Ireland in Bismarck Archipelago.

26 Japanese put more troops ashore on Bougainville.

27–31 Rommel wins big tank battle, forces British retreat, captures Benghazi.

28 F.D.R. sets up Office of Civilian Defense under Fiorello La Guardia, mayor of New York.

30 F.D.R. sets up Office of Price Administration under Leon Henderson, to control rents in defense areas and maintain ceilings on commodity costs.

31 Japanese advance in Southeast Asia retains momentum. In Burma, British pull back from Moulmein (city of Kipling's "pagoda"), and in Malaya, they abandon peninsula, taking refuge on island of Singapore, which seems safe after destruction of causeway.

FEBRUARY

1 U.S. task forces bomb and strafe enemy installations in Gilberts and Marshalls.

7 F.D.R. sets up War Shipping Administration under Emory Land. Germans appoint Norwegian head of occupation regime—Vidkun Quisling, whose name has become a synonym for traitor.

9 First formal meeting of Joint Chiefs of Staff is held in Washington: General Marshall (Army), General Arnold (Army Air Corps), Admiral Stark (Chief of Naval Operations) and Admiral King (Commander in Chief).

10 Japanese troops pour into Singapore after repairing causeway. Defense blunder is now apparent —guns point to sea, leaving the island's landward side exposed to enemy assault.

15 General Yamashita receives surrender of Singapore and captures some seventy thousand prisoners, entire British force in the fortress.

19 F.D.R. orders relocation of enemy aliens, which results in transfer of one hundred thousand nisei Japanese from West Coast to interior.

20 Japanese overrun Timor Island in Dutch East Indies.

23 Japanese submarine shells oil refinery near Santa Barbara, California—obviously a gesture rather than a serious attack.

27–March 1 Battle of the Java Sea results in loss of entire Allied-Australian - British - Dutch - U.S. fleet of cruisers and destroyers.

28 Japanese land on Java.

MARCH

3 Washington conference of U.S. and British leaders divides the western Pacific. From Sumatra west will be Britain's responsibility. East of the line will be America's responsibility.

6 Japanese capture Batavia, capital of Dutch East Indies.

7 Japanese advance through Burma forces British back from Rangoon.

8 Japanese land at Salamaua and Lae on New Guinea.

9 Admiral King becomes Chief of Naval Operations as well as Commander in Chief.

10 Dutch, British, and American troops on Java surrender unconditionally to Japanese.

11 MacArthur leaves Philippines on direct order from Roosevelt. New American commander is Lieutenant General Jonathan Wainwright.

17 MacArthur arrives in Darwin, Australia, to take command of Allied forces in southwest Pacific. Asked about the Philippines, he replies: "I shall return."

20 Russians capture Rzhev.

22 Sir Stafford Cripps arrives in India for talks with Mahatma Gandhi.

26–27 British commandos raid St. Nazaire on French coast, blow up docks and battleship berths.

31 India Congress rejects Dominion status after war, tells Cripps that it wants "independence now."

APRIL

2 *Luftwaffe* begins aerial campaign against Malta, key island between Europe and North Africa.

3 Admiral Nimitz receives central Pacific command, balancing MacArthur's command in western Pacific.

8 Rommel resumes probing operations in preparation for showdown battle.

9 Wainwright withdraws to Corregidor as Bataan falls to Japanese. Bataan Death March begins for over twelve thousand Americans, sixty thousand Filipinos. Ten thousand of them will die from the ordeal.

10 Japanese shell Corregidor.

14 Vice-President Henry Wallace becomes head of Board of Economic Warfare, which is assigned control of stockpiles essential to the war effort.

18 Colonel James Doolittle leads sixteen B-25's from the carrier *Hornet* on bombing raids over Tokyo, Yokohama, Kobe, and Nagoya. Most of the attacking planes fly on to China. MacArthur takes command of southwest Pacific. F.D.R. sets up War Manpower Commission under Paul V. McNutt to channel men (and women) into most effective positions.

26 Britain and Russia sign twenty-year treaty of friendship and aid.

28 Japanese increase tempo of their shelling of Corregidor.

29 Hitler and Mussolini meet at Berchtesgaden to plan further moves in the Mediterranean.

30 Japanese capture Lashio in Burma and close Burma Road.

MAY

3 Japanese capture Mandalay in Burma, and Tulagi and Gavutu in the Solomons. Their island strategy is to encircle the Coral Sea.

5 Japanese, having hammered Corregidor with continual artillery bombardment, cross over from Bataan and land in force.

6 Facing overwhelming numbers, with ammunition running out, and hoping to spare his men any further suffering, Wainwright surrenders Corregidor to Lt. Gen. Homma.

7–8 Battle of the Coral Sea is waged entirely by planes against ships; for first time in history, surface vessels fight without ever seeing one another. U.S. suffers heaviest loss when carrier *Lexington* goes down, but Japanese invasion convoy is turned back from Port Moresby, New Guinea.

12 Russians attack near Kharkov.

15 U.S. establishes Women's Auxiliary Army Corps under command of Colonel Oveta Culp Hobby.

17 Germans counterattack against Russians in Kharkov area.

18 U.S. forces with artillery and tanks land in Northern Ireland.

20 "Vinegar Joe" Stilwell arrives in India after trek with Chinese troops out of Burma. He tells newsmen: "We got a hell of a beating."

26 Powerful Japanese task force, built around eight carriers, sails from Inland Sea of Japan under command of Yamamoto. Nagumo, of Pearl Harbor attack, is in command of Yamamoto's carrier strike force. The strategy is to take Midway Island by surprise. But U.S. having broken Japanese code, knows about the operation. Nimitz orders admirals Spruance and Fletcher to rendezvous with their carrier forces near Midway. In North Africa, Rommel launches strong attack, spearheaded by tank units.

27 Heydrich, Nazi gauleiter of Czechoslovakia, is shot by members of the Czech Resistance.

28–30 Big tank battle develops between Rommel and Auchinleck.

30 R.A.F. devastates Cologne in massive night raid involving over 1,000 planes.

JUNE

2 Spruance and Fletcher rendezvous northeast of Midway. R.A.F. bombs Krupp steel and armament works in Essen.

3–6 Battle of Midway is fought, and proves to be turning point of Pacific war. U.S. loses carrier *Yorktown*, but four Japanese carriers and a heavy cruiser are destroyed. Yamamoto breaks off and withdraws. Midway ends Japanese offensive at sea.

10 In reprisal for assassination of Heydrich, Nazis destroy Lidice in Czechoslovakia. They execute every man, carry off the women and children, and level the town.

11 U.S. pledges lend-lease to Soviet Union to extent considered by President in national interest.

12 Japanese land on American island of Attu in Aleutians. With Kiska, occupied by enemy during assault at Midway, Attu marks westward limit of Japan's Pacific conquests. U.S. bombers attack Ploesti oil fields in Rumania. *Luftwaffe* surprises two British convoys in Mediterranean and, in running fight lasting two days, sinks fifteen out of seventeen ships.

13 F.D.R. sets up Office of War Information under Elmer Davis, and Office of Strategic Services under William J. Donovan.

17 Rommel forces British to retreat from Tobruk.

19 Rommel forces Auchinleck to pull his Eighth Army all the way back to the Egyptian frontier.

21 Tobruk falls after a brief siege. Rommel captures twenty-five thousand men and huge quantities of supplies. The invasion of Malta is postponed.

25 Rommel presses on into Egypt. Axis leaders look to a great triumph in the Nile Valley almost any day.

25–27 Churchill and Roosevelt confer in Washington. They agree to attack Hitler first in North Africa instead of on the Continent, and also reach an accord on going ahead with atom bomb research.

27 FBI Director J. Edgar Hoover reveals arrest of eight German saboteurs who landed from submarines on coasts of Florida and Long Island.

28 Auchinleck establishes defensive line at El Alamein.

30 Rommel's momentum runs out within a hundred miles of the Egyptian city of Alexandria.

JULY

1 Germans capture Sevastopol.

9 German Army Group South is divided into two sections. One section is to seize Rostov and continue through the Caucasus; the other is to attack and capture Stalingrad. This is the beginning of the German catastrophe at Stalingrad.

15 Rommel launches a last-ditch drive to break British line.

21 Rommel's drive fails. He protests lack of reinforcements and supplies.

22 Japanese land at Buna Mission on New Guinea's northern coast.

AUGUST

4 Churchill arrives in Cairo to look over desert war first hand.

6 Operation Torch gets a commanding general: Dwight Eisenhower. Gandhi prepares civil-disobedience campaign unless India is accepted as "independent partner" of Britain.

7 U.S. Marines invade Guadalcanal in Solomons and begin first American land offensive of the war.

9 Japanese sink four Allied cruisers in Battle of Savo Island and threaten to seal off Guadalcanal. Germans capture Maikop oil fields in Caucasus, one of Hitler's prime targets. British imprison Gandhi, and rioting breaks out in Indian cities. Units of Royal Navy arrive in Mediterranean for Operation Pedestal—defense of convoys to Malta.

10 Churchill announces from Cairo sweeping changes in Middle East command. Alexander gets top command of Middle East forces. Montgomery will take over the Eighth Army.

11 *Gestapo* executes ninety-nine hostages in Paris in retaliation for Resistance attacks on Germans.

12–16 Churchill confers with Stalin in Moscow. Stalin wants a second front in Europe, but Churchill says North Africa has been chosen because cross-Channel attack is not yet a feasible operation.

13 General Leslie Groves is given command of Manhattan Project —development of atomic bomb.

18 Japanese begin landing reinforcements on Guadalcanal, the first of those who will challenge the Marines in a savage battle for the island.

19 Six thousand commandos, mainly Canadian, raid Dieppe, only to run into murderous German fire. Within a few hours, over half the invaders are killed, wounded, or taken prisoner.

20 Germans cross Don River where it curves east toward the Volga, only some forty miles from Stalingrad.

22 Germans open full offensive toward Stalingrad. Initial bombardment destroys more than half of city's buildings.

23 Germans break through to Volga north of Stalingrad.

30 Germans reach outskirts of Stalingrad in fierce fighting.

SEPTEMBER

1 Seabees land on Guadalcanal to develop the airfield.

3 Germans break through to Volga south of Stalingrad.

15 U.S. carrier *Wasp* is torpedoed off Guadalcanal.

21 Violent fighting rages in suburbs of Stalingrad. Russians advance northeast of that city.

25 Hitler fires Franz Halder and appoints Kurt Zeitzler Chief of General Staff. Zeitzler finds headquarters atmosphere "not only weird but positively incredible." Hitler blames setbacks in Russia on his generals.

OCTOBER

1 Russians advance southeast of Stalingrad. Their strategy is becoming apparent to Nazi generals. They will try to hold Stalingrad while their forces in north and south push toward a juncture behind German Sixth Army.

5 General Friedrich Paulus keeps attacking in Stalingrad. Battle is one of savage man-to-man duels fought in the wreckage of the city. Germans call it "Rat War."

11–12 U.S. forces win Battle of Cape Esperance in Solomons, sinking one Japanese carrier and four destroyers. Victory keeps supply lines open to Guadalcanal, where Japanese are attempting to break through to the American airfield.

14 General Chuikov calls this day "the bloodiest and most ferocious in the whole Battle of Stalingrad." Both sides suffer terrible losses as Germans open assault to capture tractor factory in northern part of city.

23 Montgomery opens Battle of El Alamein against Afrika Korps. Rommel is in Germany on sick leave.

25 British armor makes deep penetration into German line—"real crisis in the battle," according to Montgomery. Rommel returns to find his troops shattered and confused.

26 U.S. forces engage Japanese in Battle of Santa Cruz in Solomons. U.S. carrier *Hornet* is lost. Only two Japanese destroyers are sunk, but two carriers and two battleships are damaged.

27 Montgomery wins furious tank battle with Afrika Korps.

NOVEMBER

2 Montgomery launches full-scale attack in bid to turn the tide and force Rommel to retreat.

3 Hitler orders Rommel to "hold at all costs," but Rommel does not have the men or supplies to meet Montgomery's massive assault.

4 Montgomery makes major breakthrough at El Alamein. General von Thoma, Rommel's deputy, is captured. Rommel orders general retreat back from Egypt.

6 British take thousands of Axis prisoners as Afrika Korps continues headlong retreat into Libya.

7 Marine Corps commandant approves establishment of women's reserve.

8 Operation Torch begins as General Eisenhower sends his men ashore in North Africa. Admiral Cunningham of Royal Navy shepherds 850 ships to their destinations—biggest amphibious operation up to that time. R.A.F. provides air cover. Landings are made in Algeria and Morocco, mainly at Algiers, Oran, and Casablanca. Pétain breaks off diplomatic relations with U.S.

9 Hitler tells Nazi meeting that Stalingrad is his "except for a few enemy positions still holding out." In Stalingrad, Paulus suffers fearful losses as his Sixth Army grinds

slowly forward. Germans begin rushing troops into Tunisia.

10 Admiral Jean François Darlan, Vichy representative in North Africa, agrees to armistice and orders his troops to cease hostilities. Hitler scraps his agreement with Pétain and sends German forces into Unoccupied France.

12–15 Naval Battle of Guadalcanal is strategic victory for U.S. as Japanese efforts to shell Marine positions on Guadalcanal and to land reinforcements are foiled in a series of night actions. Among U.S. losses is cruiser *Juneau* with five Sullivan brothers.

13 Montgomery captures Tobruk, the last time this fortress city on coast changes hands. Afrika Korps retreats into Tripolitania. Rommel is now trapped between Allied armies advancing from two directions.

15 Darlan names General Henri Giraud commander of French armed forces in North Africa. Eisenhower's men move into Tunisia.

16 De Gaulle says in London that he will not accept "a Vichy regime in North Africa." Allied drive into Tunisia gains momentum.

17 Pétain appoints Pierre Laval his deputy and successor.

19 Russian forces north and south of Stalingrad launch offensives in beginning of gigantic pincers movement around the German Sixth Army.

20 Montgomery captures Benghazi.

22 Paulus informs Hitler that he is now encircled by Russian forces. Germans at Stalingrad have to be supplied by air. Göring tells Hitler this is possible.

24 Hitler forbids Paulus to break out of Stalingrad encirclement and link up with German forces to the west.

27 French crews scuttle ships at Toulon naval base just in time to keep them from Germans who have overrun Unoccupied France as far as Mediterranean.

DECEMBER

1 Darlan becomes chief of state in French North Africa.

2 At University of Chicago, Enrico Fermi achieves first nuclear chain reaction, key to exploitation of atomic power, development of atomic bomb.

12 Marshal Erich von Manstein launches offensive to break through to Stalingrad and save the Sixth Army.

18 Manstein, violating Hitler's instructions, orders Paulus to break out and meet him. Paulus refuses to disobey the *Führer*'s orders.

24 Assassin murders Darlan in Algiers. Giraud becomes high commissioner of French Africa, but de Gaulle still will not accept new regime.

25 Russians stop Manstein's offensive. Paulus and his entire Sixth Army are now trapped in Stalingrad.

1943

JANUARY

2 Germans begin withdrawal from Caucasus as failure at Stalingrad threatens their flank.

5 Germans begin to pull back from Stalingrad area, conceding destruction of Sixth Army.

8 Marshal Rokossovski urges Paulus to surrender. Paulus refuses.

9 U.S. and Australian troops begin drive on Japanese-held Buna and Gona in New Guinea.

10 At Stalingrad Russians begin final drive to destroy German Sixth Army, with opening barrage from 5,000 cannon.

14 Roosevelt makes surprise flight to Casablanca, Morocco, for meeting with Churchill and other leaders.

14–24 Casablanca Conference decides future war strategy. Sicily is to be invaded, air offensive against Germany stepped up, Japanese checked in Pacific until general offensive can be mounted by Allies. Controversial demand for "unconditional surrender" of Axis is agreed on. De Gaulle is persuaded to shake hands with Giraud when they meet during the conference.

18 Moscow announces Soviet forces have broken through to Leningrad, ending the longest siege of the war. Germans are retreating toward Baltic States.

19 Paulus holds conference of corps commanders in Stalingrad.

They agree that their situation is hopeless.

24 Paulus, describing pitiful condition of Sixth Army, asks Hitler for permission to surrender. "Surrender is forbidden," Hitler replies. Montgomery takes Tripoli in westward advance.

27 Germans are now definitely retreating in Russia for fear of having more armies cut off.

30 R.A.F. hits Berlin with big daytime raid, start of massive air assault on German capital. Hitler promotes Paulus to field marshal.

31 Russians burst through to Sixth Army headquarters. Paulus surrenders with most of survivors.

FEBRUARY

2 Last small pocket of Germans in Stalingrad surrenders, bringing the battle to a complete end. Only some 90,000 Germans remain from original 300,000 in Sixth Army. Hitler berates Paulus for not committing suicide. Paulus later repays the *Führer* by denouncing him in German-language broadcasts from Moscow. As Paulus says, Hitler doomed the Sixth Army by forbidding retreat, and allowed the Russians to win their biggest victory of the war.

4 British Eight Army crosses border into Tunisia. Italian African empire is finished.

5 Churchill meets Eisenhower in Algiers for briefing on military and political situation.

6 Mussolini fires Count Ciano and personally takes over running office of foreign minister.

8 Russians capture Kursk.

9 Japanese abandon Guadalcanal after defeat by Americans in long, bitter jungle warfare.

12 Churchill reports to Commons on agreements with Roosevelt, reveals that Eisenhower has been appointed to command all Allied forces in North Africa, with Alexander as his deputy and British Marshal Tedder in charge of combined Allied air forces.

14 Rommel drives Americans back from Kasserine Pass in Tunisia. Russians capture Rostov.

16 Russians capture Kharkov.

19 Americans retake Kasserine Pass after counterattack.

22 Afrika Korps begins new offensive in Kasserine Pass. Manstein halts Russian winter drive and begins limited attacks in order to keep his line from disintegrating.

23 Eisenhower commits enough men to halt Rommel's advance.

25 Americans recover lost ground in Kasserine Pass and push on.

MARCH

1–3 In Battle of the Bismarck Sea, Allied planes from New Guinea destroy all eight transports and four of the eight escorting destroyers of a Japanese troop convoy.

2 R.A.F. hits Berlin with another in series of devastating raids.

9 Japanese land on New Georgia

in Solomons and entrench themselves around Munda.

10 Germans attack near Kharkov.

14 Germans capture Kharkov.

16 Russians attack near Smolensk.

19 Americans, striking from Algeria, take El Guettar in Tunisia.

20 Biggest convoy battle of Battle of the Atlantic ends with twenty-one Allied ships lost to U-boats operating in wolf packs.

21 Russians capture Belgorod.

23 Montgomery breaks Rommel's Mareth Line in Tunisia.

28 Afrika Korps abandons Mareth Line as British advance.

29 British occupy Mareth Line.

APRIL

7 Eisenhower's forces link up with Montgomery's Eighth Army in Tunisia.

11 Americans retake Faïd Pass, from which they had retreated during Rommel's counterattack.

12 Montgomery captures Sousse, last German-held supply port on Tunisian east coast.

13 Germans claim to have found at Katyn, Poland, mass graves of Polish officers murdered by Russians. Soviets claim Nazis carried out the executions. Responsibility is still subject of debate.

18 Admiral Yamamoto is killed when his plane is shot down over Solomons. American intelligence knew about the flight, and American pilots on Guadalcanal were ordered to attack.

23 Russians retake Kharkov.

26 Stalin breaks relations with Polish government-in-exile because of alleged anti-Russian conspiracy with Germans.

MAY

6 Rising of Jews in Warsaw Ghetto is followed by Nazi massacre.

7 In Tunisia, British take Tunis, and Americans take Bizerte.

11 U.S. forces land on Attu, against desperate Japanese resistance. Churchill arrives in Washington.

12 Rommel flies back to Germany, leaving Afrika Korps to surrender.

12–25 "Trident" conference (in Washington) agrees on invasion of Italy after Sicily. Tentative date for France invasion and plans for stepping up war in Pacific are discussed.

13 Last Germans surrender in Tunisia, ending all Axis resistance in Africa.

19 Churchill addresses Congress, says Allies have been aided by "military intuition of Corporal Hitler," and promises that when Hitler is finished, we shall "lay the cities of Japan in ashes."

22 Stalin dissolves Comintern as gesture to his Western allies.

30 Battle of Attu ends with island again in American hands.

JUNE

3 French Committee for National Liberation is formed. It includes de Gaulle in London and Giraud in North African territories.

11 Pantelleria, near Sicily, becomes first island ever to surrender to air and naval bombardment.

12 Lampedusa, another Mediterranean island, surrenders to Allies.

30 U.S. troops land on Rendova Island in New Georgia.

JULY

2 Allies capture Rendova.

4 Germans open offensive at Kursk salient, which is stopped and turned into retreat by Russian counteroffensive.

10 Invasion of Sicily begins as over two thousand vessels take part in landing 160,000 soldiers. Alexander is in charge; Patton and Montgomery are top field commanders. Americans land at Gela, British at Cape Passaro. Both forces establish beachheads.

11 Americans stop German counterattack and move inland.

12 British capture Syracuse.

15 F.D.R. sets up Board of Economic Warfare under Leo Crowley.

19 Allied planes raid Naples and hit pin-pointed military objectives in Rome. U.S. planes bomb Japanese Kurile Islands. Hitler and Mussolini meet in Feltre to discuss their crisis.

22 Patton captures Palermo.

24–August 3 R.A.F. hits Hamburg with four attacks so shattering that Germans refer to results as "the catastrophe."

25 Fascist Grand Council forces Mussolini to resign, and he is at once arrested. Badoglio becomes head of Italian Government.

28 Badoglio declares Fascist party dissolved and opens negotiations for immediate armistice.

AUGUST

1 Japanese destroyer runs down and sinks PT-109 off New Georgia. Lieutenant John Fitzgerald Kennedy saves eleven of his thirteen men. U.S. bombers hit Ploesti oil fields and refineries in Rumania.

5 Admiral Spruance takes command of U.S. Fifth Fleet in preparation for great offensive against Japan.

6–7 Battle of Vella Gulf is defeat for Japanese, who are attempting to reinforce troops in Solomons. Allies take Munda on New Georgia.

15 U.S. and Canadian forces land on Kiska, find it deserted.

17 Roosevelt and Churchill arrive in Quebec for strategy talks. Sicilian campaign ends with American capture of Messina.

17–24 Quebec Conference decides that an American will command invasion of Continental Europe and a Briton will command the Southeast Asia theater. In Pacific, Gilberts and Marshalls are to be taken as start of full drive on Japan.

18 R.A.F. hits Peenemünde with raid that smashes rocket factories.

23 Russians retake Kharkov.

24 Lord Louis Mountbatten is appointed Supreme Allied Commander in Southeast Asia by Churchill.

27 Japanese, defeated on land and at sea, evacuate New Georgia.

29 Danish crews scuttle most ships in Copenhagen harbor. Germans seize King Christian as hostage.

SEPTEMBER

1 U.S. task force attacks Marcus Island, 1,100 miles from Tokyo.

3 British Eighth Army invades Italy by crossing Strait of Messina from Sicily. Armistice signed in Algiers ends hostilities with Badoglio regime.

7 General Maxwell Taylor makes secret visit to Rome and finds German strength too great for an Allied air drop on city.

8 Italy surrenders unconditionally.

9 General Mark Clark's Fifth Army lands at Salerno, thirty miles below Naples. British airborne troops seize naval base at Taranto. Iran joins the nations at war with Hitler's Germany.

10 Germans seize Rome and begin occupation of main cities in northern Italy, from Genoa to Trieste. Salamaua in New Guinea falls to Allies.

12 In daring exploit, Nazi commando Otto Skorzeny leads glider operation that rescues Mussolini

from captivity in Abruzzi Mountains. Allies cross Volturno River. Most of Italian Navy escapes from Nazi-held ports and joins the Allies.

13 Chiang Kai-shek is elected President of Chinese Republic.

15 Mussolini proclaims foundation of Republican Fascist party in alliance with Germans.

16 U.S. forces capture Lae on New Guinea, completing conquest of area vital to MacArthur as he develops his island offensive.

18 Mussolini founds Republican Fascist State in northern Italy. Germans retreat from Salerno.

21 House of Representatives adopts Fulbright Resolution calling for U.S. participation in international organization after war.

25 Russians capture Smolensk and Bryansk in continuing offensive.

OCTOBER

1 Fifth Army enters Naples.

7 Japanese complete evacuation of New Georgia in Solomons.

9 Yugoslav partisans attack Axis forces near Trieste. Partisans are led by Tito, a Communist who has seized control of anti-German guerrilla war in mountains.

12 Allied planes hit Rabaul with huge raid in support of operation against Bougainville.

13 Italy declares war on Germany. Portugal grants U.S. and Britain the right to use bases in Azores.

19 Marshal Kesselring, German

commander in Italy, pulls his forces back from Volturno as Allied troops advance.

NOVEMBER

1 U.S. Marines land on Bougainville and gain a beachhead about six hundred yards long in the face of savage Japanese resistance.

2 Battle of Empress Augusta Bay off Bougainville ends in Japanese defeat. Instead of Americans being isolated on one island, enemy forces in Solomons are cut off. MacArthur has cleared his flank for drive on Philippines.

5 Marines steadily break Japanese resistance on Bougainville, while Seabees rush work on airfield.

6 Russians capture Kiev, dislocating German line in Ukraine.

9 UNRRA is set up in Washington. United Nations Relief and Rehabilitation Administration will be joined by forty-eight nations before it ends in 1947. It will spend four billion dollars (more than half from U.S.) to help war-torn nations with food, medicine, machinery, and farm supplies.

19 Allied planes raid Gilberts and Marshalls as invasion fleet draws near. Nimitz wants these islands as he climbs "up the ladder" toward Japanese homeland by way of Gilberts, Marshalls, Marianas, Bonins.

20 U.S. forces land on Makin and Tarawa in Gilbert Islands. Makin falls quickly, but bloody battle develops on Tarawa. Assault wave suffers about one-third casualties as Japanese machine guns sweep the beachhead from pillboxes of concrete and logs. Marines attack pillboxes with grenades and flame throwers.

21 Reinforcements come ashore on Tarawa despite appalling losses. This is critical day of battle. Marines expand beachhead against Japanese soldiers who prefer to die rather than surrender.

22 Tanks break through Japanese defenses beyond Tarawa beachhead. Roosevelt, Churchill, and Chiang Kai-shek begin Cairo Conference.

23 Marines are now mopping up Japanese on Tarawa.

24 Battle of Tarawa ends. Small atoll has cost Americans about one thousand lives. Almost all of four thousand Japanese defenders are dead.

26 Cairo Conference ends with agreement to have MacArthur and Nimitz advance on converging lines toward Japan. A British-American campaign is to be mounted in Burma with a view to reopening the supply route to China. After the war, Japan is to be forced to give up all conquests made in this century.

28 First "Big Three" conference begins at Teheran with Roosevelt, Churchill, and Stalin attempting to coordinate offensives against Hitler. Stalin promises to join the war on Japan after Germany is defeated.

29 Roosevelt tells Teheran Conference that postwar world should be ordered by "Four Policemen" —U.S., Britain, Russia, and China.

30 Roosevelt and Churchill tell Stalin that Second Front is set for June.

DECEMBER

1 Teheran Conference ends in "preliminary agreement" about postwar political arrangements. Germany is to be partitioned.

6 In Cairo, Roosevelt tells Churchill he has decided that Eisenhower will command Operation Overlord, the cross-Channel assault on Hitler's "Fortress Europe." General Marshall was thought to have been the obvious choice, but Roosevelt decides he is too valuable at home as Chief of Staff. "I could not sleep at night with you out of the country," F.D.R. tells him.

7 Fifth Army enters town of Monte Cassino, below hill with famous Benedictine abbey.

21 Stilwell begins his campaign against Japanese in northern Burma.

24 Eisenhower is officially named commander of Overlord.

25 Allies stabilize a front along Garigliano and Sangro rivers.

26 U.S. forces land at Cape Gloucester in New Britain.

31 U.S. forces capture airfield and quickly gain control of New Britain.

1944

JANUARY

4 Fifth Army launches attack east of Monte Cassino. Allied commanders believe the abbey is being used as an enemy command post.

11 Indian troops take Maungdaw after resuming Burma campaign. Red Army enters Poland, and Moscow says 1939 border will remain.

15 Russians open new offensive in Leningrad and Baltic area.

16 Eisenhower arrives in Britain to begin planning for Operation Overlord. His first task is to set up interlocking command structure of Allied officers.

20 Russians capture Novgorod.

21 Eisenhower holds first meeting of SHAEF—Supreme Headquarters Allied Expeditionary Force. He is Supreme Commander. His subordinates are: Arthur Tedder, Deputy Supreme Commander (British); Walter B. Smith, Chief of Staff (American); Bernard Montgomery, operational command (British); Omar Bradley, U.S. ground forces (American); Bertram Ramsey, naval forces (British); Harold Stark, U.S. naval forces (American); Trafford Leigh-Mallory, air forces (British); Carl Spaatz, U.S. air forces (American).

22 Allied forces make amphibious landing at Anzio, south of Rome. Pause to consolidate beachhead allows Kesselring to bring up forces around perimeter. Invaders are pinned down by artillery fire. Long, costly stalemate ensues.

29 U.S. task forces begin wide-ranging attacks on Japanese in Marshall Islands. Stalin announces Moscow-Leningrad area has been cleared of Germans.

30 Germans throw back attempt to widen Anzio beachhead and capture hundreds of Americans.

31 U.S. forces land in Marshall Islands, of which Kwajalein is the prize. Kwajalein is scene of utter destruction after constant bombardment by planes and ships. But Japanese are dug in and wage bitter defensive battle.

FEBRUARY

2 Russian forces in Estonia start campaign against Nazis in Latvia.

3 U.S. forces capture Namur and Roi in Marshall Islands.

4 Nimitz takes control of Marshall Islands as "military governor."

6 Battle of Kwajalein ends in annihilation of Japanese defenders. Allied command admits that the Anzio attack is stalled. German force Allies back on Cassino front.

10 New Guinea's Huon Peninsula falls to U.S. and Australian troops. New Britain is declared safely under Allied control.

14 Eisenhower takes charge of all Second Front operations. Allied planes drop leaflets on Monte Cassino abbey warning everyone there that it will be bombed.

15 Allied bombing leaves Monte Cassino abbey in ruins.

17 Spruance commands task force in major air raid against Truk, Japanese Pacific stronghold. U.S. Marines land on Eniwetok in Marshall Islands and advance despite stiff Japanese resistance.

20–25 "Big Week," during which R.A.F. and U.S. Air Force put some 6,000 bombers and thousands of fighter planes over Germany and virtually wipe out the *Luftwaffe* as an effective force.

21 U.S. flag is raised over Eniwetok. Shake-up in Tokyo makes Tojo "military czar" of Japan.

22–23 U.S. task force hits Marianas and obtains photographs of installations on Saipan and Tinian.

23 Japanese commander at Rabaul receives order to withdraw.

29 Strategy of "island hopping" leads to American invasion of Los Negros in Admiralties. Islands to the rear can be ignored because of Japanese naval and air defeats.

MARCH

4 Zhukov directs offensive from the Ukraine into Poland.

6 American Flying Fortresses drop two thousand tons of bombs on Berlin.

11 Neutral Eire's Prime Minister de Valera rejects U.S. request to close Axis ministries in Dublin, which are considered intelligence hazard.

13 London suspends all travel between Ireland and Britain.

15 Allies launch big assault designed to break through at Cassino.

20 Russians enter Rumania. Germans send reinforcements to Hungary to try to stop Red tide in Balkans.

22 U.S. forces land at Hollandia in New Guinea. Japanese cross from Burma into India, push through Manipur toward Imphal. Heavy Allied raid hits Frankfurt am Main. Tempo of air assault grows in preparation for D-Day.

24 British Brig. Gen. Orde Wingate, colorful leader of Chindit raiders, is killed in plane crash while leading Burma campaign.

28 Allied commanders call Cassino assault "a temporary failure."

APRIL

4 American command announces occupation of ten more atolls in Marshall Islands without opposition.

5 Charles de Gaulle becomes head of Provisional Government of the French Republic. Russians capture Tarnopol, Nazi base in Poland.

10 Russians capture Odessa.

11 Russians begin drive to retake Crimea from Germans.

12 Allies throw thousands of planes into heaviest attacks yet on German cities. Doolittle commands powerful U.S. Eight Air Force in this operation.

18 Allies mount thirty-hour, wide-ranging air assault on airfields, railroads, and factories in Germany and France. Indian and British troops drive Japanese back in Manipur, India. Russians take Balaklava, scene of "charge of the Light Brigade" during Crimean War.

22 MacArthur goes ashore at Hollandia as his men advance from their beachhead on New Guinea.

MAY

5 British release Gandhi from detention. He is ill, and they are afraid he might die on their hands.

9 Russian troops take Sevastopol.

10 James Forrestal becomes Secretary of the Navy.

11 In Italy, Alexander directs assault on German Gustav Line. Japanese forces in China seize Peiping-Hankow railroad.

16 Eisenhower decides D-Day for Operation Overlord—June 5.

17 Allies smash Gustav Line. British throw bridgehead across turbulent Rapido River. Japanese battle Chinese in streets of Loyang. Tojo expands China conquest to deprive Americans of airfields from which to bomb Japan. Merrill's Marauders advance in Burma and seize Myitkyina airstrip.

18 Allies capture Monte Cassino after two months of fighting.

23 Clark's Fifth Army breaks out of Anzio beachhead.

25 Fifth Army links with Alexander's forces. Germans concede Italian coast from Anzio to Terracina.

27 U.S. forces land on Biak Island, off coast of New Guinea.

JUNE

3 Eisenhower postpones D-Day one day because of bad weather and rough seas predicted for June 5.

4 Allies enter Rome, which the Germans abandon rather than wage destructive battle. Eternal City is for the most part undamaged, except for bombed railroad yards.

5 Eisenhower makes crucial decision to launch Overlord the next day. Rundstedt commands German defense, with Rommel as his lieutenant. Allied planes smash French ports and German defenses in endless raids.

6 D-Day. Overlord begins. Terrific naval and air bombardment rocks French coast. Paratroopers drop behind German lines at 2 A.M. to isolate area to be hit by invasion forces. Six hundred warships and four thousand other vessels bring 155,000 men to assigned beaches. Assault wave goes ashore at 6:30 A.M., despite barbed wire, mine fields and enemy fire. Rundstedt is hampered by Hitler, who holds up counterattack until too late. British are on left, Americans on right, and both establish solid beachheads from mouth of Seine to Cotentin Peninsula.

8 British capture Bayeux, home of famous "Bayeux Tapestry" depicting another cross-Channel invasion, Norman conquest of England. Americans cut railroad to Cherbourg. Fifth Army is more

than thirty miles north of Rome.

10 Allies begin using first airfield in Normandy. Russians begin second Finnish campaign of war.

11 British and Americans link up beachheads into single continuous front seventy miles long and up to fifteen miles deep. U.S. task force bombards the Marianas.

12 By this date, Eisenhower has over three hundred thousand men and fifty thousand vehicles ashore.

13 First of Germany's V-1's— "Buzz Bombs"—fall on London.

14 U.S. task force raids Iwo Jima and nearby islands in deepest penetration of Japanese waters. De Gaulle visits Normandy areas held by Allies, first time he has been in France in four years.

15 U.S. forces land on Saipan and establish beachhead against tenacious Japanese defense. Admiral Halsey takes command of Third Fleet. American Superfortresses, flying from bases in China, begin air war against Japanese cities by bombing Kyushu.

17 Iceland declares itself independent republic, no longer under political control of Denmark.

18 V-1 launch sites in France are declared top priority targets for Allied bombing missions.

19 Japanese defenders of Saipan retire to limestone caves to make a suicidal last stand.

19–20 Battle of Philippine Sea prevents Japanese from sending reinforcements through to Marianas.

Americans sink three carriers, knock down some five hundred planes, and send the enemy into retreat. Admiral Spruance and Vice-Admiral Mitscher are the heroes of this crucial victory, which ends the threat of Japanese carrier attacks.

21 Germans hit London with V-1 number one thousand.

22 F.D.R. signs "GI Bill of Rights" authorizing benefits for veterans after war. Special clause provides money for education.

24–July 4 U.S. task force attacks Volcano and Bonin Islands, again bombarding Iwo Jima.

26 Bradley takes Cherbourg after breaking fierce German defense.

27 Republican Convention, meeting in Chicago, nominates Governor Thomas E. Dewey of New York as 1944 candidate for President. Allies capture Cherbourg. U.S. warships begin bombarding Guam in softening-up for invasion.

28 Montgomery launches attack on Caen on left of his beachhead.

30 In China, Japanese advance forces the American abandonment of air base at Hengyang. Russians break German line en route to Warsaw and Berlin.

JULY

2 Rundstedt is fired after telling Marshal Wilhelm Keitel, his superior: "End the war, you fools!" Allied directive orders Operations Anvil—invasion of southern France. Churchill argues for drive from Adriatic through Yugoslavia to Vienna in order to get there before the Russians. But Eisenhower considers this too risky.

3 Russians capture Minsk.

6 De Gaulle arrives in Washington for conference with Roosevelt. Marshal von Kluge arrives in France to take Rundstedt's command.

7 Allied planes smash Caen, where advance is being held up. Lt. Gen. Saito, commander on Saipan, commits suicide. Japanese civilians kill themselves by hundreds in mass suicide.

9 Montgomery's Canadian and British forces capture Caen and move on. Saipan is declared under U.S. control.

11 U.S. recognizes de Gaulle's French Committee of National Liberation as de facto government of France in liberated areas. Eisenhower warns Germans that French "underground" forces are combatants subject to rules of war. Red Army enters Latvia. In plot known to Rommel and Kluge, Count Claus von Stauffenberg goes to Berchtesgaden to assassinate Hitler. Plot fails because Hitler is away.

12 Russians advance toward East Prussia as Nazi radio warns: "The enemy is at the gates of the Reich!" Bradley's men reach St. Lô, fortress city of German defense line.

13 Russians capture Vilna in Lithuania after bitter street fighting. This removes roadblock in their campaign through Baltic States.

14 Russians take Pinsk, German

stronghold in Pripet Marshes. Five Soviet armies are now cooperating in gigantic offensives aimed at Warsaw and Berlin.

16 Stauffenberg goes to Hitler's headquarters in second assassination attempt. Again Hitler is away.

17 Rommel is gravely wounded when his command car is strafed by Allied plane on French road. U.S. battleships bombard Japanese installations on Guam.

18 Tojo, calling Saipan "great disaster," resigns. General Kuniaki Koiso becomes Premier of Japan. Bradley's men capture St. Lô. British break through beyond Caen.

20 Democratic Convention in Chicago renominates Franklin D. Roosevelt. Harry S. Truman is his running mate. Stauffenberg conceals bomb in Hitler's "Wolf's Lair" headquarters in East Prussia. Explosion leaves the *Führer* "burned and bruised," but alive. He and Mussolini, meeting for last time, inspect the scene. Some of conspirators are shot or commit suicide.

21 U.S. forces land on Guam, biggest of the Marianas. Hitler broadcasts word of his escape to German people. Nazis begin ferocious massacre of all suspected of complicity in the assassination attempt. Of those rounded up by the *Gestapo*, some 5,000 are put to death.

23 Russians take Lublin in Poland.

24 U.S. forces land on Tinian. Russians capture Pskov, last important Russian city taken by the Germans during the war.

25 Hundreds of Allied bombers wipe out German front beyond St. Lô. Patton's tanks burst through.

27 Hitler orders Göring to mobilize all Germans for war. Goebbels will assist him. Himmler becomes dictator of home front. Russians capture Lvov in Poland.

27–28 F.D.R. meets MacArthur and Nimitz at Pearl Harbor. He asks: "Douglas, where do we go from here?" MacArthur replies: "Leyte, Mr. President; and then Luzon!" Nimitz prefers frontal drive to Formosa, but F.D.R. agrees on liberation of Philippines.

28 Russians take Brest-Litovsk, Polish stronghold they lost to Germans in early days of war.

31 Patton's tanks advance past Avranches, anchor of German line. Hitler orders panzer counterattack. Russians reach outskirts of Warsaw.

AUGUST

1 Patton's tanks break out into open country and enter Brittany. Nearness of Red Army triggers Warsaw rising under General Bor (Tadeusz Komorowski), who expects Russian aid; but Marshal Rokossovski halts his troops outside the Polish capital.

2 Russians Reach Baltic west of Riga, cutting off Germans in Latvia and Estonia. Finnish President Ryti resigns, and Mannerheim takes his place amid talk of peace.

3 Hitler sends Dietrich von Choltitz to Paris with orders to defend or destroy the city. U.S. forces secure Tinian.

4 Americans take Rennes and Dinan on Breton Peninsula, and Mortain, only 150 miles from Paris.

5 Churchill asks cancellation of southern France invasion and use of troops in northern France. Eisenhower refuses. Allied planes hit Riviera and Rhone Valley in preparation for Allied landings on the coast.

7 Kluge's panzers attack Avranches. U.S. forces capture Brest.

8 Allied planes shatter Kluge's offensive, first time in history that air power alone stops ground attack. Americans turn east toward Canadian troops advancing on Falaise. In Italy, Allies reach Florence.

9 Eisenhower moves his headquarters from England to Normandy. Canadians and British advance toward Falaise. Americans reach Le Mans, 110 miles from Paris. Buzz bombs cause women and children to leave London.

10 Battle of Guam is declared over as organized Japanese resistance ends.

11 Churchill meets Tito in Naples, and they agree on partisan attack along Istrian Peninsula. Last Japanese units retreat from India to Burma. Giant tank battle rages on Riga-Warsaw sector of Eastern Front.

12 Germans retreat to Gothic Line, leaving Florence almost unscathed. Allied line now extends across Italy from Leghorn to Ancona.

13 Kluge, fearing entrapment, begins to pull back from Falaise

pocket, on which Allies are converging from both east and west.

15 American Seventh Army and French units under General Alexander Patch land between Marseilles and Nice in Operation Dragoon, so-called by Churchill "because I was dragooned into it."

16 Canadians capture Falaise. German noncombatants leave Paris.

17 Hitler fires Kluge, who writes him letter saying war in the west is lost. Germans retreat as Allies advance in south of France. Street fighting in Paris causes mass flight by Vichyites.

18 Kluge commits suicide. In Paris, Resistance occupies public buildings. Patch now holds coast from Cannes to Toulon, and his advance units are thirty miles inland.

19 Americans link up with Canadians, closing Falaise pocket.

20 Russians attack in Balkans. General von Choltitz, commanding in Paris, ignores Hitler's order to destroy that city and negotiates terms by which he and his garrison will be able to surrender to regular Allied troops instead of French resistance fighters.

21 Dumbarton Oaks Conference opens in Washington, D.C., to study postwar problems.

22 Ordered by Hitler to carry out "widest possible destruction in Paris," Choltitz sends Bradley a warning to enter city quickly. Eisenhower approves, and Bradley give assignment to French forces. Eighty thousand Germans in Falaise pocket surrender to Allies.

23 French units capture Marseilles as Americans sweep 140 miles from Mediterranean. Belgians and British capture Deauville on Channel coast. King Michael of Rumania arrests Antonescu and forms new government to make peace.

24 Americans capture Bordeaux. Rumania surrenders, allowing Russians to cut off German naval units in Black Sea.

25 French tanks enter Paris, led by General Leclerc, who made epic march from Lake Chad to North Africa to join Allies against Afrika Korps. Choltitz surrenders city to Allies. Bulgaria abandons Axis.

26 De Gaulle arrives in Paris amid wild rejoicing. Hunt for collaborationists is on as French patriots seek revenge for four years of humiliation. Allies attack Gothic Line in Italy, and one general calls fighting "some of the bloodiest in the history of the British Army."

27 Eisenhower arrives in Paris.

28 Americans take Château-Thierry and cross Marne. Historic battlefields of World War I are being overrun. Russians cross the Carpathians into Transylvania.

29 Patch's forces race northward through the Rhone Valley. Parisians cheer American parade down Champs-Élysées. In Italy, Allies break Gothic Line. Red Army captures Constanta, major Rumanian port on Black Sea.

30 British and Canadians take Rouen. Americans take Laon. Red Army enters Bucharest, and Rumanians declare war on Germany.

31 Americans reach Maginot Line, which had been so useless to the French in 1940. British capture Amiens and seal off buzz-bomb launching sites on coast of northern France.

SEPTEMBER

3 Allies moving up Rhone Valley take Lyons, near Swiss border.

4 British take Brussels and Antwerp and move into Holland. Cease-fire in Finland forces Germans to make hurried retreat.

5 Russia declares war on Bulgaria.

6 Americans take Namur and cross Meuse. Hungary declares war on Rumania over Transylvania.

8 First German V-2 falls on London. This is a true rocket, ancestor of vehicles used later in space programs. Allies capture Liège. Bulgaria accepts Soviet armistice conditions.

11 French forces from south link up with Patton's Third Army at Dijon. U.S. First Army reaches German frontier near Trier and captures Luxembourg.

12 Americans cross German border. British push through Holland. Patton captures part of Maginot Line intact. His juncture with Patch gives Allies line from Switzerland to Belgium.

12–16 Roosevelt and Churchill meet in Quebec (Octagon Conference) to discuss strategy in the war with Japan and postwar plans for Germany.

13   British capture Le Havre.

14   Americans take Aachen, first great German city to fall to the Allies. Five thousand planes fly over Germany, hitting targets from the Siegfried Line to Berlin.

15   Nimitz's men land on Peleliu, MacArthur's on Morotai, only three hundred miles from Philippines.

16   Russians take Sofia. Germans start evacuating Estonia.

17   Montgomery drops paratroopers and gliders—one British and two American divisions—on Arnhem in Holland. He wants his armor to link up with airborne forces and cut off Germans to the west. Japanese advance in China compels Americans to give up big air base at Kweilin.

18   Montgomery's armor is unable to break through to Arnhem, and British airborne division is surrounded.

19   First U.S. supply convoy docks at Le Havre. Finland cedes territory to Soviet Union.

21   Arnhem perimeter contracts under heavy German pressure.

22   Montgomery's armor attacks as Arnhem situation becomes critical.

24   Ground attack toward Arnhem is an admitted failure. American planes begin using Peleliu airfield behind battlefront. U.S. forces take Ulithi in Carolines. Russians enter Czechoslovakia.

25   Montgomery calls off Arnhem operation and orders survivors to be flown out of trap.

28   Battle of Arnhem ends. Almost seven thousand men of British airborne division are lost, less than two thousand rescued. Allied forces liberate Calais.

29   Russians invade Yugoslavia.

OCTOBER

1   Canadians capture five thousand Germans in Calais. Red Army units join Tito's partisans in Yugoslavia.

2   Americans smash two miles into Siegfried Line. Warsaw uprising ends. "Lublin government," Polish puppet government in Moscow, condemns it as "futile."

3   Battle of Morotai ends. British forces land in Greece.

5   Russians reach Baltic near Riga.

7   Keitel orders Rommel to Berlin. Rommel refuses, telling his family: "I'd never get to Berlin alive."

7–14   Mitscher's carriers raid into Japanese waters, pounding the Ryukus and Formosa and destroying eight hundred enemy planes.

9   Dumbarton Oaks Conference ends with plans for United Nations.

9–20   Churchill confers with Stalin in Moscow on eastern Europe. Poland cannot be agreed on because Stalin backs Lublin faction against Polish government-in-exile in London.

10   British and Greek forces enter

Corinth. Russians capture Memel, isolating Nazis in Latvia.

11 Advance units of Red Army occupy German soil in East Prussia.

14 Nazis force Rommel to commit suicide because he had known of plot against Hitler, then report he died of a stroke. Allies take Athens.

17 U.S. forces occupy three islands in Leyte Gulf, completing first phase of this campaign.

19 Hitler orders devastation of Warsaw as Russians move on city.

20 Powerful American armada enters Leyte Gulf and lands massive invasion force on Leyte. Beachhead twenty miles long is established. Filipino President Osmeña goes ashore with MacArthur, who begins a brief speech with the words: "People of the Philippines, I have returned."

23 Tacloban on Leyte becomes temporary capital of Philippines. Japanese commit most of their naval strength in supreme bid to regain control of sea around Leyte.

23–26 Battle for Leyte Gulf, greatest naval engagement in history, is fought in Philippine waters. U.S. Third and Seventh Fleets batter Japanese in four major battles— Sibuyan Sea, Samar, Surigao Strait, and Engaño. Enemy loses twenty-six combatant ships, U.S. loses only six. Americans encounter first kamikaze suicide pilots.

28 Stilwell is called home because of clashes with Chiang Kai-shek.

NOVEMBER

3 German commanders are briefed on Hitler's plan for counteroffensive in Ardennes. Rundstedt has been ordered from retirement to take charge of the operation.

5 U.S. planes bomb Singapore and destroy four hundred Japanese aircraft on the ground in Philippines.

7 F.D.R. wins fourth term, with Truman as Vice-President. Dewey carries only twelve states. French Consultative Assembly holds first session in Paris.

11 Hitler orders his generals to break through Ardennes and drive on Antwerp. Strategy is to divide and demoralize Allied armies.

12 R.A.F. destroys German battleship *Tirpitz* near Tromso, Norway.

15 British move against Greek rebels who threaten take-over.

20 Patton's men enter Metz.

22 Americans close down Omaha Beach, great D-Day beachhead, as French ports are now available.

24 Superfortresses from Saipan bomb Tokyo in first raid from Marianas base.

25 Americans break through Hürtgen Forest after fierce fighting. Peleliu is declared secure.

26 Americans abandon Yungning air base in China under enemy pressure.

27 Edward R. Stettinius becomes Secretary of State as Hull retires because of poor health.

28 Patton's Third Army drives deep into Saar basin.

30 Canadians smash across Dutch border and invade Germany.

DECEMBER

2 De Gaulle arrives in Moscow.

3 Civil war starts in Greece as rebels reject British ultimatum to surrender their arms.

7 Montgomery urges concentration of Allied forces for thrust into northern Germany, but Eisenhower adheres to his strategy of advancing across Rhine on a broad front.

11 De Gaulle and Stalin agree to mutual assistance pact.

15 U.S. forces land on Mindoro Island in Philippines.

16 "Rundstedt offensive" catches Allies by surprise and smashes forward in Ardennes. Skorzeny leads Operation Greif—German soldiers in American uniforms infiltrate American lines. Bad weather grounds Allied air forces.

17 Germans push into Belgium and Luxembourg. Eisenhower orders reinforcements into area where Battle of the Bulge is developing.

18 Bastogne, key road center, is reinforced by U.S. 101st Airborne. Japanese retreat from Burma.

19 German troops reach Bastogne, which they are ordered to take.

20 Bastogne is isolated as Germans drive toward Liège.

21 German officer, under flag of truce, demands Bastogne surrender.

General Anthony McAuliffe answers with a single word: "Nuts!" Garrison is supplied by air drops.

22 Patton's tanks hit southern flank of the Bulge, while McAuliffe launches local attacks.

23 Clearing weather allows Allied planes to resume bombing and strafing missions over the Bulge.

24 Patton dents German flank as Allied planes hammer Germans in the Bulge. Rundstedt, stalled at Bastogne, abandons his drive toward the Meuse and commits units to a last attack on McAuliffe's defenses.

25 Churchill flies to Athens to try to end Greek civil war.

26 Patton's armor breaks through to Bastogne. MacArthur announces that Leyte is secure.

27 Superfortresses from Marianas hit Tokyo in growing air assault on the Japanese capital.

31 Battle of the Bulge ends in liquidation of the Bulge. More than one hundred thousand men on both sides are killed, wounded, or missing. Fifty thousand Germans are captured, and Rundstedt has lost six hundred tanks.

1945

JANUARY

1 France joins Allies in full partnership, culmination of de Gaulle's long wartime desire for equality.

3 Americans counterattack in Ardennes, moving toward line they held before Battle of the Bulge. Germans are in full retreat. House approves Congressman Dies's Committee on Un-American Activities.

4 Kamikaze plane sinks U.S. escort carrier off Luzon's Lingayen Gulf.

5 Kamikazes in force hit six Allied warships off Luzon, causing many casualties and much damage.

6 Kamikazes attack Allied force clearing Lingayen Gulf. One ship is sunk, eleven damaged, and casualties are high. Twenty-eight of the suicide planes are shot down.

7–8 Kamikaze attacks continue as task force bombards shore installations on Luzon invasion beaches. Eisenhower announces change in his command structure. Montgomery receives command of all Allied units north of Bulge, while Bradley takes over those to the south.

9 U.S. invasion forces land on shore of Lingayen Gulf despite desperate kamikaze attacks. MacArthur's men establish firm beachhead.

11 U.S. build-up on Luzon continues at rapid pace as Japanese withdraw inland to fight there rather than on the beaches. Greek rebels accept truce with British after six weeks of fighting.

12 Kamikazes return in force over Lingayen Gulf but fail to slow the invasion. Russians begin final drive on wide front, with Berlin as ultimate objective.

13 MacArthur goes ashore on Luzon. Japanese hurl last big kamikaze blitz at invasion.

14 Zhukov attacks from Vistula bridgehead in center of Russian advance toward Germany.

15 MacArthur widens Luzon beachhead to forty-five miles.

17 Zhukov captures Warsaw.

19 Konev captures Cracow.

20 Konev invades Germany as Nazis withdraw in full retreat. Hungary surrenders to Russia.

21 Allies re-establish line broken by Battle of the Bulge.

22 Russians take Tannenberg, scene of great Hindenburg victory over Russians in World War I. Hungary accepts armistice conditions.

23 Konev reaches the Oder and regroups for drive on Berlin. Germans begin frantic mass sea evacuation of East Prussia.

28 Allies reopen Burma Road.

30 Mopping up on Mindoro is turned over to Filipino forces.

FEBRUARY

1 MacArthur's men launch drive to wrest Manila from Japanese.

2 Roosevelt and Churchill confer in Malta. Churchill urges Allied occupation of Austria to save as much as possible from Red Army.

3 U.S. forces enter suburbs of Manila, liberate Allied inmates of prison camp.

4 Roosevelt, Churchill, and Stalin open major conference at Yalta in the Crimea. Approaching defeat of Germany necessitates agreement on main international problems.

5 Yalta Conference agrees to partition Germany after unconditional surrender of Hitler's shattered Reich.

6 Big Power veto in U.N. Security Council is agreed on at Yalta. MacArthur declares Manila liberated after three years of Japanese occupation.

10 Stalin agrees to free elections in Poland. Roosevelt agrees to Soviet expansion into Japanese and Chinese territory in return for Soviet attack on Japan. Ninety Superfortresses bomb Tokyo. Zhukov reaches Oder and regroups for drive on Berlin.

11 Yalta Conference ends. Most decisions depend on Stalin's good faith, and some are kept secret. Hence the controversy about this conference, which begins soon afterward.

13–14 Eight hundred R.A.F. planes at night and 1,300 U.S. bombers the next day attack refugee-crowded Dresden, until now almost untouched by the war. High explosives and catastrophic fire storms kill some 135,000 and devastate six square miles of the city.

15 Roosevelt and Churchill meet for last time aboard U.S. cruiser in Alexandria harbor. F.D.R., "placid and frail" in Churchill's words, confers with Farouk of Egypt, Haile Selassie of Ethiopia, and Ibn Saud of Saudi Arabia. De Gaulle refuses to meet him at Algiers.

16 U.S. paratroopers land on Corregidor after heavy bombardment of the Rock. U.S. task force raids Japanese island of Honshu.

19 U.S. Marines land on Iwo Jima. Himmler approaches Count Bernadotte about possible peace in West.

21 Reinforcements are committed on Iwo Jima as heavy casualties result from savage enemy defense.

23 Marines raise flag on Suribachi while Iwo Jima battle rages. Photograph of this incident is the best known of the war. Allied armies on Germans border open new offensive.

26 Corregidor is captured after ten-day assault from air and sea.

MARCH

1 F.D.R. reports to Congress on Yalta Conference and appeals for approval of its decisions.

2 MacArthur returns to Corregidor.

3 Marines advance on Iwo Jima by flushing Japanese soldiers out of caves and pillboxes.

4 Fighting ends in Manila with reduction of final last-ditch resistance.

7 Americans seize Remagen bridge over the Rhine, thwarting German demolition team. Troops and vehicles pour across. Cologne falls.

9–10 U.S. planes turn Tokyo into

inferno with incendiaries. One quarter of the city is destroyed, almost one hundred thousand people are killed.

14 U.S. Navy military government is established on Iwo Jima.

16 Main battle ends on Iwo Jima. U.S. has base 750 miles from Yokohama. Cost: almost twenty thousand casualties, four thousand dead.

17 Remagen bridge collapses, but Allies are now smashing deep into Hitler's Reich. Coblenz is taken.

18 Hitler says if war is lost, "the nation will also perish."

19 Hitler issues order for total scorched-earth policy. Food supplies, water works, railroads, and all other facilities are to be destroyed so that invading armies will find only a wasteland.

19–25 U.S. task force batters Ryuku Islands in preparation for invasion of Okinawa. Shipping is sunk, airfields knocked out.

23 Churchill and Eisenhower watch American troops crossing Rhine. Hitler orders German population to move into the center of Germany, but Albert Speer, munitions minister, countermands the order to prevent "an unimaginable catastrophe."

26 Entire Allied front is now east of the Rhine, and German defenses are disintegrating. Many Germans express relief at the advance, hoping the Allies will occupy as much of Germany as possible and keep the Russians out. On Iwo Jima, Japanese holdouts launch futile suicide attack. Americans are preparing the airfield for Japan raids.

27 Last V-2 hits London. Patton's Third Army races into Frankfurt.

28 Montgomery proposes an all-out drive on Berlin. Eisenhower says "no." Hitler fires Guderian as Army commander in chief after violent disagreement in *Führer*'s Berlin bunker.

APRIL

1 U.S. invasion force lands on Okinawa. Stalin tells Eisenhower that Berlin is of no importance —then orders Zhukov and Konev to take Berlin before the Allies.

2 Churchill urges Eisenhower to "shake hands with the Russians as far to the east as possible."

3 Army and Navy commands in Pacific are divided between MacArthur and Nimitz for assault on Japan.

5 Okinawa battle develops as Americans reach entrenched Japanese defense. Admiral Suzuki replaces Koiso as Premier of Japan.

6–7 Fighting is violent on Okinawa. American planes sink battleship *Yamato* along with a cruiser and four destroyers in flotilla trying to reach island for a suicide attack. Some 350 kamikaze planes attack ships off beachhead and do great damage.

7 Bombers from Iwo Jima hit Tokyo.

9 Russians enter Königsberg in East Prussia and take Vienna.

10 Eisenhower's men capture concentration camp at Buchenwald and reveal worst horrors of Hitler's Reich.

11 General Simpson's Ninth Army reaches Elbe River. Allies have taken three hundred thousand prisoners in two weeks.

12 Franklin Delano Roosevelt dies in Warm Springs, Georgia. Harry S. Truman becomes President. Patton forces mayor and citizens of Ohrdruf to walk through concentration camp of which they had disclaimed any knowledge.

14 Eisenhower orders his troops to halt at the Elbe instead of going on to Berlin. He fears Hitler is setting up fortress in Bavaria. This "National Redoubt" is one of war's big myths.

16 Russians begin final drive on Berlin. Zhukov concentrates twenty thousand guns to blast a path, but General Heinrici brings him to a temporary halt at Seelow heights.

17 Ernie Pyle, the "G.I.'s war correspondent," is killed on Ie Shima near Okinawa in the Ryukus. Americans take Nuremberg. Stalin gives Konev permission to turn his tanks north toward Berlin. Zhukov breaks through at Seelow heights.

18 Allies, racing through Germany, capture Magdeburg and Leipzig.

20 Hitler receives top Nazis on his fifty-sixth birthday, last time he emerges from bunker into Reichschancellery gardens. He predicts Russian defeat at gates of Berlin but appoints two commanders should Germany be split by invading armies. Admiral Doenitz will have command in the north, General Kesselring in the south.

21 Americans crack key Okinawa defense on "Sugar-Loaf Hill."

22 Hitler decides to stay in Berlin as Konev's tanks beat Zhukov's into the city by one day. Allies take Bologna on "forgotten front."

25 Churchill and Truman reject Himmler's offer of surrender to western Allies only. Hitler fires Göring for asking to take over German leadership. Americans and Russians link up on the Elbe. The two Russians armies join in Berlin and encircle the heart of the city. San Francisco Conference begins work on a Charter for United Nations.

27 Allies capture Genoa and Verona and sweep through the Po Valley.

28 Mussolini, trying to escape to Switzerland, is caught and shot by Italian partisans. Russians reach center of Berlin.

28–29 Hitler marries his mistress, Eva Braun, learns of the death of Mussolini, and dictates a "Political Testament" bequeathing his authority to Admiral Doenitz. Russian shells are now falling in the Reichschancellery gardens above Hitler's personal bunker. German forces in Italy surrender.

30 Adolph Hitler shoots himself. Obeying his orders, members of his staff cremate his body in the Reichschancellery gardens, along with the body of Eva Braun, who took poison. Churchill urges Allied liberation of Prague. Tito's partisans enter Trieste.

MAY

1 Doenitz announces that Hitler is dead. Australian troops land on Borneo.

2 Doenitz takes over as head of German regime. Berlin surrenders. British troops land near Rangoon.

4 Montgomery receives surrender of German forces in northwest Germany, Holland, and Denmark. Nazi generals try to capitulate to western Allies only but are refused.

6 Doenitz orders all German forces to lay down their arms and all U-boats at sea to return to port.

7 Jodl signs unconditional surrender at Eisenhower's headquarters at Rheims. Russians are represented, but Moscow later will ignore this surrender in its propaganda.

8 V-E Day is celebrated in U.S. and western Europe as Churchill and Truman broadcast word of the end of the war against Germany. Crowds surge wildly through streets of New York, London, and Moscow.

9 Keitel signs unconditional surrender at Zhukov's headquarters near Berlin. Stalin proclaims victory over the Germans. Russians take Prague.

11 Churchill urges Truman to keep

U.S. troops in advanced positions in Germany until assured of Stalin's intentions in eastern Europe.

12 Churchill sends Truman "Iron Curtain" telegram, warning about Stalin's "misinterpretation of the Yalta decisions." Russian activity in Poland worries him most. Tito's aggression in Trieste causes Italian Premier to appeal to the Allies.

15 U.S., Britain, and Russia disband Doenitz regime. Göring and other Nazi leaders are being held for trial as war criminals. Goebbels has committed suicide (along with his wife and six children). Himmler is missing, so is Bormann, who is never discovered.

16 Truman protests to Stalin that Allies are being barred from Vienna by Soviet commander.

18 Stalin says Allies can visit Vienna, but demands an agreement on Austrian occupation.

22 Himmler, *Gestapo* head, is captured by British troops while trying to escape in disguise.

23 Churchill resigns as Prime Minister, forcing a general election in Britain. Himmler poisons himself while being searched and is buried secretly.

23–26 U.S. planes carry out heavy incendiary raids on Tokyo. Fires are visible for days afterward.

29 Incendiary attack sends flames whipping through Yokohama as strategy of fire-bombing all major cities continues.

JUNE

5 Allied Control Commission assumes authority over Germany at meeting in Berlin. Eisenhower, Montgomery, Zhukov, and Tassigny represent their nations. Four occupation zones are set up in pre-war German territory. Berlin is to be run jointly, but no provisions have been made for Allied control of access routes across the Soviet zone of occupation.

9 Western Allies agree with Tito to have military administration of Venezia Giulia, including Trieste.

10 Soviet commander orders British missions to leave Vienna.

12 Western Allies agree with Stalin to set up tripartite commission to help organize Polish government.

18 General Simon Bolivar Buckner is killed in action on Okinawa.

19 Eisenhower returns home and receives a hero's welcome. Four million New Yorkers cheer his ticker tape parade up Broadway.

22 Resistance on Okinawa ends. Japanese have lost more than one hundred thousand men, Americans some 7,500 in land fighting and about 5,000 Navy men, almost all from kamikaze attacks.

26 Truman observes signing of United Nations Charter in San Francisco. Forty-six nations agree to international organization where disputes can be settled peacefully.

27 Luzon is declared secure despite pockets of Japanese holding out. Kamikaze plane hits U.S. carrier *Bunker Hill*, killing almost four hundred of crew.

JULY

1 Allied troops begin pull-back from their advanced positions, which are in Russian zone in east Germany.

3 Tripartite control of Berlin replaces single Soviet authority.

4 MacArthur announces liberation of all the Philippine Islands.

5 General Carl Spaatz is appointed head of Strategic Air Forces in the Pacific. Air conquest of Japan is to be attempted, to make invasion of the home islands unnecessary. British hold general election.

10 More than one thousand U.S. planes batter Tokyo.

14 Eisenhower disbands SHAEF.

16 U.S. scientists explode the first atomic bomb in test at Alamogordo, New Mexico.

16–17 British warships join Americans in bombardment of Japan.

17 Churchill, Truman, and Stalin open Potsdam Conference. Truman has favorable impression of the Soviet dictator at first meeting.

21 U.S. tells Japan by radio to make peace or face total destruction.

23 Stalin proposes Russian control of Turkish Dardanelles. Truman and Churchill object. Nagoya, Osaka, and Kure are bombed by U.S. planes.

24 Stalin insists on recognition of his east European puppet regimes. Truman and Churchill reply they want democratic governments. Truman calls this the "bitterest debate of the conference."

25 Churchill leaves Potsdam to return home for general election results.

26 Churchill loses the election. Truman, with Britain and China, issues "Potsdam Declaration" calling for "unconditional surrender" of Japan, but promising no enslavement of Japanese.

28 Clement Attlee arrives in Potsdam as British Prime Minister. Stalin reveals having received peace feeler from Tokyo. Senate ratifies United Nations Charter by vote of 89 to 2.

29 Japan rejects Allied ultimatum.

31 Truman formally asks Stalin for Soviet war against Japan.

AUGUST

2 Superfortresses drop six thousand tons of bombs on Japanese cities. U.S. shifts Tenth Air Force from Burma to China in preparation for final onslaught on Japan. Potsdam Conference ends with communiqué containing harsh terms for Germany, including vast reparations demanded by Stalin. Truman leaves with unfavorable opinion of the Soviet dictator, who has been evasive on key issues.

3 U.S. air and sea forces complete blockade of Japanese home islands. Focus is on Honshu, main island where landing will be made in case of invasion. Some experts believe the cost will be one million American casualties on the beaches.

6 Superfortress "Enola Gay" drops a single bomb, the first atomic bomb, on the city of Hiroshima. Over half the city is wiped out. There are over one hundred thousand casualties in addition to widespread suffering from radiation sickness.

8 Truman signs U.N. Charter. Russia declares war on Japan, and Soviet armies attack in Manchuria. Tokyo Government remains silent on question of capitulation.

9 U.S. plane drops second atomic bomb on Nagasaki, which is devastated like Hiroshima. Japanese now know U.S. has superweapon capable of destroying their nation.

10 Tokyo sues for peace with one condition: Hirohito must remain on the Imperial throne of Japan. Russians invade Korea.

11 Truman tells Tokyo that Hirohito can stay but he will be subject to U.S. Supreme Commander, who will have full authority in Japan.

14 Tokyo War Council deadlocks in vote on surrender. Emperor Hirohito decides for immediate capitulation, accepts U.S. terms.

15 Emperor Hirohito broadcasts news of Japanese defeat to his people. Truman announces cease fire, with MacArthur named to accept surrender for all Allied powers.

16 Stalin demands surrender of Japanese Hokkaido Island to Soviet forces to be landed there.

18 Truman replies that all Japanese islands will surrender to MacArthur.

19 Japanese surrender delegation arrives in Manila for briefing on mechanics of surrender. Truman has decided to have the ceremony on deck of battleship *Missouri*.

22 Japanese garrison on Mills Island in Marshalls is first of war to surrender without fighting.

27 Halsey's Third Fleet sails into Tokyo Bay and drops anchor.

29 Nimitz arrives in Tokyo Bay and tells Halsey to begin rescue of Allied prisoners of war. Truman defends Hull and Marshall from criticism in newly released report on Pearl Harbor. Allies publish list of twenty-four German leaders who will be defendants at war crimes trial to be held in Nuremberg. Twenty-one eventually are indicted.

30 US. occupation forces begin landings on shores of Tokyo Bay. Japanese surrender Yokosuka Naval Base and First Naval District of Honshu. MacArthur lands at Atsugi airfield and sets up headquarters in Yokohama before move to Tokyo.

SEPTEMBER

1 Occupation forces extend control around Tokyo Bay. Military men on hand for formal capitulation of Japan include General Wainwright, a prisoner of war ever since the Japanese forced him to give up at Corregidor in 1942, and General Percival, commander who surrendered Singapore.

2 With concourse of Allied representatives at hand, MacArthur presides at capitulation ceremony on board *Missouri*, anchored in Tokyo Bay. Premier Suzuki signs for Japan and delivers his country to MacArthur's administration. In an address to the American people, President Truman proclaims V-J Day. World War II is over.

ACKNOWLEDGMENTS

The Editors make grateful acknowledgment for permission to quote from the following works:

Barbarossa by Alan Clark. Copyright © 1965 by Alan Clark. The quotation by a Nazi lieutenant on page 129 reprinted by permission of William Morrow and Company, Inc.

Berlin: Story of a Battle by Andrew Tully. Copyright © 1963 by Andrew Tully. The excerpt from a German officer's diary on page 268 reprinted by permission of Simon & Schuster, Inc.

Brave Men by Ernie Pyle. Copyright 1943, 1944 by Scripps-Howard Newspaper Alliance; copyright 1944 by Holt, Rinehart and Winston, Inc. The excerpt on page 188 reprinted by permission of Holt, Rinehart and Winston, Inc.

Calculated Risk by General Mark Clark. Copyright 1950 by Mark Clark. The quotation on page 181 reprinted by permission of Harper & Row, Publishers, Inc.

Closing the Ring by Winston S. Churchill. Copyright 1951 by Houghton Mifflin. The quotation on page 178 reprinted by permission of Houghton Mifflin Company.

Crusade in Europe by Dwight D. Eisenhower. Copyright © 1963 by Doubleday and Company, Inc. The quotations on pages 135, 227 and 265 reprinted by permission of Doubleday and Company, Inc.

Defeat in the West by Milton Shulman. Copyright 1948 by E. P. Dutton & Company. The quotation by von Rundstedt on pages 34–35 reprinted by permission of Secker & Warburg Ltd.

The First and the Last by Adolf Galland, translated by Mervyn Savill. Copyright 1954 by Henry Holt and Company, Inc. The excerpt on page 200 reprinted by permission of Holt, Rinehart and Winston, Inc.

The Gathering Storm by Winston S. Churchill. Copyright 1948 by Houghton Mifflin Company. The quotations on page 31 reprinted by permission of Houghton Mifflin Company.

The Grand Alliance by Winston S. Churchill. Copyright 1950 by Houghton Mifflin Company. The quotations on pages 49–50, 102, 134 reprinted by permission of Houghton Mifflin Company.

The Hinge of Fate by Winston S. Churchill. Copyright 1950 by Houghton Mifflin Company. The quotations on pages 137, 159, 161 and 162 reprinted by permission of Houghton Mifflin Company.

Japan and Her Destiny by Mamoru Shigemitsu, translated by Oswald White, edited by Maj. Gen. F. S. G. Piggott. Copyright 1958 by E. P. Dutton & Co., Inc. The quotation on page 216 reprinted by permission of E. P. Dutton & Co., Inc.

The Labyrinth: Memoirs of Walter Schellenberg, translated by Louis Hagen. Copyright 1956 by Harper & Brothers. The quotation on page 28 reprinted by permission of Harper & Row, Publishers.

The Memoirs of General Lord Ismay. Copyright © 1960 by The Viking Press, Inc. The quotations on pages 134 and 139 reprinted by permission of The Viking Press, Inc.

Men at War edited by Ernest Hemingway. Copyright 1942 by Crown Publishers, Inc. The quotations on pages 70–71 reprinted by permission of Crown Publishers, Inc.

The Rommel Papers edited by B. H. Liddell Hart. Copyright 1953 by Harcourt, Brace and Company. The quotations on pages 114–115 and 183 reprinted by permission of Harcourt, Brace & World, Inc.

Roosevelt and Hopkins by Robert E. Sherwood. The excerpt on page 66 reprinted by permission of Harper & Row, Publishers.

Royal Air Force, 1939–1945 (Vol. II) by Denis Richards and Hilary St. George Saunders. The quotation by Guy Penrose Gibson on page 197 reprinted by permission of H. M. Stationery Office, London.

See Here, Private Hargrove by Marion Hargrove. Copyright 1943 by Marion Hargrove. The excerpt on page 185 reprinted by permission of Marion Hargrove.

A Soldier's Story by Omar N. Bradley. Copyright 1951 by Henry Holt and Company. The quotation on page 236 reprinted by permission of Holt, Rinehart and Winston.

Their Finest Hour by Winston S. Churchill. Copyright 1949 by Houghton Mifflin Company. The quotation on page 86 reprinted by permission of Houghton Mifflin Company.

A Torch to the Enemy by Martin Caidin. Copyright © 1960 by Martin Caidin. The account by a factory worker on page 280 reprinted by permission of Ballantine Books.

Up Front by Bill Mauldin. Copyright 1945 by Bill Mauldin and Henry Holt and Company, Inc. The quotation on pages 189–190 reprinted by permission of Holt, Rinehart and Winston, Inc.

PICTURE CREDITS

INDEX

Italic page numbers refer to illustrations.

A

345

the B-29, 208–9; XX Bomber Command, 208; XXI Bomber Command, 208–9; raids on Japan, 209; Japanese attacks on Chinese airfields, 247; losses in Formosa, 249; in liberation of the Philippines, 249; massive bombing of Japanese cities, 279–80; Hiroshima and Nagasaki, 282, 283

Air Force, Yugoslav, 50

Air Transport Command, 163

Aisne River, 36

Ajax (cruiser), 87

Alamagordo Air Base, New Mexico, 281

Alaska, 80; *See also* Aleutian Islands

Albania, 102; Italian invasion of, 22; 92; Greek invasion of, 49; resistance movement, 142, 175, 225

Aleutian Islands, 98, 147, 158, 243

Alexander III, Czar of Russia, 8

Alexander, Gen. Sir Harold, 106; command in Italy, 176, 179

Alexandria, Egypt, 90, 92, 102

Algeria, 110–11; map, *104–5*; Algerians, in Italian campaign, 165, 179

Algiers, Algeria, 112

Allies: after WWI, 7, 9; and Hitler's rise to power, 15; war strategy, 133–34, 136; propaganda, 141–42, 144, 167, 170; division of responsibilities in Pacific front, 159; U.S. as arsenal for, 219, 221; and Normandy invasion, 226–32; on the offensive against Japan, 243–55; synchronizing assault on Germany, 258; occupation of Germany, 289–90; war trials, 290–91; demobilization, 291; Cold War, 291, 293–95; *See also* Conferences; Operations; *and specific countries*

Ambrosio, Gen. Vittorio, 170

America First Committee, 58–59

American Persian Gulf Service Command, 130

American Volunteers Group (AVG), 206

Amery, Leopold, 43

Ammunition, *See* Armament

Amphibious warfare, 47, 96; at Guadalcanal, 147, 150; island-hopping in Pacific, 154–55; at Betio, 155; at Kwajalein, 155, 158; at Attu, 158; Sicilian campaign, 166–67; DUKW, 166; at Salerno, 172–73; at Cuzio and Nettuno, 178; in Normandy, 226, *228*, 229, 232; in Asia, 243; at Lingayen, 273; at Iwo Jima, 274, *276*; at Okinawa, 275, 277; *See also* Marines, U.S.

Andalsnes campaign, 31

Andaman Islands, 78

Anders, Gen., 179

Anderson, Jane, 141

Anti-imperialism. *See* Nationalist movements

Anti-Semitism: German, 15, 175, 211, 165; American, 59

Antwerp, Belgium, 237, 239; bombing of, 145, *238*

Anzio, Italy, 165, *169*, 178

Apennines, *168*

Apsheron Peninsula, U.S.S.R., 140

Arab petroleum resources, struggle over, 140–41

Aramco, 141

Ardennes campaign, 32, *231*, 239, *240*, 241, 262

Argentina, 87, *91*

Argentina Bay, *56*

Arizona (battleship), *68*, 74

Armament: post-WWI rearmament of Germany, 8–9; rearmament of Soviets, 121, 124, 130–31; espionage and research, 144; German production, 213–14; U.S. as arsenal of Allies, 219, 221; *See also* Aircraft; Atomic weapons; Lend-Lease program; tanks; V-weapons

Army, Australian, 109, 147, 153

Army, Belgian, *35*

Army, British: at Dunkirk, 34, *37*;

munist control of, 262
Bulge, Battle of the, 239, 241, 257, map, *240*
Buna, New Guinea, 153
Bunker Hill (ship), *279*
Burma, *146*, 147, 217, 277, 279; Japanese invade, 70, 76; Chiang on importance of, 161; campaign in, 161-62, 163; AVG in, 206; Allies in, 243, 246, 247; Japanese offensive, 247
Burma Road, 162
Burmese Hump, 162
Bush, Dr. Vannevar, 62, 145
Bushy Park, England, 197
Butcher, Capt. Harry C., 264-65
Byrnes, James F., 281, 283, 289, 290

C

"C" rations, 185–86
Cairo, Egypt, 101
Cairo Conference, 139, 276
Calabria, Italy, 172
California (battleship), 74
California Arabian Standard Oil Company (Aramco), 141
Callaway (transport), *253*
Canada, 59; *See also* Army, Canadian
Canaris, Adm. Wilhelm, 142
Cannes, France, 236
Capa, Robert, 189
Carentan, France, *235*
Carol, King of Rumania, 49
Caroline Islands, 155, 158
Cartoonists, war, *33, 132, 182,* 189–90
Casablanca, Morocco, 111, *138*
Casablanca Conference, *135*, 136–137, *138*; and Burma campaign, 161; and Sicilian campaign, 165
Case White, Operation, 26
Case Yellow, Operation, 32, 34
Cassino, Italy, 82, *169,* 177, 178–79
Castellano, Gen. Giuseppe, 172

Casualties: Allied, 34, 155, 167, 190, 201, *235*; Axis, 114, 162, 167, 204; British, 52; German, 28, 36, 52, 114, 120; Italian, 114, 175; Japanese, 245, 248, 255, 274, 277, 280, 283, 284; Soviet, 120, 126, 284; U.S., 190, *228, 245,* 246, 248, 252, 253, 255, 274, 277, *279; See also* Concentration camps
Catania, Italy, 167
Caucasus, *122-23*, 127; Hitler's Directive No. 45 against, 127
Central Aircraft Manufacturing Company (CAMCO), 206
Ceylon, 153; Japanese threat to, 78
Chamberlain, Neville: appeasement policy, 22; censure and resignation of, 41, 43
Chang Ching-hui, 217
"Chanson d'Automne," (Verlaine), 229
Chelyabinsk, U.S.S.R., 125
Chennault, Maj. Gen. Claire, 161, 206, 247
Cherbourg, France, *230–31*, 234
Chiang Kai-shek, *21*, 76, 133, 134, 206, 247, 266, 279, 294; at Cairo Conference, 139; role of, with Allies, 159, 161
Chiang Kai-shek, Madame, 139
China, 8, 208, 217, 243, 291; Japanese invasion of, 17–18, 64; Allied strategy for, 139; Japanese war in, 153; as special American interest, 159; 161, 163; as base to bomb Japan, 244; Japanese offensive in, 247; Yalta Conference and future of, 258; Japanese on defensive in, 277, 279; Japanese surrender, 286; Communist control of, 294-95; *See also* Chiang Kai-shek; Formosa; Manchuria; Mao Tse-tung
Chinese-American Combat Wing, 206
Cho, Lt. Gen., 277

Choiseul Island, 154
Choltitz, Gen. Dietrich von, 237
Christian X, King of Denmark, 31
Chromium resources, 141
Chuikov, Gen. Vasili, 129
Churchill, Winston, 22, 31, *51, 56, 132*; becomes Prime Minister, 32, 43; offer of British-French union, 38; resolve after French surrender, 39, *51*; character of, 41, *51*; Admiralty experience, 43; Hitler's peace offer to, 44; on Hitler, 46; and German invasion of Russia, 55; early communications with Roosevelt, *56*, 59; and Lend-Lease program, 63; Hopkins mission to, 66; meeting with Roosevelt at Newfoundland, 66–67; on Pacific losses, 76; promise of independence to India, 78; on battle of Oran, 86; on German sea losses, 95; in Cairo, 106; and battle of El Alamein, 110, *113*; voted out of office, 133, 145; and European balance of power, 134; war strategy of, 134, 136; on relations with Stalin, 134, 136; and sphere of influence in the Balkans, 136, 165; and Curzon Line, 136; at Casablanca Conference, 136–37, *138*; relations with de Gaulle, 137; at Cairo Conference, 139; at Teheran Conference, 139–40; on China, 159; against Burma campaign, 161; on Gen. Wingate, 162; and Italian campaign, 165, *168*; on Anzio assault, 178; and propaganda, *180*; on Molotov-Ribbentrop conference, 196; on cost of day bombing, 199; and morale of British, 218, 219; and second front plans, 225; and Operation Overlord, 226; and Operation Dragoon, 236; at Yalta Conference, *256*, 257–58; requests Stalin's aid on western front, 259; on Roosevelt's death, 266; and use of A-bomb, 283; and UN, 291, 293

Ciano, Count Galeazzo, 18, 36, 49
"Cicero" (Elyesa Bazna), 142, 144
Cinema on war, 221
Cinnabar resources, 141
CIO, 221
Citadel, Operation, 130
Civilians, agreement on exchange of, in Yalta Conference, 258–59
Clark, Maj. Gen. Mark W., 110–11, 112, 165, 172–73, 175–76, 181
Clark Field, Philippines, 273
Clausewitz, Gen. Karl von, 47
Clemenceau, Georges, 7
"Clubmobiles," 186
Coast Guard, U.S., *253*
Cold War, 257, 289, 291, 293–95
Collins, Gen. Joseph ("Lightning Joe"), 234
Cologne, Germany, 262; British bombing of, 195, 196
Colonialism, 7, 44, 75, 78; Roosevelt's opposition to, 134, 136; Allied plan to strip Japan of colonies, 139; Japanese exploitation of nationalist movements in Asia, 216–17; *See also* Nationalist movements
Combined Chiefs of Staff, 133, *138*
Combined Operations, 47
Comic strips, war, 189–90; *See also* Cartoonists
Command of the Rear of the Red Army, 124
Commando units, 47
Commissar Order, 117
Committee to Defend America by Aiding the Allies, 58
Communists: sabotage in Germany, 121; Allied views of, 133; guerrillas, 133; control of eastern Europe, 259, 262, 293–94; in China, 279, 294–95; *See also*

Union of Soviet Socialist Republics

Compton, Arthur, 145

Conant, James B., 145

Concentration camps, Nazi, *215, 263*, 265; Italians in, 175; and Nuremberg Trials, 290–91

Conferences: Casablanca, *135*, 136–37, *138*, 161, 165; Cairo, 139, 276; Dumbarton Oaks, 293; Newfoundland, 66–67; Potsdam, 279, 283; Teheran, 136, 139–40, 276; Trident, 161, 201; Yalta, 136, *256*, 257–59, 289, 291

Congress, U.S.: establishes draft, *65*; declares war, 75; *See also* Isolationism

Construction battalions (Seabees), 154, 155, 221–22

Convoys: Allied, 63, 93, 95, 103, 130, 150, 158; Axis, 153

Coral Sea, Battle of the, *94*, 96, 98, 153

Corregidor, Philippines, 80, 254, 273–74

Corsica, 173

Cotentin Peninsula, Normandy, 226, 229, *230–31* (map)

Coughlin, Father Charles E., 58

Coventry, England, 47, *48*

C.P.R., 193

Crete, 101, 142; British in, 50; German invasion of, 52, 92

Crimea, U.S.S.R., 257–58

Cripps, Sir Stafford, 47, 49, 55, 124; mission to Delhi, 78

Croatia, Yugoslavia, 52

Crosby, Bing, 186

Cunningham, Gen. Sir Alan, 103

Cunningham, Adm. Sir Andrew, 90, 92

Curzon Line, 136, 258

Cyprus, 53

Cyrenaica, Libya, 102

Czechoslovakia: German invasion of, 20, 25; Communist control of, 262

D

"D" bar, 186

D-Day, *228, 229,* 232

Dachau concentration camp, 265

Dairen, China, 284

Daladier, Edouard, 22

Danube River valley, 165

Dardanelles, 49

Darlan, Adm. Jean Louis, 38, 111, 115, 133

Darwin, Australia, 79

Davies, Joseph, 221

Dawes, Charles G., 9

de Gaulle, Gen. Charles, 133, 159; assumes command of French resistance, 38, 39; exclusion from Operation Torch, 110–11; assumes leadership of Free France, 111–12, 115; *135*; on German offensive at Leningrad, 129; at Casablanca Conference, *135*, 136–37; and liberation of Paris, 236, 237

Delhi, India, 247

Denmark: German invasion of, 31; and German surrender, 269

Depression, *10*, 11, 14

Derevyanko, Lt. Gen., 286

Derna, Libya, *108*

Desert Rats, 103

Desert War. *See* North African campaign

Detachment, 101, 162

Dieppe, France, 225, 226

Dill, Sir John, 49

Dimitrov, Georgi, 20

Directive No. 45, 127

Disposal Squads, 47

Dnieper Dam, U.S.S.R., 126

Dobruja, Rumania, 49

Dodecanese, Greece, 101

Doenitz, Grand Adm. Karl, 268–69; on U-boat losses, 93, 95

D'Olier, Franklin, 211, 213–14

Dollmann, Col. Friedrich, 264

Doolittle, Col. James, 214;

Felix, Operation, 92
Fermi, Enrico, 145, 281
Fermor, Patrick Leigh, 142
Ferrara, Italy, 264
The Fighting Lady (film), 221
Finland, 22, 293; Soviet invasion of, 28–29, *33;* "transit agreement" for German troops, 50
Fletcher, Rear Adm. Frank, 96, 99
Florida Island, 147
Flying Fortress, B-17, 197, 199, 200, *207*
Flying Tigers, 206
Foch, Marshal Ferdinand, 38
Foggia, Italy, 165, 176
Forced labor camps, Nazi, 212–13, 265
Formosa, 139, 248, 274, 286; plan to invade, 244; Allied air raids on, 249
France: after WWI, 7–8; appeasement of Hitler, 15, 20, 22, 25; and Spanish Civil War, *19;* on Germany, 26; support for Belgians, *35;* German defeat of, 36, 38; under Pétain, 38; de Gaulle assumes leadership of resistance, 39; resistance movement, 47, 142, 175, 225, *230–31,* 236; Operation Torch, 110–11; Roosevelt on future of, 140; weaponry research in, 144–45; GI behavior in, 193; the Maquis, 225, *230–31,* 236; Normandy invasion, 226–32; map of liberation, *230–31;* liberation of Cherbourg, *230–31,* 234; Operation Dragoon, 236; liberation of Paris, 236–37; role assigned at Yalta, 258; and UN, 259; *See also* Allies; Conference; de Gaulle; Free France
Franco, Francisco, *19,* 92; and Spanish Civil War, 18, 20
Frank, Hans, 291
Free France, 134, *135,* 265; *See also* de Gaulle
French Forces of the Interior

(F.F.I.), 236; *See also* Resistance movement, French
Frick, Wilhelm, 291
Friedenburg, Adm. Hans von, 269
Fritsche, Hans, 291
Fröbel, Julius, 8

G

Galahad Force, 162
Galbraith, John Kenneth, 11
Galland, Adolf, 200
Gamelin, Gen. Maurice, 36
Gandhi, Mahatma, 78
Garcia Lorca, Federico, 20
Garibaldi Partisan Division, 175
Garigliano River, 165, 179
Gavutu Island, 147
Gela, Italy, 167
Geneva Convention, 212, 217
Genoa, Italy, 264
Genocide, German, 265
German-American Bund Organization, 80
Germany: after WWI, 7–8; *Truppenant,* 8; "Special Group R," 9; relations with U.S.S.R., 8–9; post-WWI rearmament, 8–9; post-WWI debt and economy, 9, 11; rise of Hitler, 14–15; and Spanish Civil War, 18, *19,* 20; invasion of Czechoslavakia, 20, 22; invasion of Poland, 25–26, *27, 28, 30;* partition of Poland, 28; invasion of Norway, 29, 31; invasion of Denmark, 31; invasion of Holland, Belgium, and Luxembourg, 32, *35;* defeat of France, 36, 38; propaganda, 36, 86, 141, 142, 144, 214; occupation of Balkan states, 49–53; invasion of Yugoslavia and Greece, 50, 52; control of northern Mediterranean, 52–53; drawbacks to success in Balkans, 53; Tripartite Pact, 64; V-weapons program, 144, 145, 204–5, 208, 233, 257;

Churchill; Conferences; London; Navy, British; Operations, Allies
Greater East Asia Co-Prosperity Sphere, 69–70; 217
Great Marianas Turkey Shoot, 244
Greece, 133, 142, 165, 166, 293, 294; invasion of Turkey, 17; Italian invasion of, 49; invasion of Albania, 49; British forces in, 49–50; German invasion of, 50, 52; partitioning of, 52; resistance in, 175, 225; *See also* Crete
Greenwood, Arthur, 43
Greif, Operation, 239
Grenade ("potato masher"), *24*
Grew, Joseph Clark, 70, 283, 284
Groves, Gen. Leslie R., 145, 281
Grozny, U.S.S.R., 140
Guadalcanal Island, 147, *148–49*, 150–151, 153, *161*; map, *156–57*; Marine grave marker at, 190
Guadalcanal, Naval Battle of, 150–51
Guam, 80; Allies take, 246
Guderian, Gen. Heinz, 26, 121
Guerillas, 101, 129, 225; Communist, 133; Allied use of, 142; Balkan, 165; Corsican, 173; Italian, 175; *See also* Resistance movements
Gusen concentration camp, *263*
Gustav Line, 178, 179

H

Haakon VII, King of Norway, 31
The Hague Convention, 212
Hahn, Otto, 144
Haile Selassie, Emperor of Ethiopia, 18, 101
Halban, Hans von, 145
Halder, Gen. Franz, 117, 121, 125, 127
Halsey, Adm. William F., 180, 243, 249, 251, 254
Hamburg, Germany, 196, 200–201

Hamilton, Duke of, 53
Hanford, Washington, 281
Hara-kiri (Japanese ritual suicide), 244, 246, 254
Hargrove, Marion, 185
Harriman, Averell, 66
Harris, Sir Arthur ("Bomber"), 196
Harrodsburg, Kentucky, 190
Harz Mountains, Germany, 290
Hatta, 217
Hawaii, 70, 80; *See also* Pearl Harbor
Haw Haw, Lord (William Joyce), 141
Heavy water research, 144–45
Heisenberg, Werner, 145
Hellcat, F6F, 243
Helsinki, Finland, 28
Hemingway, Ernest, 7, 19, 70–71, 189
Henderson Field, 150, 151
Herblock (Herbert Lawrence Block), *33*
Herkules, Operation, 103
Hersey, John, 189
Hess, Rudolf, 38, *54*; mission to Britain, 53, *54*
Heusinger, 234
Hewitt, Vice-Adm. H. Kent, 166
Higashikuni, Prince, 186
Higgins, Andrew, 96
Highlanders, 109; *See also* Army, British
Hillary, Richard, 46
Himmler, Heinrich, 117, 290; seeks settlement with Italian Resistance, 264; Hitler expels, 268
Hirohito, Emperor, *97, 282*, 283, 284, 294
Hiroshima, Japan, 209, 280, *282*, 283
Hitler, Adolf, *54*, 69, 140, 145, 290; rise of, 14–15; alliance with Mussolini, 17; and Spanish Civil War, *19;* invasion of Czechoslovakia, 20, 22; nonagression pact with Stalin, 22, 25; desire for war in 1939, 25; invasion of

Influenza epidemic, *10*
Inouye, Vice-Adm. Shigeyoshi, 96
Iran, 101, 294; Teheran Conference, 139–40
Iraq, 53, 101
Ironbottom Sound, 151
Ismay, Gen. Lord, 134, 139
Isolationism, U.S., 57–59, *60–61*, 63, 80
Italian campaign, 165–81; strategy of, 165; Sicilian campaign, 165–67, 170, *171, 174;* map, *168–69;* Mussolini's fall from power, 170; Italy joins Allies, 172, 173; German retaliations against Italians, 175; liberation of Naples, 175–176; transfer of command to Alexander, 176; Casino, *177*, 178–79; Anzio and Nettuno assaults, 178; liberation of Rome *180*, 181; bombings, *207*
Italian Somaliland, 101
Italy: Mussolini's rise to power, 15, 17; invasion of Ethiopia, 18; and Spanish Civil War, 18, *19;* joins Germany in war, 36; and partition of eastern Europe, 49; invasion of Greece, 49; and partitioning of Yugoslavia and Greece, 52; Tripartite Pact, 64; losses in Albania and Libya, 102; resistance movement, 142, 225; Mussolini's fall from power, 170; joins Allies, 172, 173; German retaliation against, 175; Fascist Republic, 175; GI behavior in, 192–93; American Army in North, 237; Allies complete liberation of, 264; settlement after war, 290; *See also* Air Force, Italian; Army, Italian; Italian campaign; Mussolini; Navy, Italian
Iwo Jima, 252; taking of, 274–75, *276*

J

Japan, 133, 140; invasion of Manchuria and China, 17–18, 64, 69; deteriorating relations with U.S., 63–64, 69–71; Tripartite Pact, 64, 69; invades Indochina, 64, 75, 76; the Greater East Asia Co-Prosperity Sphere, 69–70, 217; U.S. blockade of, 69; attack on Pearl Harbor, 70, 71, 74–75; taking of Philippines, 75; advance on Asian mainland, 75– 76, 78; propaganda, 75, 78, 214, 216–17; Doolittle bombing raid on Tokyo, 82–83; as sea power, 85, 99; Allied plans to divest of colonies, 139; nonaggression treaty with U.S.S.R., 133, 163; extent of control in 1942, 147; defeat at Guadalcanal, 147, 150–51; and nationalist movements in Asia, 163, 216–17; American air raids on, 209; morale on the home front, 214–17; effect of bombing on morale, 214, 216; shortages, 216; racism, 216–17; military code, 217; Allies take the offensive against, 243–55; Allied plans to bomb, 243–44; Koiso replaces Tojo government, 247–48; Yalta and fate of, 257, 258; U.S.S.R. to enter war against, 259; peace overtures by, after German defeat, 279; massive bombing of cities, 279–80; Potsdam Declaration, 283; Hiroshima and Nagasaki, *272, 282*, 283; U.S.S.R. declares war on, 284; surrender, *272, 284, 285*, 286; war crime trials, 291; under Allied military rule, 291; *See also* Air Force, Japanese; Army, Japanese; Navy, Japanese; Operations, Axis
Japanese-Americans: internment of, 80, *81*, 82; in Italian campaign, 179

117, 118, 279, 284, 289; on bombing of Berlin, 196

Monastir Gap, Yugoslavia, 52

Monnet, Jean, 39

Monte Cassino, Abbey of, *177*, 178–79

Montevideo, Uruguay, *91*

Montgomery, Rear Adm., Alfred, 248

Montgomery, Field Marshal Bernard L. ("Monty"), 227, 254; and Battle of El Alamein, *104–5*, 107, 109, *113*; character and reputation of, 106–7; takes Tunis, 112, 114; on Hitler's errors in North African campaign, 114; and Italian campaign, 166–67, 172, 173, 175, 176; and Liberation of France and Belgium, *230–31* (map); at Caen, 234, 236; conflict over invasion of Germany strategy, 237; and Battle of the Bulge, *240*; in Germany, 262

Morgan, Gen. Sir Frederick, 226

Morgenthau, Henry, Jr., 289

Morison, Samuel Eliot, *168*

Morocco: map, *104–5*; Operation Torch, 110–11; Casablanca Conference, 136–37; Moroccans in Italian campaign, 165, 179

Mortain, France, 234

Moscow, U.S.S.R., 117, *122–23;* shock at German offensive, 118, 120; camouflaging of, 120; evacuation of, 124–25; Germans outside of, 125–26; mobilization of civilians, 217; life in, 217–18; celebration at German surrender, 271

Moselle River, 262

Motion films and propaganda, 221

Mountbatten, Adm. Lord Louis, 47, 279, 286; and Southeast Asia Command, 161, 247

MPs, 187

Mrs. Miniver (film), 221

Mueller, Heinrich, 213

"Mulberries," 226

Munich Agreement, 17, 22, 25

Murmansk Run, 95

Murphy, Robert, 14, 111

Murrow, Ed, 189

Musashi (battleship), 85, *97*, 251

Mussolini, Benito, *16*, 117, 145; rise to power, 15, 17; alliance with Hitler, 17; invasion of Ethiopia, 18; and Spanish Civil War, *19;* invasion of Albania, 22; joins Germany in war, 36; and Desert War, 107; and losses in North African campaign, 114; relation with generals, 133; Allied propaganda against in Italian campaign, 167, 170; loss of power and arrest, 170, 172; on German occupation of Italy, 173; German rescue of, 175; Fascist Republic, 175; death of, 266

Mussolini, Vittorio, 18

Mustang, P-51, 200, 208, 274

Myitkyina, Burma, 162

N

Nagasaki, Japan, *272*, 280, *282*, 284

Nagoya, Japan, 209, 280

Nagumo, Vice-Adm. Chuichi, 246

Namsos campaign, 31

Naples, Italy, 165, 172–73; liberation of 175–76

Narvik, Norway, 29, 31

National Defense Research Committee, 62

Nationalist movements, 75, 79, 163; Japanese exploitation of, 163, 216–17; *See also* Resistance movements

Nationalist Socialist party. *See* Nazi party

Navy, British, 31, 43, 44, 59, 75, *84*; at Dunkirk, 34; radar system, 44; sinking of *Repulse* and *Prince of Wales*, 76; weakness of, 85; U.S. ships to, 85; Battle of Oran, 86; victories over *Graf*

O

P

Panama, 80
Pantelleria, Italy, 166
Papen, Franz von, 291
Papua, New Guinea, 153
Paris, France: WWI peace treaties at, 7; German conquest of, 36, 38; liberation of, *231*, 236–37
Pas de Calais, 227
Pasha, Enver, 8
Patch, Lt. Gen. Alexander, *230–31*, 236
Patton, Maj. Gen. George S., Jr., 112, 125, 188, 254; and Italian campaign, 165–66, 167, *171*, 176; and liberation of France, 234, 236, 237; at Bastogne, 239; in Czechoslovakia, 262
Paul, Prince of Yugoslavia, 50
Paulus, Sir Friedrich, 109, 127, 129
Pearl Harbor, 43, 64, *72–73*, 206, 286; Japanese attack on, *68*, 70–71, 74–75
Peenemünde, Germany, 144, 205
Percival, Lt. Gen. Sir Arthur, 76, 248, 286
Perry, Commodore Matthew, 69
Persian Gulf, 140–41
Petacci, Clara, 266
Pétain, Marshal Philippe, 110, 111; assumes power, 38
Peter, King of Yugoslavia, 50
Petlyakov, Vladimir, 131
Petrie, Gen., 214
Petroleum resources, struggle over, 140–41
Philippines, 70; Japanese invasion of, 75, 79–80; Allied plans to invade, *148–49*, 244; Japanese puppet government in, 248; resistance movement, 248; strategic importance of, 248; return of MacArthur, 254–55
Phillips, Sir Tom, 76
Phony War, 32
Photographers, war, 189
Picasso, Pablo, 20
Piccolo Peak, Italy, 173
Pipinellis, Panayotis, 124
Pius XII, Pope, 14, 26

Ploesti, Rumania, 200–1
PLUTO (Pipe-Line Under the Ocean), 226
Plutonium bomb, 283
Poland, 133, *215*, 290, 293; Soviet-German plan to partition, 22–23, 25; German invasion of, 25–26, 27, 28, *30*; government in exile, 26; partition of, 28; resistance movement, *30*, 47, 225, 259; and Curzon Line, 136, 258; Red Army in, 257; Provisional Government, 258; uprising in Warsaw, 259; Communist control of, 262
Poles in Italian campaign, 179
Political refugees, agreement to return to U.S.S.R., 259
Political Warfare Executive (PWE), 141–42
Politics of WWII, 133–45
Ponza, Italy, 170, 175
Popski's Private Army, 101
Po River, 264
Port Arthur, Manchuria, 284
Port Moresby, New Guinea, 96, 98, 147, 153
Port Said, Egypt, 102
Portsmouth, England, 233
Portugal, 141
"Potato masher" grenade, *24*
Potsdam Conference, 279, 283
Potsdam Declaration, 283, 284
Pownall, Rear Adm. Charles, 243
Press coverage (U.S.) of war, 188–89
Prince of Wales (battleship), 76, 87
Prinz Eugen (cruiser), 87
Prisoners of war: German mistreatment of, 213; Japanese mistreatment of, 217
Propaganda: Allied, 141–42, 144, 167, 170, *180*; Axis, 141, 142, 144, 179; British, 47, 50, 53, 87; German, 36, 86, 141, 142, 144; Japanese, 75, 78, 214, 216–17; U.S., *210*, 217, 221
Psychological pressure of war, 192–93

Purple Heart, 179
Pyle, Ernie, 189, 192

Q

Qattara Depression, Egypt, 107
Quezon, Manuel, 254
Quisling, Vidkun, 31

R

Rabaul, New Britain Island, *148–
49*, 150, 153, 248
Racism: German, *30*, 216; Japanese,
216–17; *See also* Anti-Semitism;
Colonialism
Radar: British, 44; German, 201
Radek, Karl, 9, 17
Radford, Rear Adm. Arthur W.,
243
Radio propaganda. *See* Propaganda
Raeder, Adm. Erich, 85–86
Rangoon, Burma, 286
Rankin, Jeannette, 75
Rapallo, Treaty of, 9, 22
Rapido River, 179
Rationing: Britain, 218–19, *220*;
U.S., *220*, 221
Red Army. *See* Army, Soviet
Red Cross, 186, 213
Refugees, political, agreement to
return to U.S.S.R., 259
Regensburg, Germany, 199–200
Reichenau, Field Marshal Walther
von, 26, 126
Relocation camps, U.S., 80, *81*,
82
Remagen, Germany, 262, 264
Rentenmark, 11, 14
Reparations, German, 258
Repulse (cruiser), 76
Resistance movements: in Albania,
142, 175, 225; in Balkans, 101,
165, 225, 237; in France, 39,
47, 142, 175, 224, *230–31*, 236;
in Germany, 211, 233–34; in
Greece, 175, 225; in Hungary,

225; in Italy, 175, 225; in the
Netherlands, 47, 225; in Nor-
way, 47, 225; in the Philippines,
248; in Rumania, 226; in Yugo-
slavia, 142, 225; *See also* Nation-
alist movements
Reuben James (destroyer), 93
Reuter, Ernst, 211
Reynaud, Paul, 36, 38
Rheims, France, 269
Rhine River, 237, 257, 262, 264
Ribbentrop, Joachim von, 22, 26,
28, 38, 49, 291; conference with
Molotov, 196; exploring com-
promise between Germany and
U.S.S.R., 264
River Plate, Battle of the, 87
Riviera, France, 236
Rjukan, Norway, 144, 145
Rockwell, Norman, *210*
Roebling, Donald, 96
Roer River, 262
Rokossovski, Konstantin, 131, 259
Rome Italy: Allied bombing of,
170; plan for parachute landing
in, 172; liberation of, *164*, *180*,
181
Rommel, Field Marshal Erwin,
32; in Egypt, 85, 92; character
and reputation of, 102; in Desert War, 102–3, *104–5*, 106–7,
109, 114; Battle of El Alamein,
104–5, 107, 109, *113*, 114–15;
Operation Torch against, 110;
recalled, 112; in Italian campaign, 173, 176; on building of
American Army, 183; and Normandy invasion, 227, 229, 232,
235; forced suicide of, 234
Roosevelt, Franklin Delano, 26,
32, 43, *56*, 69, *132*, 145, 254,
289; New Deal, 14; University
of Virginia speech, 36, 59; prepares U.S. for war, 58–59, 62–
63; early communications with
Churchill, *56*, 59; declares state
of emergency, 59, 62; Lend-
Lease program, 62–63; meeting
with Churchill at Newfound-

land, 66–67; and declaration of
war, 75; orders MacArthur out
of the Philippines, 79; and concentration of war effort in
Europe, 80; and bombing raid
on Tokyo, 83; war strategy of,
134; relations with Stalin, 136;
at Casablanca Conference, 136–
37, *138*; on de Gaulle, 137; on
unconditional surrender of
Axis, 137; at Cairo Conferenc,
139; at Teheran Conference,
139–40; on France's future and
obligations, 140; and atomic
bomb research, 144–45; support of Chiang, 159; and propaganda, *180*; and U.S. armament
of Allies, 219, 221, 222–23;
and second front plans, 225;
and Operation Overlord, 226;
on D-Day, 232; at Yalta Conference, *256*, 257–58; ill health
of, 257–58; death of, 265–66;
and UN, 289, 291, *292*
Rosenberg, Alfred, 291
Rosenthal, Joe, 274
Rostov, U.S.S.R., 127
Rotterdam, Netherlands, 50
Roundup, Operation, 136
Royal Air Force. *See* Air Force,
British
Ruhr River Valley, Germany,
264–65
Rumania, 22; Russian occupation
of Bessarabia, 22, 25, 39, 47,
49; partitioning of, 49; Hitler's
"military mission" to, 50;
bombing of Ploesti, 200–201;
resistance movement, 226; Red
Army in, 257; loss of Bucovina
and Bessarabia, 293
Rundstedt, Field Marshal Gerd
von, 32, 34, 36; and Operation
Barbarossa, 118, *122–23*, 125,
126; and Normandy invasion,
227, 232, *235*; and Ardennes
campaign, 239; Hitler dis-
misses, 264
Rupel, Fort, 54

Russell Islands, 154
Russia. *See* Union of Soviet Social-
ist Republics
Russian front. *See* Barbarossa,
Operation

S

Saar, Germany, 15, 291
Saboteurs, 121, 142, 144, 145. *See
also* Espionage; Resistance
movements
"Sad Sack" comic strip, 189
Sagan camp, 213
Saint-Lô, France, *230–31*
St. Lo (carrier), 252
Saipan, Marianas, *242*, 244, *245*,
246, 247
Saito, Lt. Gen. Yoshitsugu, 244,
246
Sakhalin Island, U.S.S.R., 279,
284, 291
Salamaua, New Guinea, 153
Salerno, Italy, *169*, 172, 173, 175
Salinas, Calif., 190
San Antonio Bay, Philippines, 273
San Bernardino Strait, 251, 254
San Francisco, Calif., 271
Sangro River, 165
Santa Cruz Islands, Battle of, 150
Santee (carrier), 252
Sardinia, 166, 173
Sato, Ambassador, 284
Sauckel, Fritz, 291
Saudi Arabia, 141
Savo Island, Battle of, 150
Scandinavian neutrality, 29, 141
Schacht, Hjalmar Horace Greeley,
11, 14, 291
Schellenberg, Walter, 28
Schmidt, Maj. Gen. Harry, 274
Schulenberg, Count Werner von
der, 118
Schumann, Maurice, 39
Schuster, Ildefonso, Cardinal, 266
Schweinfurt, Germany, 199–200
"Screaming meemies," 178
Seabees, 154, 155, 221–22

Sea Lion, Operation, 44, 46–47
Security Council of The United Nations, 259
Seeckt, Hans von, 8–9, 15, 17, 39
See Here, Private Hargrove (Hargrove), 185
Selective Service, U.S. *See* Draft, U.S.
Senegalese in Italian campaign, 179
Serbia, 52
Sevastopol, U.S.S.R., 126
Seyss-Inquart, Artur von, 291
SHAEF, 226, 236, 237
Shepheard's Hotel, Cairo, 101
Sherman, Rear Adm. Frederick C., 243
Sherwood, Robert, 58, 67
Shigemitsu, Mamoru, 216, 286
Shipbuilding, U.S., 95–96
Sho-Go, Operation, 249
Shoho (carrier), 98
Sholokhov, Mikhail, 124
Shoup, Col. David, 155
Shuri, Okinawa, 277
Shute, Nevil, 44
Siam. *See* Thailand
Sibuyan Sea, Battle of the, 251
Sicily, Italy, 136; Allied invasion of, 92, 112, 165–67, 170, *171, 174,* map, *168–69*
Simović, Gen. Dušan, 50
Singapore, 70, 248, 279, 286; Japanese capture, 75–76, 78
Skorzeny, Otto, 175, 239
Slave labor camps. *See* Concentration camps
Sledgehammer, Operation, 111
"Slot, the," 150
Slovakia (German puppet state), 87
Smigly-Rydz, Marshal Edward, 26
Smith, Lt. Gen. Holland M. ("Howling Mad"), 188, 246, 274
Smolensk, U.S.S.R.: Germans take, 120; Soviets retake, 130
Sofia, Bulgaria, 262

Solomon Islands, 147, 150–51, 154, 243. *See also* Guadalcanal Island
Somaliland, Italian, 101
Somme River, 229; Battle of, 36
South Africans: in North African campaign, 109; in Italian campaign, 179
Southampton, England, 233
South Asia: British responsibility for, 159, 161. *See also specific countries*
Southeast Asia Command, 161
Spaatz, Lt. Gen. Carl ("Tooey"), 188, 197, 199, 283
Spain, 111, 166; civil war in, 18, *19,* 20, 58; Operation Felix, 92
Spam, 186
Spatha, Cape, Crete, 90
Special Operations Executive, 47
Speer, Albert, 200, 213–14
Speidel, Lt. Gen. Hans, 106, 232
Spies. *See* Espionage
Sprague, Rear Adm. Clifton, 251, 252
Sprague, Rear Adm. Thomas, 252
Spruance, Adm. Raymond, 99, 155, 243, 244, 274, 275
Stafford, Jo, 186
Stalin, Joseph, 14, 117, 133, 134, *143;* consolidation of power, 17; nonaggression pact with Germany, 22, 25; desire for war in 1939, 25; invasion of Finland, *33;* discredits Hitler's plan to invade U.S.S.R., 55; Hopkins's mission to, 66; satisfaction over Pearl Harbor, 71; unprepared for German offensive, 118, 120; scorched-earth policy, 120; creation of special army units, 124; orders evacuation of Moscow, 124–25; and loss of Kiev, 126; and loss of Kharkov, 127; creation of generals and marshals, 131; on relations among Allies, 133; and Casablanca Conference, 136; at Teheran Conference, 139–40; and oil resources, 140; support

for Chiang, 159; and sphere of influence in Balkans, 165; tyranny of, 217; demand for second front, 225; and invasion plans for France, 226; at Yalta Conference, *256*, 257–58; and uprising in Warsaw, 259; self-confidence of, 258; desire to take Berlin, 262; at Potsdam Conference, 279; and use of A-bomb, 283; and Soviet development of A-bomb, 289; and UN, 293; China policy, 294

Stalingrad, U.S.S.R., 127; Battle of, 109–10, 127, *128*, 129; Hitler's Directive No. 45 against, 127

Stalin-JS tank, 131

Stalin Line, 118

Stars and Stripes (newspaper), 189

Stauffenberg, Lt. Col. Count Klaus von, 233–34

"Steam," 192

Stein, Gertrude, 57

Steinbeck, John 189

Steinhardt, Laurence, 124

Stettinius, Edward, 258

Stilwell, Gen. Joseph, 139, 247; loss of Burma, 76; Command of China-Burma-India Theater, 159; and Burma campaign, 161

Stimson, Henry L., 18, 63, *65*, 281, 284, 289

Stirling (plane), 199

Stormovik (plane), 204

Streicher, Julius, 291

Stumme, Gen. Georg von, 109

Submarines: German (U-boats), 44, 63, 82, 85, 86, 93, 95, 96; and espionage, 142

Suez Canal, Egypt, 90, 92; mining of, 102

Suicide, Japanese ritual (hara-kiri), 244, 246, 254, 277. *See also* Kamikaze attacks

Sukarno, 217

Sultan, Lt. Gen. Daniel I., 247

Sumatra, 147, 279

Superfortress, B-29, 208–9, 214, 247, 274, 275, 277, 279–80, 283

Supreme Headquarters, Allied Expeditionary Force (SHAEF), 226, 236, 237

Suribachi, Mount, Iwo Jima, 274, *276*

Surigao Strait, 251

Suwanee (ship), 252

Suzuki, Adm. Kantaro, 283; at Japanese surrender, 284, 286

Sverdlovsk, U.S.S.R., 125

Sweden, 29, 141; iron mines of, 29, 31

Switzerland, 265

Sword beach, Normandy, 232

Syracuse, Italy, 167

Syria, 53, 101

T

Tacloban airport, Philippines, 254

Taffy 3, 251, 252

Tanaka Memorial, 69

Tanks, *100*, *164*, *171*; French, 34; German, 34, *100;* Soviet, 121, 130–31

Taranto, Italy, 92

Tarawa atoll, *152*, 155

Tasigny, Gen. Jean de Lattre de, 236

Taylor, Maj. Gen. Maxwell, 172, 232

Teheran Conference, 136, 139–40, 226

Tempelhof airfield, Germany, 268

Tennessee (battleship), 74

Terauchi, Field Marshal Hisaichi, 248, 255

Thailand, 279; Japanese invade, 70, 76

Thoma, Gen. Ritter von, 109

Thunderbolt, P-47, 200

Tibbets, Col. Paul W., Jr., 283

Timor Island, 147

Timoshenko, Marshal Semën Konstantinovich, 118, 120, 125, 127

Tinian Island, 246

Tito, Marshal (Josip Broz), 20,

occupation of Germany, 289–90; development of A-bomb, 289; and Cold War, 291, 293–95; control of eastern Europe, 293–94; China policy, 294; *See also* Air Force, Soviet; Allies; Army, Soviet; Conferences; Navy, Soviet; Stalin

United Kingdom. *See* Great Britain

United Nations, 134, 258; Security Council, 259; creation of, 271, *292;* and Cold War, 291, 293

United States: post-WWI economy, collapse, and Depression, 11, 14; and Spanish Civil War, *19;* evolution of foreign policy, 57–58; in WWI, 57–58; isolationism, 57–59, *60–61*, 63, 80; Roosevelt prepares ofr war, 58–59, 62–63; arms sales to Britain and France, 58, 59; election of 1940, 62; Lend-Lease program, *60–61*, 62–63, 66, 158; deteriorating relations with Japan, 63–64, 69–71; embargo on Japan, 64, 69; attack on Pearl Harbor, 71, 74–75; declaration of war, 75; mounting of war effort, 80, 82; impact of early Japanese successes, 82; neutrality of, 133; war strategy, 134; interest in Mideast oil resources, 141; responsibility for Pacific front, 159; home front, 183–93, 219–23; propaganda, *210, 221;* relative comfort and security at home, 219; as arsenal of Allies, 219, 221; rise in national debt, 221; taxes and war bonds, 221; rationing, *220*, 221; mobilization of civilian population, 221–22; women in work force, 222; black market, 222; exuberance during war, 222–23; plans in 1942 for second front, 225; Truman succeeds to presidency, 261; testing and use of atomic weapons, 281, 283; and Cold

V

Volturno River, 176, 178
Voroshilov, Marshal Kliment
    Efremovich, 118

W

Wainwright, Lt. Gen. Jonathan
    M., 286; and Bataan, 79–80
Wakde Islands, 249
Wake Island, 80
Walcheron Island, Netherlands,
    237
"Walkyrie" plot, 233
Wang Ching-wei, 217
War bonds, U.S., 221
War crimes trials: Germany, 290–
    91; Japan, 291
War Production Board, 80, 219
Warsaw: German capture of, 28;
    uprising in, 259
Washington, George, 57
Washington, D.C.: Trident Con-
    ference, 161, 201; growth dur-
    ing war, 222; Dumbarton Oaks
    Conference, 293
Wasp (carrier), 92
Watch on the Rhine, Operation,
    239
Watson-Watt, Sir Robert, 44
Wavell, Gen. Sir Archibald, 102,
    103, *108*
Weapons. *See* Armament; Atomic
    weapons; V-weapons
Wedemeyer, Maj. Gen. Albert C.,
    247
Wehrmacht. See Army, German
Western Desert campaign, 102, *108*
West Virginia (battleship), 74
West Wall, German, *231*
Weygand, Gen. Maxime, 36
Wheeler, Burton K., 59, 80
White, William Allen, 58
Wilhelm II, Kaiser of Germany,
    58
Willkie, Wendell L., 62
Wilson, Gen. Sir Henry
    ("Jumbo"), 176
Wilson, Woodrow, 57; self-

determination policy, 7; and
    League of Nations, 8
Wingate, Maj. Gen. Orde, 101,
    162–63, 246
Wingate's Chindits, 162, 246
Wolff, Gen. Karl, 264
Wolfram resources, 141
Women in work force: in Britain,
    219; in U.S., 222; in U.S.S.R.,
    217
World War I: peace treaties follow-
    ing, 7; Depression following,
    10; U.S. in, 57

Y

Yahagi (cruiser), 277
Yak fighter (plane), 204
Yakovlev, Alexander, 131
Yalta Conference, 136, *256*, 257–
    59, 289, 291
Yamamoto, Adm. Isoroku, 158;
    and attack on Pearl Harbor, 71;
    and Battle of Midway, 98–99
Yamasaki, Col. Yasuyo, 158
Yamashita, Gen. Tomoyuki, 248,
    254, 255, 273
Yamato (battleship), 85, 277
Yank (magazine), 189
Yawata, Kyushu Island, 208
Yelnya, Battle of, 131
Yonai, Adm. Mitsumasa, 248
Yorktown (carrier), 96, 99
Yugoslavia, 133; German invasion
    of, 50, 52; partitioning of, 52;
    resistance movement, 142, 225;
    under Communist control, 262

Z

Zaibatsu (Japanese industrialists),
    216
Zero (plane), 208, 243
Zhukov, Gen. Georgi, 125, 127, 129,
    130, 131, 259; at Berlin, 262, 268;
    and German surrender, 269
Zog, King of Albania, 22